ETHNOTEK®

Threads of Change

An Essential Guide To Weaving Traditional Art & Modern Business

The Ethnotek Story

By Jake Orak

Published by Ethnotek LLC, Minnesota, USA, in collaboration with Far Books, a division of Far Features Ltd.

Dedication

For Phạm Hữu Ái and Cao Thanh Tú,
my Vietnamese brothers who took a chance on me.
Ethnotek wouldn't have been possible without you.

Contents

Artisan Countries

GUATEMALA GHANA INDIA INDONESIA VIETNAM

Handmade Processes

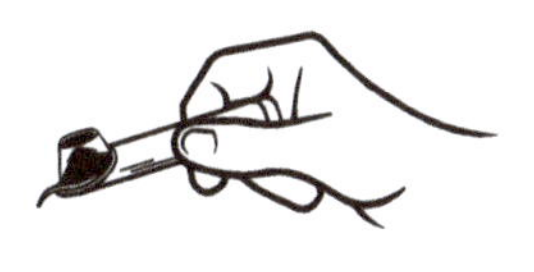

BATIK WEAVING EMBROIDERY

Prologue

Social Entrepreneurs Change The World

"Every time you spend money, you're casting a vote for the kind of world you want.

— Anna Lappe

Before we start our journey into the Ethnotek story, I feel it's essential to set the stage to explain what a social entrepreneur is and why their work is important, as well as share some facts and stats about the artisan economy. Hopefully, you'll see why social entrepreneurs and conscious consumers can change the world together.

Social entrepreneurs are the unsung heroes of positive change, innovators who blend business acumen with a burning desire to make a difference. These visionary individuals create profitable companies that support livelihoods while tackling real-world social and environmental issues. Picture them as the guardians of a sustainable and compassionate future, weaving threads of impact through ethical business philosophies and practices into the fabric of our global society. As Kyle Westaway wrote in his book *Profit & Purpose*, "Imagine combining the heart of Gandhi and the mind of Henry Ford."

While sometimes confused with non-government organizations (NGOs) or non-profit organizations (NPOs), social entrepreneurship is a for-profit endeavor, even though a greater emphasis is on creating social or environmental changes.

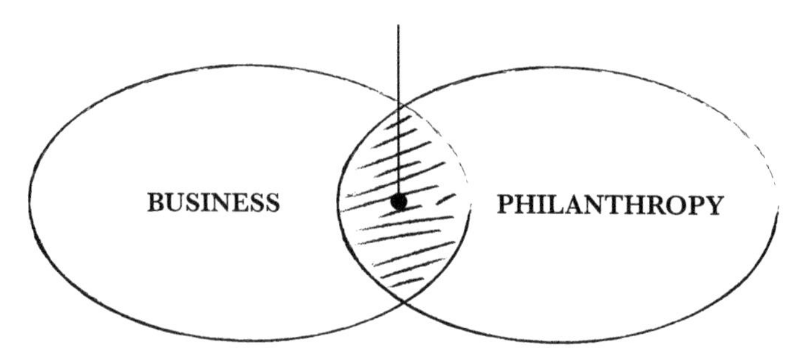

Trades in goods and services to generate income to solve the world's social and environmental issues.

Most modern societies are built upon a capitalist foundation with trade at its core — buying and selling. We work and get paid. We buy things to make life more comfortable and enjoyable. Today, capitalists are celebrated as much as they're vilified. From tech titans being idolized like cult heroes to Wall Street bankers facing waves of protests and backlash over how much political sway they hold — it's a turbulent time when politics, power, and big business are ever-more entangled.

Companies and industries drive the economy, creating jobs and producing consumer goods and services that steer global markets. In our interconnected global economy, companies are the fuel that keeps our great big capitalist show on the road. The bigger they get, the louder their voice and influence reach as a result. We need an ever-growing number of social entrepreneurs entering the global marketplace to spread ethical and responsible consumption ideas and products. Every one of them has an impact — and a voice that can echo worldwide.

Positive change doesn't happen on its own. We need more people to take up the challenge of social entrepreneurship with the intent of tipping the balance of business from a model where people and the planet profit. That's an optimistic horizon we can all reach for.

I also want to clarify that profit is not bad — it's good. For social enterprises, profit is imperative to invest and grow the mission. Social entrepreneurs shouldn't worry about living like starving artists. That's not beneficial for anyone. We have to abandon the outdated idea that profit is bad for a company focused on doing good — it's simply not true. We can keep our morals and bank balances in good health. In fact, to be successful social entrepreneurs, we must because everyone in the value chain will benefit.

At the time of writing, the impact investing market is valued at more than US$1 trillion, according to the Global Impact Investing Network (GIIN). This whopping figure is a testament to the growing realization that profit and purpose can coexist harmoniously.

Social entrepreneurs march to a different beat in the dynamic dance of supply and demand. They recognize that success isn't solely measured in profits but also in the positive footprints they leave behind. According to a report by the Global Entrepreneurship Monitor, social entrepreneurship is on the rise, with approximately 72% of entrepreneurs globally expressing the intention to create companies with social or environmental goals. This isn't a passing trend. It's a seismic shift.

These change-makers act as catalysts for progress, tackling issues ranging from poverty and healthcare to education and environmental sustainability. The stats show that social enterprises are a powerful force for good. A study by the British Council estimates that social enterprises contribute around 2–3% of the Gross Domestic Product

(GDP) in many countries and employ millions of people globally. This isn't just business; it's a movement rewriting the world economy.

So, why should you care about social entrepreneurs? Because they are the dreamers who refuse to accept the status quo, the architects of a more equitable future, who stitch together a tapestry of change, making business better and nudging the needle of positive progress.

For our case study of social entrepreneurship in this book, we will deep dive into the company I founded and helped nurture for more than a decade: Ethnotek.

What started as a simple idea has spread further than I could have imagined. Ask me what we do, and it's simple. We design, produce, and sell customizable bags that fuse artisanal traditional threads with high-tech materials to customers worldwide. But why we do it is more important to us. Ethnotek's chosen method of social entrepreneurship is to help grow the artisan economy, particularly focused on traditional handmade artisan textiles.

Our durable, high-tech laptop and travel bags feature traditional handmade textiles. We partner with artisan communities in Ghana, Guatemala, India, Indonesia, and Vietnam to make this happen. Through the sale of our bags, money flows back to communities via textile purchase orders. As our social enterprise grows, so do the profits and opportunities of our artisan partners' small businesses. It's a simple and symbiotic supply chain model and trade relationship.

There's so much opportunity for aspiring social entrepreneurs working in the artisan space. A recent study published by Powered By People found that the sector turns over US$500 billion in annual revenue today and is projected to grow by 20% per year, reaching US$1 trillion in 2024.

The sector is currently dominated by 76% female-led businesses, with 64% of workers under 35 and 62% of the whole industry living and working in rural areas. Interestingly, artisan production is already the second-largest employer globally (after agriculture). Yet the sector has chronically under-served investment, digitalization, and access to business finance and markets. Despite its enormous scale and potential, the artisan industry remains undervalued as a vehicle for economic, social, and environmental impact.

At the same time, the sector also plays a massive role in achieving many of the United Nations Sustainable Development Goals (SDGs). Artisan livelihoods in rural areas underpin progress toward "No Poverty" (SDG 1). High participation rates by women and youth are critical to "Gender Equality" (SDG 5). Artisan production's scale and global growth potential deliver "Decent Work and Economic Growth" (SDG 8). Digital, finance, logistics, and training activities for artisans contribute to "Industry, Innovation, and Infrastructure" (SDG 9) and help bridge income gaps, contributing to "Reduced Inequalities" (SDG 10). These artisan businesses protect and safeguard the world's cultural and natural heritage, Sustainable Cities & Communities (SDG 11), and inspire Responsible Consumption & Production (SDG 12). Finally, sector-wide artisan collaboration is a powerful contributor to the "Partnership For The Goals" (SDG 17). Indirectly, social enterprises working in the artisan sector also help achieve goals related to "Zero Hunger" (SDG 2), "Good Health and Well-Being" (SDG 3), "Quality Education" (SDG 4) and "Clean Water and Sanitation" (SDG 6).

While there is much promise, many challenges face the artisan sector worldwide. Here are just the top five:

1. 60% struggle with access to finance, finding means to fund projects via loans, investment, or customer demand.

2. 59% struggle with access to markets outside the local region.

3. 37% lack social media skills needed to reach and promote their craft on social media.

4. 36% face merchandising problems: Knowledge of how to package, display, price, and sell products effectively.

5. 34% face marketing issues: Learning to create content to promote their product, process, and mission.

I can vouch for all of these points as I've witnessed them first-hand. We encountered them in the early stages of Ethnotek, and a primary reason behind many was the unfortunate reality that demand for artisanal-made weaved products was in decline at the time.

In 2011, after meeting with some of the artisans, I made the following journal entry:

The top three factors reported that have impacted reduced demand for their handmade textiles are:

1. Scalability Issues: The long lead time for production and high costs due to the complex weaving process deters many local and international customers.

2. Market Access: Makers need help getting their goods online, as well as packaging, marketing, selling, or finding new customers outside their local regions.

3. Knowledge Transfer Issues: Motivating and empowering the younger generation of weavers to adopt local traditions.

I circled back to these points while researching this book to see if they were still relevant. Despite our considerable efforts over the past decade, they are. The artisans and social entrepreneurs I interviewed for this book explained that this is so important to address through commerce because when crafts like these fade, so does the cultural identity woven into them. Their rich art forms help make our planet such a beautiful, colorful, exciting, and unique place. As expressions of diverse beliefs, values, and creativity, without them, we face a mass-produced world of homogeny, which we must work hard to stop from transpiring.

The artisans we partner with never wanted charity. They always wanted trade. They wanted to sell their art at a fair price and have a sustainable relationship. Purchasing finished goods upholds two important pillars in their communities: purpose and perpetuation. Buying traditional textiles that are made through a process that proudly embodies cultural identity is more than a job; it's a purpose. Consistently financing this process through textile purchase orders creates a platform for hiring others in the community and teaching the method to youngsters. This perpetuates the education and continuation of handmade textiles and the surrounding culture. These two pillars are sacred foundations for the artisans we work with and have served as cornerstones of our relationships for all these years.

My job became easy once I learned about the essential needs of the artisans we partner with early in our relationships. My responsibility was to help bring a wider global audience to the artisans' craft by combining the fabrics with robust outdoor-grade materials. This means my role has always been to design, produce, and connect our awesome products to our customers worldwide, who then help drive the entire impact cycle — more customers, more business, more impact. That's how it works — supply and demand.

The artisans are not our employees. We are trade partners. With their permission, we buy what they sell and celebrate their creative cultural expressions with our community. The same goes for our production family in Vietnam, where all Ethnotek bags are produced. What enables our artisan and production partners to be self-employed and continue their craft is the amazing people who buy our bags that feature the artisans' incredible work.

We are just one of hundreds, possibly thousands of other social enterprises collaborating with artisans in many creative ways, such as homewares, ethical fashion, footwear, and more. We'll talk about some examples of more brands later in this book, and you can find more reading in the Acknowledgments.

Finally, to end our brief but essential mini-adventure through social entrepreneurship in the artisan space, let's touch upon some incredible stats from the Powered By People study.

For most growing artisan businesses, exports and international sales are key drivers of market access. Artisans exporting internationally see an average 37% increase in sales within the first two years, with the potential to increase to an average of 700% in five years. Wowza! Small and medium-sized enterprises (SMEs) also play a crucial role in the artisan sector. Most Artisan enterprises are SMEs — an often hidden branch of the business universe in many low-income economies. Once highlighted, supported, and connected, they can be given prominence and allowed to flourish. Of those surveyed, 86% were "small-scale brands" with sales under US$250,000 per year. In comparison, the remaining 14% surpassed that figure, achieving the category of "growth-scale brands". With the right digital tools, backed by financing solutions and enhanced export-driven market access, many small-scale artisan businesses can climb the ladder to become growth-stage exporters, commanding a widening global retail market share.

With this in mind, I encourage you to buy from small brands with transparent artisan supply chains. Conscious consumers are vital in fueling demand and growth, which helps small businesses reach growth scale. Our digital age makes this beautiful world much smaller and empowers us to drive support and collaborate with global communities with just a few clicks.

As we begin our journey into the Ethnotek story, keep this idea in mind: Social entrepreneurs are redesigning the blueprint for a business landscape where success is measured in social and environmental positive outcomes — then profit. That's a destination we can all jump on for the ride.

Introduction

A Founder's Journey

"If you want to understand the entrepreneur, study the juvenile delinquent. The delinquent is saying with his actions, 'This sucks, I'm going to do my own thing.'"

— Yvon Chouinard

Minneapolis, Minnesota
2011

It was a gloomy Minneapolis Tuesday morning when my world brightened up in ways I couldn't have imagined —and it was such a simple thing, too. Or maybe I should say a stranger who brought this sunshine into my day. I was sitting in traffic watching the rain streak down the window when, suddenly, a splash of color slowly moved by on the sidewalk outside. Immediately, a flash of recognition sparked in me.

"No way," I said aloud as this wonderful stranger strolled effortlessly along the sidewalk like she was in slow motion. I had no idea who this person was, but I knew exactly what she was wearing, where it was made, who designed it, whose artisanal fabric she was sporting, what village it was woven in, what it represented to the people, family, and community who threaded it together — I knew everything there was to know about what she was carrying on her back. A bright and colorful rainbow-striped backpack. The Guatemala 1 Raja Pack! This was the first time I had seen someone wearing one of the Ethnotek bags I had designed in the world. And so, on this dreary wet morning, while I was stuck in bumper-to-bumper traffic inside my nearly broken down Volkswagen Passat Wagon, my world was glowing warm with good vibes. I could have leaped out of the car and run in the rain to hug that stranger and thank her for buying one of our bags. I didn't because I was too shy, but as I rolled on by grinning ear-to-ear, I felt tears of joy welling up inside. It was such a simple yet powerful thing. To witness for the first time that there were people out there who believed in what our company was creating and the values woven into our mission. Simple but impactful moments like these make the journey of a social entrepreneur meaningful.

There have been many moments like this on the Ethnotek journey. In this book, I will tell you about some things in the hope that you will also be lucky enough to enjoy similar experiences on your travels along the entrepreneurial path, in whatever flavor that may be.

This book is for dreamers, doers, and creatives who believe small businesses can change the world. And specifically, a guide for social entrepreneurs working at the intersection of traditional arts and modern business. You may already work within a social enterprise or are thinking about starting your own. You may already have an artisan-based business and are experiencing problems scaling up, or you may want to learn how to start a small business and manage its operations. If you can identify with any of these roles, then I hope you will find something in the following pages that resonates with you. At the very least, I hope you will find some companionship and insights along the creative entrepreneurial trail.

I am also writing this book to help the current Ethnotek team fully understand the founding vision and hopefully spark a reconnection with our existing distributors and retailers. Furthermore, I want to speak directly to the loyal and passionate customers who have supported us over the years by giving insights into our company's inner workings and stories. Lastly, this is a long-form welcome letter to those new to the Ethnotek family. So welcome, and come on in. Learn all there is to know about who we are and what we do. I hope you find some connection and a few strands of inspiration to bring us closer together. So, what will you get from reading this book? Well, because Ethnotek is a company that is always on the go, this book has been written in a guide format. This is an unconventional companion for social entrepreneurs. It's mostly anecdotal because businesses are themselves a collection of stories. And so I will share stories, learnings, experiences, and lessons from my founder's journey, as well as real-world examples, trends, reportage, some factoids, figures, diagrams, and doodles to give you a complete picture of the Ethnotek story.

Also, I will lay out a roadmap of Ethnotek's design principles, direct trade methods, core values, and philosophies so that you can apply some or all of them to your own social enterprise, creative process, community project, or way of working.

By the end of this book, you will have a guide of what we did, how we did it, and what we got right (and wrong) on our company journey. There will be a lot of recommendations and future vision-questing before we say goodbye —and, of course, a few laughs along the way. Specifically, I want to talk to you about the nine most important big ideas from Ethnotek's journey.

We'll begin our adventure by addressing a simple but essential question: Why is combining traditional handmade art and modern business important? I will then discuss the importance of differentiating as a business and the value of what our artisan partners taught me and passed along. Then, we'll take a long celebratory road trip into the culture of our artisan partners. Next, I will look at our approach by going to the source and meeting our collaborators to build trust and long-lasting relationships. We'll explore the motivations behind putting our community first, ahead of brand image, before touching upon my design philosophies and belief in slowing down at the design stage to avoid adverse downstream social and environmental effects. Then, we'll venture across the sometimes treacherous intersection of cultural inclusion and misappropriation before emerging refreshed with positive vibes to discuss adapting to the ever-changing nature of traditional weaving before opening the door to the future of Ethnotek. Finally, I will provide some useful resources at the back of the book for further reading.

I believe that small businesses can change the world. Why? Because we are more agile and innovative than large corporations or policymakers. But we must tread lightly. Be radically committed to our causes and lift each other up. We're more powerful together when we share knowledge and nurture an ecosystem of positivity as opposed to competing with each other. Together, we can move mountains!

The inception of Ethnotek, before it had a name, legal registration, and product, came from four distinct waypoints in my personal life.

The first was the realization that I felt bored by the banality and homogeneity of growing up in the Midwest United States. Sorry to make such a cynical statement, but it was how I felt then. The flat plains were dominated by harsh winters and scattered with strip malls and fast food franchises. Consumer culture and a politically charged feeling of divisive fear seemed to guide much of the cultural psyche of that time in my life. Add into the mix that I had a problem with authority and tended to get into trouble while on home turf in the USA. Again, it was more of an issue that I was trying to rebel against the culture I was surrounded by. I felt like a bit of a misfit and dreamed about something else.

I grew up with white privilege and little ethnic diversity around me. And that's where the second waypoint sticks its pin in the map for me. Thankfully, in 2000, I got to study abroad for a trimester in high school in Costa Rica at the School of Environmental Studies and again for a semester in Singapore during college at the University of Wisconsin-Stout.

While in Singapore, my fellow Stouties Nick, Paul, and I traveled all over Southeast Asia. Those initial experiences expanded my mind and broadened my horizons to the beauty and diversity of this incredible part of the world. Not only to the realization that the world is not a big scary place but also to the visceral experience and diversity of all things human rushing through me. The bright colors, rich textures, delicious food, diverse languages, difficult-to-calculate currencies, music, and art were all different, all new, and I was hooked. I knew I needed to break out on my own by using my creativity to bring me closer to the art and culture I was relishing in Southeast Asia – but how? I had no idea then.

The third waypoint was where the concept for Ethnotek's products came from. In 2005, I graduated college, worked a corporate job as a junior designer at 3M Corporation for a year, and had a cushy salary and benefits. From there, in 2006, I took a downward career move to be an intern at a bag company called Crumpler, which required me to move to Ho Chi Minh City, Vietnam, but at a quarter of the salary I was already making.

It was perfect, just the adventure I was looking for. I happily took the downgrade in remuneration to get back to Southeast Asia. By the time 2007 rolled around, I had been promoted, and during Vietnam's Hung Kings' national holiday, things were clicking into gear. I had a week off work and traveled to the northern highlands near the southern border of China through Sa Pa, Bắc Hà, Lai Châu, and Hà Giang. During this solo motorbike trip, I spent time with the various Hmong tribes that populated the region, which blew my mind. Most Hmong communities still wear their traditional attire and primarily work in agriculture throughout the breathtaking landscape. In their free time, they handmake the most stunning and intricate embroidered textiles I had ever seen.

One day around this time, after a long day of trekking, I remember sitting at a cafe in Bắc Hà with muddy shoes, a cold beer in my hand, and exhilaration running through my veins from a day on the road. I jotted down some ideas and sketches in my journal.

Most of them were chicken scratchings, but the one doodle I circled, underlined, and bolded was to "Collaborate with artisans worldwide to combine their traditional handmade textiles with high-tech bags and backpacks." Eureka!

I remember being so inspired by the cultural interactions I was having during that trip that a wave of emotion washed over me. I felt an overwhelming sense of collective creativity to celebrate traditional craft and culture and share this love far and wide. But as things turned out, that idea sat in my notebook for three years, gathering dust.

The fourth waypoint took place one week in 2010. I was looking to buy a backpack for myself, something I never really had to do in most of my adult life because I was a bag designer for six years and always used samples from bags I was developing and testing. When I decided to buy my own, I couldn't find anything that met my needs but, more importantly, embodied my values. I need variety in my life to stay inspired and express myself, and I cringed at the idea that I'd have to spend so much money on a bag that always looked the same. I searched long and hard for something customizable — nothing. I also wanted something environmentally friendly, socially responsible, and that looked unique. I kept coming up empty-handed. I remember thinking, fuck it. I'll just design it myself. I have contacts at factories and sample rooms in Vietnam; it could work! Then, the idea that I scribbled in my notebook all those years ago shot right back into my head with such clarity and electricity that I might as well have shot laser beams out of my eyes.

I spent nights and weekends after my day job designing what is now known as the Raja Pack. After several months of iteration, I was delighted with the design. It had checked all the boxes for the backpack I wanted and couldn't find anywhere else. I had what I felt confident could be the best backpack for the planet. Or at least something very different and unique to me.

After shopping my bag samples around to other people, it seemed to have the potential to become a business. Not all feedback was positive, though. Fellow bag designers told me the combination of soft, natural hand-loomed cotton fabrics and stiff, waterproof nylon and polyester tech fabrics felt mismatched and might cause complications and quality issues in the future. Other logistics colleagues said the artisan supply chain in the locations where I wanted to work would be a nightmare and should be avoided. I remember someone saying if this idea were feasible, someone would have already done it. I used that skeptical but valid feedback as fuel and went for it anyway.

I borrowed some money from my parents and grandparents, combined that with my life savings, and got to work. I registered the company in Pasadena, California, took many photos and videos of the product in use, built a website and a press release, and launched Ethnotek in July 2011. We got lots of press right out of the gate. The media loved the artisan story. The bags were customizable and looked so different from everything else on the market.

Two weeks after launching, I got calls from two well-known national outdoor and lifestyle retailers, REI (Recreational Equipment Incorporated) and Urban Outfitters, who wanted to carry our line. Wowza!

Let's back up a bit before the launch for full transparency. I wanted to be honest with my boss and tell him about my burgeoning artisan company idea. My plan, which I communicated to him, was to honor his business and my job with him and only work on Ethnotek on the weekends so I wasn't distracted. I told him on a Friday afternoon and was fired Monday morning. In hindsight, he did me the biggest favor anyone could have at that early stage because it forced me to be all in. I had no choice.

So that's a neatly packaged bio of who I am and how I ventured into the artisan bag space. While it's a strange and rewarding feeling to look back, I hope it also sets us up nicely for getting to know me a little bit as we head off on this journey together.

Before we get into it, let me tell you what this book is not. It's not a how-to book or an instructional manual. It's not a beat-my-own-chest book about how great Ethnotek is as a company and how we got everything right. It's not that because we are not that. We (I) made many mistakes starting, creating, building, and managing Ethnotek, but all those are learnings worth sharing.

This is an unconventional guidebook, but it's the truth. That said, it's not a memoir, far from it! I hope it's a book of learning that can be a valuable and actionable resource for readers. Dog-ear it, use it, trash it, carry it, please use it however it may serve you. That's my only wish.

This book also serves a slightly selfish purpose. To examine and explore why Ethnotek succeeded despite its many challenges, setbacks, and seemingly odd pairing of materials in its products and complicated supply chain. What made it tick, how did it work, and how did we endure so many problems, avoid backlash, and come out ahead? How the hell did this happen? Surely, there's a replicable recipe somewhere that can also benefit others. Maybe. We shall see.

From that initial sketch in my notebook in 2007 to today, Ethnotek has more than 150,000 loyal customers across 52 countries. We're collaborating with over 500 artisans in five countries and have generated over US$10 million in revenue. Not bad for an idea that a dirtbag hiker with muddy boots scribbled down in his notebook while sipping a beer far from home. This book is for the creative misfits who can and will do the same.

Jake Orak
Founder of Ethnotek
2024

1

Be The Only

"In a world full of pebbles, dare to be a diamond."

— Matshona Dhliwayo

Salt Lake City, Utah
2012

We made it! The thought floated into my mind as I stared in awe at the long line of customers still waiting patiently at our booth at the end of a long, exhilarating day. It was the moment the realization hit me that people *really* wanted what we were selling. When fear and anxiety transformed into confidence and optimism for the future, it was also the day I learned one of the most valuable lessons on my Ethnotek journey: **Don't Be Different, Be The Only**.

This lesson would stay with me long after this joyous moment in our company's history, which materialized like magic at the Outdoor Retailer trade show in Salt Lake City, a destination that would have great meaning on the Ethnotek journey even if I didn't know it at the time.

It was our first-ever trade show, with a lot of nervous preparation and a bumpy road trip across the country that ended with a broken-down van we had to abandon. We spent money we didn't have and invested a lot of sweat and effort to get our brand and team out West. Would the gamble pay off? I had no clue.

Thankfully, the existential dread and cash concerns — *how the heck are we gonna pay for this trade show?* — immediately subsided upon arrival at our booth on the first morning. I remember it like it was yesterday. It was 8:30 am, and the show officially opened in thirty minutes. Our small ragtag team of Megan, Steph, Josh, Brad, Aaron, and I wandered through the huge conference center's labyrinth wearing colorful Ethnotek-branded T-shirts. As we rounded the last corner, we all stopped in our tracks. A crowd had gathered near our small booth. At first, we thought they must be queuing for one of our exhibitor neighbors, but as we got closer, we saw it was for us. We tried to play it cool and greeted the people who had arrived early and patiently waited, looking eager to talk to someone — to us!

As our team began to mingle and chat with the waiting crowd, I noticed a magazine on our table that wasn't there the previous night. It was the trade show publication *OR Daily*, and a little colorful flag was sticking out from one of the pages. I instinctively turned to it and couldn't believe my eyes. It was a full two-page spread, followed by three more pages highlighting our company as the featured brand of the new exhibitor hall. Holy shit! This would explain the curious crowd waiting for us. We knew about this publication and that copies were delivered to key buyers' hotel rooms the morning before the show started. A few weeks earlier, we submitted a multi-page press release and some lifestyle and product photos to the show organizers, but we had never heard back and forgotten about it until that morning.

Five Japanese men standing first in line at our booth were the earliest of the early birds holding copies of our brand catalog with some dog-eared pages — yet another great sign! We had left out a stack of brand catalogs the night before, and these fine gentlemen hadn't hesitated to grab some copies and find what they were looking for.

Our operations and customer service guy, Josh, first greeted the exceptionally polite Japanese group. They handed him the catalog and said simply, "We like your bags. We're one of Japan's biggest outdoor distributors, and here's our test order. We hope you'll consider us to be your exclusive distributor in Japan."

Then they walked away. After a quick Google search, we discovered they were massive. A&F Corporation was the name on their card, and we later found out that the man who did the talking was Mr. Akatsu himself (the "A" in A&F Corporation), which was a huge honor for us to have the owner so excited about our brand. At the end of a whirlwind day and incredible turnout, our finance guy at the time, Brad, crunched the numbers.

"Guys, we just made US$12,000!" he said, looking at us with excitement and shock.

"Holy shit!" was all I could reply. This was beyond anything we could have hoped for from our first-ever trade show.

It was also a fun moment because just before the show, Brad had been freaking out about how expensive it was to exhibit and that we couldn't afford it, which, to be honest, he was right. We spent 90% of our available cash and took a huge gamble. I remember his warning to me.

"Jake, this isn't like that movie *Field Of Dreams*, where if you build it, they will come. We have to be smart."

But I felt in my gut it was the right thing to do. We needed some international exposure, and the show was where that might happen. It was a great opportunity for someone to discover us.

Brad looked up at me, still holding the US$12,000 invoice, and I winked back.

"I told you so," I said.

We both laughed, and in true Japanese fashion, he bowed at me ceremoniously. You gotta love the magic and adrenaline that keep the good vibes flowing in the early start-up days.

Those first orders paid for the whole trade show for us. From that moment on, we could breathe a sigh of relief. Our only job for the next few days was to have fun and share Ethnotek's story — a new one-of-a-kind brand working with artisans worldwide to create truly unique products.

The orders kept coming, and so did the hype. The next day, we had another press write-up, and people loved hanging out with us at our booth. We pumped music and kept the good vibes flowing as more people came to mingle with the happy-go-lucky Minnesotans. They mainly came because we had products unlike anyone had seen before and were creating media buzz at the show. That was partly due to our incredible marketing gals at the time, Megan and Steph, who were actively crawling the show, recruiting people with their magnetic personalities to come check us out.

Another massive help was that we also had the street-cred of customers like REI and Urban Outfitters carrying our line, who had signed up the previous year (more on them in a minute). Yet, despite having these big retailers on our customer list, I was still blown away by the quantity and quality of the media exposure and the genuine interest and enthusiasm from people who discovered our brand for the first time at the show. They were excited and inspired by what we were doing, which begs the question, *why*?

The reason was because we were offering something entirely fresh in the market. Since inception, we had garnered media exposure due to our business model and unique bags, meaning journalists who would generally hard-pass on promoting commercial enterprises were happy to write about us because of our artisan mission. Our story was hopeful, colorful, new, and exciting, plus the products spoke for themselves. Right off the bat, the incredible media buzz was further proof-of-concept that people were excited about what we were creating. It was another lesson learned early on that building the mission into the product itself is not only desirable, but it's also what resonates with people. We weren't delivering the journalists' marketing speak. We were giving them a true story about a company launching something never seen before that was on a great mission to promote artisans' work. We simply showed them what we were doing. Show, don't tell, as the idiom goes.

A good question to stop and think about is *why* we were seen as a new and exciting brand and *how* we achieved this. It comes back to my first point at the beginning of this chapter: Don't Be Different, Be The Only. At a big-picture level, this idea begins by embracing the concept of **Interfusing**, which can help your business carve out a niche by being the only one doing what you are doing. This has the potential to revolutionize your brand and the industry.

It means to be truly original, don't compete. Create new categories and business threads born from a place of originality. In fact, some of the world's greatest innovations were born of seemingly weird combinations of things that didn't belong together; and yet combined, they created something world-changing.

Looking at Interfusing through the lens of our brand, Ethnotek is the fusion of two entities: "ethnology" and "technology." Ethnology is a branch of anthropology that analyzes cultures, especially their historical development. Meanwhile, technology is the study and constant evolution of techniques, tools, and machines that allow us to achieve practical goals and play an essential role in our daily lives.

My eureka moment to combine these two disciplines after that long, sweaty day's hike through the muddy trails of the Bắc Hà highlands years earlier was only the beginning of our company's journey along the beautiful and scenic path of Interfusing.

But from day one of the inception of our company, this seemingly strange but wonderful combination sparked interest, curiosity, and demand for what we produced. We weren't different. We were the only ones doing what we were doing. And sometimes, to find a slice of success in a highly competitive world, being different simply isn't enough. Sometimes, you must find your own untrodden path to blaze a trail.

Because we were the only brand making customizable backpacks, combining artisan textiles with tech fabrics and high-end features, this simple yet powerful merging of ideas had a wide-reaching effect on all areas of our business, just like it can for yours, too, if you embrace this often overlooked yet impactful concept of Interfusing.

First, our unique example of Interfusing created magic that all start-up brands need: **Media Buzz**, just like the first trade show example at Salt Lake City.

But the show wasn't the first time we had received Media Buzz. It's just a great example to highlight how our Interfusing product philosophy won us media coverage that translated directly into real-world excitement and direct sales, all in a matter of hours! That's the power that a compelling and authentic story can have for a start-up business in the early days.

In fact, our first exposure to media buzz happened a year earlier. It seemed too easy, and I was as surprised as anyone to read the headlines. One month before Ethnotek's company launch, I sent out press releases to all of my favorite design and travel blogs with the hook that they'd be the first to write about our unique company. Our mission and product struck a chord with them, and all the media I pitched published our story the week we launched. Some early publications that helped us get on the map were the *Matador Network*, *Huffington Post*, *Bless This Stuff*, *Carryology*, *Vita.MN*, The Star Tribune, *LosAngelist*, *Thrillist*, *Examiner*, *Green Global Travel*, *Digital Trends*, *Change Creator*, and so many more.

This initial exposure for our launch led to one of the best phone calls I have ever received. I remember the day well, July 17th, 2011. I was pacing around my tiny apartment in Pasadena, California, slurping the first of my morning coffees when the phone rang. It was an unknown number. The friendly voice that greeted me on the other end of the line was a mythical hero figure (or, in the bag world, as close as it gets to one).

The caller introduced himself as Russell Fine, a product manager in charge of buying decisions for the travel department at REI! He spelled out the acronym (although he didn't need to) as Recreational Equipment Incorporated. I wanted to say, "Yeah, dude, I know who you guys are; I pretty much live in your store!"

Finding my composure, I asked how I could help. The next few minutes were a blur. Russell and his team had seen the Ethnotek media exposure. REI was in. They loved the mission, the freshness, the color, the story. As it turned out, he called me while on a family vacation because his friend sent him a link to one of the blogs that published us on launch week, and he wanted to jump on the distribution opportunity.

After a brief chat, he said, "Let's have a proper in-depth meeting when I'm back in the office next week, and don't move forward with any other outdoor retailer until then. We have big plans for your brand!"

"Amazing," I said as coolly as humanly possible before ending the call and dancing around my living room in my undies —woohoooo!

In the days following that monumental call for our little brand, I started researching moving companies to transport my life and Ethnotek inventory back to Minnesota. I then moved back into my parent's basement to save money and put every penny back into the company. Keep in mind that, as shared earlier, at this time I had just been fired from my day job. Despite being jobless, I was on a high after the REI call. They were one of North America's biggest and most well-respected outdoor retailers, and they had just become our first-ever Business-to-Business (B2B) account after that glorious early morning phone call—all thanks to the incredible media exposure due to our Interfusing approach when creating our unique products. Sometimes, in business, that's how simple big things can happen. And it was all because what we were offering was new, and the only ones doing what we were doing.

A few weeks later, now back home in Minnesota to bootstrap the company, I got a similar call from an equally enthusiastic buyer for Urban Outfitters, a big-box lifestyle fashion retailer similar in size to REI. Shortly after the call, they became our second B2B account. My head was spinning. Things were getting real serious, real fast!

Other than media buzz, in the early days of Ethnotek, our Interfusing approach opened many doors for our business. **Customer Engagement** was a huge one. Following the great media coverage, as more people learned about our brand mission, this created excitement and a growing base of fans who quickly became loyal customers, which grew into a vibrant community that fully embraced and appreciated the fresh approach we were bringing to the market. This initial excitement and connection ignited the spark that has kept the passion alight to this day, both inside and outside Ethnotek, from our team and ever-growing community. People really do love it when a newcomer on a mission brings fresh ideas to a crowded marketplace.

Consequently, our Interfusing philosophy also had the unknown (at the time) effect of inspiring a process of natural selection when finding the **Right Partners**, especially B2B. This was simply because they came to us, pulled by the originality and values we were communicating. The products spoke for themselves, and the right distributors listened to what we had to say, which had many knock-on benefits and saved us so much time and effort. We got the distributors who loved what we were doing, which meant they were excited about the brand and products, which filtered down to the customers and helped create lasting relationships with shared values at heart from the get-go. That's a perfect partnership.

Another positive effect our Interfusing philosophy had on our business was that we showed that we were a company that valued creative expression of art and traditional handcraft, which created an emotional bond and positioned us as a business for good.

But if all this talk of Interfusing sounds too good to be true, you don't need to take my word for it because **History Repeats**! We need only look at the origin of history's greatest, most innovative inventions to find evidence. A big one is the printing press.

In the pre-15th century, all books were laboriously written by hand or printed with ink and stamped woodblocks. But around 1450, in Strasbourg, a German inventor and craftsman, Johannes Gutenberg, was about to change the world. He asked the question: What if combining a novel printing method with a moveable type was possible?

His solution was to couple (Interfuse) the flexibility of a coin punch with the power of a wine press. His invention transformed moveable-type printing forever, allowing for the mass production of books and the subsequent proliferation of knowledge and ideas spreading throughout the Western World. In terms of revolutionizing communication, only the invention of the Internet comes close, and to this day, Gutenberg is regarded as one of history's most influential inventors. All because of two disparate ideas, magnetized to smash together and create something new. That's innovation and Interfusing at its best.

So, how do we begin to think about Interfusing? A great way to generate original ideas for your business is to look for weird combinations. Most new ideas are blends of other ideas. So, spending time getting lost in research, sketching, and imagining how to mix your products or services with those from different industries, sectors, markets, causes, genres, flavors, whatever, no matter how crazy — just let the ideas flow. Take a product and think of an absurd way to make it work.

Here's one **Recent Example** I love from TOMS shoes. I've long been a fan of their ethos, work, and products. The founder, Blake Mycoskie's, vision also inspired some aspects of Ethnotek. Launched in 2006, TOMS interfused the classic Argentine *alpargata* shoe design with a unique One for One® giving model. The idea came when Mycoskie traveled through Argentina and met a woman volunteering to deliver shoes to children. After encountering many shoeless children and learning of the many associated health implications, he had the idea to launch a range of traditional-style *alpargata* shoes into the American market and then donate profits back to communities needing footwear in Argentina and other countries worldwide. TOMS also pioneered the One for One® model, giving away a pair of shoes for every pair sold. This model has since been adopted by many other product-based social enterprises worldwide. Today, TOMS gives away one-third of its profits for grassroots good causes, including significant investment in mental health initiatives. We've always appreciated this example at Ethnotek because Mycoskie's original idea shows the concept of Interfusing beyond a manufacturing technique or product itself. Coupling the sale of a product with a charity model works just as well. While TOMS has faced backlash for putting local shoemakers out of business as an unintended consequence of its giving model, it's made solid efforts to balance that out. Its giving model has expanded to support many social justice and environmental causes, which still perfectly embodies its Interfusing method and core values.

Now let's shift perspective as we wander further along the Interfusing trail to wade into the **Law of Category** and **Blue Ocean Strategy**.

One of the most influential business books I've ever read is *The 22 Immutable Laws of Marketing* by Al Ries and Jack Trout. The laws that stuck with me the most were **Category**, **Mind**, and **Line Extension.** The Law of Category highlights that being first in conventional business thinking is best. But being first-to-market is very hard to do, and it is also risky. Even if you are the first, the world might not be ready and may need time to catch up. Remember that there were many MP3 players and smartphones before the iPod and iPhone, and social networks before Facebook, Instagram, and TikTok. Instead of racing to be the revolutionary first, create a new category or niche to be first in — be different! This concept helped me immensely in my early days as a designer, kept me grounded, and pushed aside any worries about rushing to be first. It also served as a springboard to another hugely helpful idea I stumbled upon one day from Kevin Kelly: "Don't aim to be the best. Be the only." In my opinion, the most effective way to be different and Be The Only is by bundling (Interfusing) seemingly disparate things together, where the sum of its parts becomes something entirely new.

Our Ethnotek customers didn't know they wanted a super colorful, high-quality laptop and travel bag that supported artisans and traditional crafts worldwide until our bags came on the scene. Essentially, we invented new demand and supplied it perfectly. Sure, it was a gamble on something highly specialized, unproven, and, at its beginning stage, a tiny or non-existent demographic, but it worked and quickly spread like wildfire.

As I mentioned in the introduction, I wasn't being smart. It wasn't a conscious and carefully plotted business strategy at the time. I was just trying to design a better bag and was lucky to receive a eureka moment that merged two ideas. Yet today, in hindsight, I realize that while it may have seemed like pure coincidence and luck that I stumbled upon my Interfusing idea for Ethnotek, I had laid the groundwork for the sparks to catch fire. All my time researching, traveling, learning new design skills, sourcing materials, drawing, doodling, and writing — were all keys to unlocking the muse. So, a key takeaway is that finding your eureka moments may take a deep dive into the creative ideation space. For you, maybe that requires a trip, research, or scouting mission —whatever opens your mind and ignites your imagination to find your own Be The Only moment.

In the early days of Ethnotek, I was also deeply inspired by the Blue Ocean Strategy, pioneered by Chan Kim and Renée Mauborgne, which also aligns with Kevin Kelly's Be The Only concept. It's about creating and capturing uncontested market space, making the competition irrelevant.

Red Oceans represent all industries today, the known market space. They are the industry boundaries that are defined and accepted and where the competitive rules of the game are known. Companies try to outperform their rivals to grab a more significant share of existing demand. As the market space gets crowded, profits and growth reduce. Products become commodities, leading to cutthroat or bloody competition. Hence, the pretty morbid term Red Oceans.

Blue Oceans, in contrast, are much more to our liking at Ethnotek. They denote all the industries not in existence today — the unknown market space, untainted by competition. In Blue Oceans, demand is created rather than fought over. There is ample opportunity for profitability and rapid growth. Competition is irrelevant because the rules of the game are waiting to be set. A Blue Ocean is an analogy to describe the broader, more profound potential in unexplored market space.

This concept further points to the idea that while being different is good, being the only one doing what you do is best. If developed, designed, and integrated into the business properly, this is the number-one leverage your entire new brand can springboard from. So remember, Blue Oceans represent freedom, smooth sailing, and rapid growth, while Red Oceans represent swimming with blood-thirsty monsters in the crowded shallows. Easy choice, right?

In the case of Ethnotek, I bundled the things I valued and couldn't find in the marketplace: high-tech backpack + customizable + artisan-made fabric = a new niche. This paved the way for us to have leverage in sales negotiations to dictate our lead times, terms, pricing, and payment methods, all of which broke fast-fashion industry standards and helped us push out into that beautiful big Blue Ocean of uncontested market space. Our simple Interfusing equation created ripples that led to our company enjoying creative freedom, prosperity, and longevity until today. So, if I haven't said it enough, friends, please consider Interfusing as a primary point of ideation in the early stages of your business.

But before we leave Interfusing and head off to explore new horizons, I have one last relevant story to share for this chapter. It was a Minnesota morning not long after the first trade show. I was doing some snooping (I mean research) at a local REI store that just happened to stock our Ethnotek bags. This was also when our bags had been given the prestigious end-cap position in the store, usually reserved for big-name brands — a huge honor for our small startup brand at the time. As I wandered into the bag area, I was happily surprised to see a young lady holding one of our Raja Pack backpacks and studying it with curiosity and interest. As I hid behind a clothes rack like a total creep, I watched the scene play out as an REI staff member, who may have been in her late 50s, with a bob of blonde hair and some well-earned wrinkles at the side of her eyes (that said she laughed a lot and spent many a day outdoors) strolled up to the customer and asked her if she had heard of this new brand, Ethnotek.

"Their bags are one-of-a-kind," she said, smiling, as she ripped off the front Thread panel, which made a delightful *kkkkkrrrriiiissshhh* sound that tough Velcro makes.

"This is their Thread system," she added as she replaced the front panel with a different-colored one, handwoven by another of our Ethnotek artisan partners.

"And just like that, it's a different bag!" the staff member added.

I watched the *ah-ha* moment wash across this young customer's face as she realized she could change the Thread to any number of other artisan handmade ones. The staff member then explained that the backpack is super rugged, water-resistant, laptop-compatible, and great for travel.

"Ethnotek also works with traditional handweaving artisans worldwide."

I heard the customer say, "Wow, cool," and a big smile spread across her face.

"I'll take one," was her sweet reply.

That was, and still is, one of my career's proudest and most rewarding moments. Even though I was being a weirdo-fly-on-the-wall, we had a moment. The brand, story, product, seller, customer (and shy creator) danced in that moment. This brief encounter was also further validation that our Thread system was special.

As we leave our brief exploration of Be The Only, I hope I've given you a few insights into our Interfusing philosophy at Ethnotek and why we feel it's been so crucial to our prolonged success. What it is, why it worked, and the positive (and far-reaching) effect it has had on our brand, business, artisans, customers, and community —and continues to do so to this day. I firmly believe this approach was one of the pillars of positivity for us and will continue to be going forward. And so, for those inside our organization and our wider community, or anyone looking to start a new business, I urge you to consider this approach, too. As you've read, I can attest that it can lead to many wonderful destinations.

When I think back to the moment all those years ago to the Salt Lake City first trade show, I can't help but smile. There are many photos from that event, and when I look at that fresh-faced entrepreneur and our team, who are all excited, I see the long road we've been on, and I'm filled with pride. I still remember the shock and joy of that long line of customers, distributors, and attendees swarming around our booth, each filled with excitement at the new, exciting brand with the artisan fabric bags. That kind of validation was, and is to this day, heartwarming, and I will never forget it.

Looking back also makes everything seem so clear. Embodying the Be The Only concept helped set us apart from the get-go, allowing us to head in our own direction. So I say don't compete. Don't even be different. You, me, and we, as socially minded business people, must think outside the box and Be The Only ones doing what we are doing. Walk to your own beat and keep the independent mindset close to hand as we head into a new community-focused territory on the next destination of our Ethnotek story: **Take Leadership From Those You Seek To Benefit.**

2

Take Leadership From Those You Seek To Benefit

"Wisdom is the reward you get for a lifetime of listening when you'd have preferred to talk."

— Doug Larson

Bhujodi, India
2015

I sat cross-legged on the floor of Shamji's workshop, eyeing the many colorful fabrics blanketing the small space in a mesmerizing veil of geometric patterns. I had come to know and love this place after many sourcing trips to meet with this legendary man, whom I was now proud to call my friend.

Shamji Valji was the head weaver for the Ethnotek India team and one of the most experienced artisans of his craft in Bhujodi. He always wore a neatly trimmed mustache that bordered an ever-present smile. His good nature and infectious laugh always kept spirits high among his team.

Wafts of fresh spices and woodfire smoke filled the air as early evening sunlight poured through the open windows. I shared stories about how our loyal customers loved the artisans' latest handmade threads and designs, and the weavers listened intently. As I took another long sip of steaming hot *chai masala* tea, Shamji motioned for me to join him on the far side of the small workshop. He seemed to have something on his mind.

"Jake, we are struggling to keep up with your fabric orders. Is it possible to change to small quarterly orders instead of big semi-annual ones?" he asked, looking concerned.

While this may sound like a small request, it had profound business implications at the time. We had been operating on big, bulk orders since the beginning of our relationship with Shamji and his team. Changing our orders could scare off distribution partners who relied on consistent stock to meet customer demand. But I had already made my decision.

"We can do it, Shamji," I said, secretly having no clue how we would make this work with our distributors. But I knew we had to find a way because Shamji only ever asked me for things he really needed. If it weren't important, he wouldn't have asked. And so the second he expressed his concerns, I knew that if I didn't act in our partnering weavers' best interests, I could not justify my position as a company leader who puts "artisan-made" and "pride" at the heart of our business and mission.

I also knew that if I didn't react to this red flag Shamji was waving, I would put him and his team under more pressure, and our relationship would suffer. I was not going to let that happen. I thanked Shamji for his simple request and agreed to make it work, pushing aside (for now) the real implications this might have on orders.

And so it was on this day that Shamji taught me an invaluable business lesson that would guide my relationship with the artisans we have worked with for many years: **Take Leadership From Those You Seek To Benefit.**

Understanding the root of Shamji's conflict he was facing is a great place to begin our exploration of this idea. During our candid discussion that day in his workshop, he walked me through his weaving teams' current work processes, painting a picture of their entire operation as it was today, not as it had been when we began working together a few years earlier. While I had become familiar with the intricacies of his operation, the cultural and business practices, and the beautiful surrounding region's vibrant weaving trade, I had missed something important. I had failed to understand how our existing seasonal order structure and payment methods affected the whole ecosystem and livelihood of Shamji's team. This realization only became clear because he voiced his concerns.

Midway through our discussion, I realized that Shamji had been building me up for this news for a few days. Before I visited him and the team, he suggested I stop by our yarn dyers in Ahmedabad along with our export and logistics partner, Ashok. I had dutifully agreed, always eager for more facetime with our artisan partners. So, a few days earlier, after a long flight from Ho Chi Minh City to Ahmedabad, I found myself sitting in Ashok's living room.

Ashok (at the time) was a semi-retired air freight coordinator at Ahmedabad Airport who moonlighted as an exporter of handmade artisanal Indian textiles. He had been working with Ethnotek for six years. He was a reliable, highly knowledgeable in-country partner who understood the history, cultural significance, and nuances of ethical business with artisans in this region. As we spent the day getting to know each other better, Ashok explained the various steps in his process and the challenges he encountered sourcing threads. He taught me about his method of gathering materials from weavers throughout the Kutch desert region where Shamji's team was based, arranging customs IMPEX (import-export) documentation, trucking, payment transfers, taxation, and much more, which gave me a new appreciation for the work he and his partner, Purnima, put into every pre-production material delivery we received from them on the other end at our production workshop Vietnam. At the end of an eye-opening day with Ashok, I had a much clearer understanding of his job and the details of his days spent helping us to export Shamji and his team's beautiful textiles.

After leaving Ashok, I took a rickshaw ride across town to visit our yarn dyers. They gave me a tour of their facility, showing me their gigantic machines that thread raw cotton and yarn spools, the dying vats, and the meticulously formulated dye chemistry they use to match the color guidebook that Shamji had created especially for them. Finally, the dyers educated me about their farm, where their cotton was organically grown, and then sent me on my way with a garbage bag full of dyed yarn spools to deliver to Shamji.

After an overnight bus journey from Ahmedabad to Bhuj, I arrived bleary-eyed at a deserted bus terminal just after sunrise, checked into my hostel, and had a shower and a bite to eat before meeting up with our facilitator, Pankaj. The two of us shared a rickshaw to Shamji's home in the Bhujodi village. By the time I knocked on his door, I was exhausted but exhilarated with a whole new appreciation for Shamji, his team, and the lengths they went to ensure what they produced and exported was of the highest quality while maintaining the traditional weaving methods that meant so much to them — and all of us at

Ethnotek. And so, by the time the steaming cups of *masala* tea were served, as the sun sank lower and the day turned to dusk when we finally sat around and talked business, Shamji's request was ready to be made, and my mind was already made up. And this was all because Shamji simply and powerfully showed me the way and opened the door to understanding his weaving world.

Shamji's story highlights the key lesson I want to share in this chapter: Take Leadership From Those You Seek To Benefit. His simple decision to show me instead of telling me his issue with our current product orders changed everything in our relationship and benefited our business for years to come.

Later in the evening, as Shamji and I drank more tea late into the night at his workshop, we had a long chat about the future of our business together. He walked through the timelines he was working with. The spooling and dying process took three to four weeks before final color checking and loom setup. Then, it took another week to deliver the dyed yarn to each of the home workshops of the artisans who carried out the weaving. Finally, it took a further week to set up the loom combs* and shedders*, which only Shamji could do due to its complexity.

All the steps in the process had to be perfectly executed; otherwise, the motifs in the finished textile would be off. After the loom was set up, one artisan could weave up to two meters daily. At that time, they were working on a 2,000-meter order for Ethnotek, which would take 33 months to complete for a single weaver. However, Shamji led a sizable interconnected community of weavers between the Bhujodi, Kandherai, Varnora, and Jambudhi villages that could handle the large volume we needed. Despite using additional weavers, the team was maxed out to complete our huge orders, causing delays for their other customers.

On the one hand, I felt proud that an idea I scribbled in a notebook all those years ago significantly impacted employment in the region. At the same time, I felt an uncomfortable pang in my stomach that I was unknowingly overworking them. I shamefully expressed this feeling to Shamji, who reassured me it was okay. He was handling it to ensure there wasn't stress on the workers, but he said with a long pause, "It's not sustainable, so we need to make a new plan."

Shamji's proposal was simple. Instead of placing large semi-annual fabric orders like we had been doing, we should make smaller quarterly ones and provide him with a seasonal forecast so they could prepare materials and workforce in advance.

Reiterating the problem, he told me his team of weavers were struggling to complete the large orders in such a short amount of time. Also, the long gaps between those orders meant their looms were maxed out for half the year and empty for the other half. He proposed keeping the looms in use for 10–12 months and requiring fewer finished meters per weaver to better balance their daily tasks with family, spiritual practices, tending livestock, and weaving for different customers.

"That sounds like a plan," I said as we shook hands on the decision.

To this day, I'm so grateful that Shamji and I had established enough trust for him to feel safe enough to propose the restructure. Because, to be fair, it wouldn't be easy for us to pull it off. Changing our production cycle with the factory in Vietnam and the purchase order dynamic with our B2B customers would be challenging and risky because we could lose business. Still, I was 100% committed to making it work. After all, it's why Ethnotek is in business in the first place: To be of service to our artisan partners, first and foremost.

Let's back up for a minute to explain where this pressure on the weavers originated. Usually, big retailers and distributors have two big seasons per year (Fall-Winter and Spring-Summer), and they hold all the leverage because of their buying power. Fast-fashion standards usually dictate lead times of 30–90 days from purchase order to delivered goods and net 30–120 payment terms, meaning that the buyer doesn't have to pay a thing until 30–120 days after you deliver the goods to them. This is fine for well-established brands with deep pockets, but for a tiny basement company like ours, it stretched us to the limits in the early days of Ethnotek.

Similarly, these big-box retailers minimize operational risk by requiring the brand to warehouse its entire order after it ships from the factory and deliver it in smaller periodic shipments to its distribution centers nationwide. Net payment terms only kick in after each of those smaller shipments are sent over several months. This can sometimes mean the brand isn't fully paid for an order until a year after producing the goods. We had to take out high-interest invoice-factoring loans, find a temporary warehouse, and learn new EDM (Electronic Data Management) systems to get our bags into the coveted big-name stores and prove to the world that we could handle it. We could meet these demands for a few years but subsequently had to walk away. It was too much for us to handle financially and put too much strain on our artisan partners. Hence, what eventually happened with Shamji and his team of weavers.

Side note: I am not putting our USA retailers (REI and Urban Outfitters) mentioned above in a bad light. On the contrary, it was simply a case of us trying to grow too big and fast and paying the price by putting strain on our artisan partners. It's just simply how big retailers work. They have an ordering system and are used to working with large, bulk orders from non-artisan-focused brands. But that wasn't us! And so trying to keep pace with the bulk orders soon began to expose cracks in our business model.

Many big retailers worldwide also operate on a payment structure incompatible with our company mission. Before publicly launching Ethnotek, I told our artisan partners that we'd pay them a 50% deposit in advance so they didn't have to finance materials and labor for our orders and a 50% balance payment immediately after receiving their fabrics at our production workshop in Vietnam. We held to this standard even when the early big customers didn't want to match that, and we still do to this day.

After my discussion with Shamji, I started enforcing a new B2B rule: payment terms from retailers and distributors that mirrored our payment terms with artisans. I also enforced delivery lead times to match what the artisans requested, which meant nearly tripling lead times. A couple of years after rolling with these more balanced terms, I stretched it even further by requiring our retail customers to forecast their semi-annual orders and place deposits on artisan fabric per those forecasts every quarter. We lost 90% of our customers due to these unique and demanding terms.

Our Japanese and German distributors went with the flow on this, so I knew we were in a game of quality over quantity. We just had to find the right partners who shared our core values and were open to taking the risk to make culture, artisan empowerment, and our colorful bags a part of their business. And though it took time, our strong approach worked.

This pivotal change to our business model was a game-changing move that allowed us to remove bottlenecks and strain throughout the supply chain and scale the business globally. After the new flow gathered momentum, things became relaxed and fun. This release of pressure freed us to do what we do best: create and inspire!

Shamji's request had many unintended benefits for Ethnotek. We gained valuable lessons that helped guide future decisions. One game-changer was the realization that by staying true to our mission, a natural selection process filtered retailers and distributors, meaning **The Good Ones Stay.** This is by no means to say that the retailers we lost were bad, but they weren't the right fit for us at that stage of our business.

And so, despite losing nearly all of our B2B accounts due to our restructured order and payment terms with our artisan partners, those two incredible distributors (A&F Corporation and Gustavo Trading) who stuck by us like glue formed an even stronger, unbreakable bond. They not only supported our new terms, but because of our commitment to the cause, they upped their orders while also being flexible and working with us to keep the pressure off the artisan supply chain and the good vibes flowing — even more validation that our risk was worthwhile. And what was the effect? Well, you can bet the team and I bent over backward to deliver on our promise after they agreed to inconvenience their business and take on a financial burden to benefit our artisan partners. Genuine shared-value partnerships are formed through equal sacrifice for a greater good and shared mission.

Sometimes, in business, it's not all about what you get right; it's about what you get wrong and the learnings from those misadventures that provide a springboard for new realization, opportunities, and self-growth. That's why **Realizing Mistakes,** especially with relationships, has been such a powerful opportunity for us as a company. In the case of Shamji and the Vankar community weavers between 2010–2015, I didn't understand their process enough to plan our sales seasons and mass production in Vietnam. I was simply conforming to industry standards. This required our B2B customers to forecast their upcoming seasonal orders, the proportion of each fabric style they estimated ordering, and place a three-month advanced deposit to get the weavers started each quarter, which we dubbed "Bridge Orders."

This was a hard sell, but our most important customers got on board, and this reduced overall lead time by 30 days, released strain on the artisans, and increased the quality of the textiles, which saved re-weaving and shipping costs all-round. So, another key learning that I took away from this whole experience was to constantly adopt the role of a student in my relationship with our artisan partners. Getting in this mindset before each in-person visit helped so much going forward by asking questions, understanding their limitations, and learning from them, radically reshaping our business for years to come.

These small learnings turned **Ripples Into Waves**. We grew an emotional bond of understanding by investing time in understanding our artisan partners' needs, pains, concerns, worries, inspirations, motivations, and the day-to-day practicalities of running their businesses. The relationship blossomed, leading to beautiful interactions that surpassed trading partners as friendships formed. In business, that's something rare and unique. And it can happen simply by taking a minute to see the world through someone else's eyes to create a real human connection.

Now, I want to make sure that I communicate that Shamji's request to change our order regularity and quantity not only transformed our company's relationship with the Indian artisans we work with but also with *all* our partnering artisans who weave the majestic threads that we proudly carry on our products. It was a lesson that transformed ripples into waves that reached distant shorelines worldwide within the Ethnotek family. When I think about how this was made possible, it's easy to see now that Shamji set up my visit so that I would be attentive and in the role of the student, not as the buyer or owner of the company.

So, a key takeaway for me, and hopefully for all you would-be social entrepreneurs, is to **Listen More Than You Speak**. This is a valuable life skill, but it's especially relevant when working in the artisan space as a social entrepreneur. I keep this in mind whenever it's time to begin the ideation process for a new collection or order. I bring them into the idea to get their insights, and I don't work in a silo on my own, working on ideas that wouldn't fly with them or hinder their work. Quite the opposite, I listen to their opinions early on, and in turn, they appreciate being part of the creative process. On so many occasions, the Ethnotek artisans taught me invaluable lessons about their process (we deep dive into this further with the Mayan Star project in Chapter 3). And so, I developed the motto **Listen, Learn, Adapt, Be Present** on all my sourcing journeys to visit our artisan partners.

By building trust and putting our artisan partners' needs first, we helped steer clear of unintended harm and **Avoid Danger** in our business, including stress, shipping delays, negatively impacting product quality, and decreasing customer dissatisfaction or bad press.

Another benefit of this listening approach with the artisans was easing tension and bottlenecks in the supply chain. With a robust relationship built on **Transparent Communication**, ambiguities were eradicated as a natural side effect, which led to more productivity and efficiency across all aspects of our relationship. Another essential learning we adopted early on with the artisans is listening to them as business partners. This may sound simple, but I can tell you from experience that this mistake often happens in cross-cultural, socially-orientated artisan businesses. There's an issue with what I would say is the "NGO mentality factor," that is, some companies treat their in-country partners not as equals, creating a company culture of "handouts" or "we know what's best for you." When, in fact, what the in-country trade partners want is reliable business partners. This kind of misunderstanding and misframing of the relationship is bad for everyone. So, I always remember a lesson I learned long ago from our artisan partners: **We Don't Want Handouts, Thanks.**

If you take one thing away from this chapter, I hope it's this: Don't presume to know the minds of your artisans, collaborators, or partners that you do business with. As entrepreneurs, we can only learn by listening to their needs. And that takes time, in-person visits, and empathy. Also, sometimes tough decisions must be made to respect artisan relationships. Not all suppliers and distributors will want to bend from the industry standards to accommodate the needs of regional artisans. Most won't, as we learned. So, it can be difficult, costly, and painful for the business to lose those (sometimes huge) clients, but this may be necessary for the company's longevity. From the examples and stories I've shared, I hope you can also see the importance of staying true to the mission and the people who live it. This approach has served us well. Hopefully, it can be for you, too.

Thinking back to Shamji's lesson, I'm grateful to him all those years ago. It was a simple suggestion he made that could have easily been ignored on our part or perhaps unsaid by Shamji if we hadn't visited in person as much. We could have said, "No, we can't operate this way; it's not industry standard, and we'll lose customers as a result."

Alas, we didn't. We stood steadfast to our word and values and rode out the storm of lost business and a briefly bleeding bank balance. And you know what? It turned out not only okay but for the better. Our ability to stand our ground and say "no" emboldened us to our community and separated the true believers in us from those who only wanted money. After all, we're a company for artisans by artisans. And it's this simple destination where we will now turn our attention to the joy of **Celebrating Culture**.

3

Celebrate Craft & Culture

"The joy of life comes from our encounters with new experiences, and hence there is no greater joy than to have an endlessly changing horizon, for each day to have a new and different sun."

— Christopher McCandless

Bắc Hà, Vietnam
2007

The higher I hiked, the clearer-headed I felt. Misty mountain air filled my lungs, and mud squelched beneath my boots as the trail snaked through the dense forest. For the past week, I'd been cruising through the highlands around Lào Cai, Northern Vietnam, on a beat-up Russian Minsk motorbike. This morning was the pinnacle of the trip: A welcome dose of respite and a relaxing hike in the lush foothills of Mount Fansipan, Vietnam's tallest peak. The region is home to the highest population of Hmong tribes, who live scattered between the giant landmass northwest of Hanoi, between Điện Biên Phủ and Cao Bằng. It had been one of the best trips of my life—a deep immersion into the culture of this beautiful part of the world. However, nothing could have prepared me for the awe and wonder I was about to experience.

As I continued along the trail, I suddenly emerged from the cool blanket of the jungle canopy. I strolled along a breathtakingly beautiful cliffside that plunged hundreds of meters on one side down to a verdant valley awash in rice terraces. Clouds meandered their way through the scene, and playful chatter of farmers far below echoed around the valley and up to meet me. I stood there on the cliff edge, drinking it all in. I watched swirls of smoke waft out of the chimneys from tiny village homes dotting the horizon in the distance. I was so intoxicated by the scene that I didn't notice a Hmong woman had emerged from a nearby thicket and was now standing beside me, also enjoying the vista. Laughing at myself for being so startled, she smiled, and we gazed curiously at each other. She was dressed head to toe in traditional hand-embroidered clothing. Her skirt's deep indigo blue base material had subtle *batik* designs embedded into it, adorned with eye-popping detail from needle-and-thread embroidery. I later learned that making one skirt takes at least six months. Shortly after this encounter, farther along the trail, I entered a market where all the tribes from the region came to trade livestock, fruits, vegetables, tools, and crafts. It was a menagerie of colors, geometric patterns, and local dialects. I bought some handmade textiles and sat down to admire their intricacies. It was clear that I held many generations of artisanal crafts handed down through time. I felt an overwhelming appreciation for bearing witness to this celebration of culture and knew at that moment my path would lead to sharing these beautiful handmade textiles somehow, someday.

Ethnotek is a company that celebrates people and the beautiful things they create. It's really that simple. In this chapter, we'll look at how we do that, why it's essential, and what methods we use to make sure this foundation of our business continues to thrive. This chapter is also the longest in the book because it deserves to be. The artisans we partner with are the beating heart of our business, so it feels right to do a deep dive into our process of collaboration together. Also, textile sourcing is my favorite part of the work we do. So buckle up and get comfortable. We're about to take an extended adventure into the world of **Meaningful Motifs** to see the world through the eyes of the artisans we work with and learn about their stunning art and what it means. We'll follow the threads to their origin as we venture to every country and workshop with our artisan partners as we go on an exploration to **Celebrate Craft & Culture.**

A brief side note before we set off on our journey: Since Ethnotek's inception, we have worked with a diverse group of artisans (more than 500 in five countries to date). We've learned a lot and been gifted a wealth of knowledge and insights into the cultural nuances and uniqueness of each culture's textile and their meaning to the communities who create them. But over the last decade, as we've dove into the origin and evolution of each country's textiles, we've also noticed something incredible: universality. Let me explain. A common observation is that entirely different cultures, sometimes separated by centuries, continents, and oceans, have produced similar motifs. Time and time again, the motifs proudly woven into textiles echo those of distant earthly ancestors without known contact or knowledge of each other. This is a living testament to the interconnectedness of creatively inclined species. Throughout history, motifs woven into textiles have represented complex scenes from daily life to the divine. While beliefs and mythologies may differ, the motifs and symbols often possess universal themes and, in some cases, appear timeless: Designs like the star, zig zag, diamond, and stripes feature in cultures from Ancient Greece to Native America or modern-day Middle East and Asia; the list is endless. It's incredible to think about how art transcends time and space to extend a hand between generations, from the distant past to the modern day. Creative expression through symbols and textiles is woven into the fabric of human nature — a fact we at Ethnotek celebrate daily. With this in mind, we have booked a return ticket and a round-the-world art adventure ahead. First stop, Ghana!

Ghana

We arrived at Kotoka International Airport in the capital, Accra, jetlagged and with sore shoulders from the yellow fever and typhoid shots required to enter the country. I traveled with Cori, my wife at the time, and Ethnotek's accounting and community manager. After making our way through customs, we exchanged U.S. dollars for Ghanaian cedis before emerging into the blazing midday heat of Accra and a waiting crowd of yelling taxi drivers, all jostling for a fare. Instantly, our jet lag subsided, and excitement washed over us — we had arrived! A large man wearing brand new Air Jordans and a hand-dyed shirt that sparkled with geometric Adinkra patterns emerged from the crowd with a glowing smile and a welcoming hug. This was our facilitator, Reiss Niih Boafo! After years of working together, this was our first in-person meeting, and we had much to catch up on. We bundled into Reiss's car and sped off into traffic as a treasure trove of heritage, food, flavor, music, and art of one of West Africa's most vibrant cultures whizzed by the window. As Reiss drove, we chatted about his life growing up in Ghana. Born in 1987 in Kukurantumi, a small town in the Eastern Volta Region of the country, he had a pleasant childhood. His parents had worked at the hydroelectric dam in Akosombo. Reiss moved to Accra for university, where he obtained a BSC in Accounting, an MBA in Corporate Governance, and where he also taught himself web design. He followed the Christian faith, and even though his father was from the Krobo tribe, he grew up predominantly influenced by Akan cultural practices from his mother's side of the family. Reiss also spoke English and Twi, a dialect of the Akan language.

As we drove, I stared out the window and let Ghana wash over me. I'd wanted to visit for so long, and finally, we were here, in one of Africa's many beautiful countries. With its welcoming beaches on the Gulf of Guinea and borders touching the Ivory Coast, Burkina Faso, and Togo, Ghana is a land of celebration, resilience, and rich heritage. It proudly holds the title of being the first African country to break free from British colonial rule in 1957 under the inspiring leadership of Kwame Nkrumah. Ghana's compelling and challenging history was a picture of triumph over the adversities of the transatlantic slave trade. The coastal forts like Cape Coast Castle and Elmina Castle are solemn reminders of that era, now serving as meaningful educational sites and monuments of remembrance. Today, the heart of Ghana beats with music, dance, and art. The country vibrates with the rhythms of traditional ceremonies and festivals that tell stories of past generations. In parallel, Ghana's highlife, raglife, and hiplife music, a blend of local Akan rhythms, western instruments, and hip-hop influence, has captured the imagination of the nation's youth. Reiss then explained the origins of a famous Ghanaian textile we hoped to see on our sourcing trip. It was made by the Ashanti people, or Asante, a royal lineage known for its splendid gold jewelry and exquisite wood carvings. Today, their vibrant *kente* cloth, initially a royal fabric, symbolizes Ghanaian pride and identity, with each color and pattern narrating a unique tale. Reiss shared stories about his homeland with a mixture of pride and optimism. There was good reason, too. Ghana stands as a beacon of democracy and economic growth in Africa. A major cocoa producer with a booming tourism and hydroelectric power sector, it's a nation marching confidently toward a future of prosperity and equality despite its challenges. The country is a mosaic of faiths, encompassing Christianity, Islam, and traditionalist African beliefs. The traditional religions, with their reverence for a supreme deity, ancestors, and spirits, are widely worshiped across the country.

After half an hour of driving and listening to Reiss' stories, he pulled over at an open-air roadside restaurant, and we piled out. Moments later, the waiter had filled our entire table with an assortment of delicious local dishes, including *fufu* (pounded cassava dough) served with *jollof* rice and *banku* (a pillow of fermented corn and cassava flour) with tilapia fish dipped in the rich and oily dark red groundnut soup—yum! Food is definitely a reason to visit Ghana.

After stuffing our faces with some fine local fare, we hit the road again, eventually arriving at our hotel for a shower and a well-earned night's sleep. Over the next few days, we drove across the country to meet weavers. We made a long, full-day drive to Kpetoe Kene Village, near the Togo border, renowned for its traditional *kente* textiles. After a long day on the road, we were tired and groggy, but on arrival at the village, the sound of beating drums and a roaring crowd awoke us from our daze. Thankfully, we had arrived as a festival parade was in full flow. This celebration was part of the Kente Weaving Festival in Agotime, organized by the Ewe community. Reiss pulled over, and we all jumped out to follow the parade. Reiss explained that festival-goers practiced *vodun*, a form of *voodoo*, and many drank local liquor to enter an entranced state. Just then, a large procession of men dressed in vibrant red ceremonial wear danced by us, performing warrior dances and carrying village chiefs on makeshift thrones above their heads. Some waved machetes in celebration in the air. Small explosions of gunpowder crackled and fizzed like clouds of fireworks. It was an intoxicating scene, and without realizing it, I got caught up in the moment and swept away with the parade. As part of the festival, there was also a weaving competition and dance at the Grand Darbar, where all village chiefs and their entourages gathered to vote for the winner of Miss Agbamevor (Miss Kente). Thousands of people from around the region traveled for the festival, and we were so lucky to witness this once-in-a-lifetime event. We attended the festivities in the Kpetoe Village to learn about *kente*, its origins, the culture and make contacts with new weavers. We did not go away empty-handed!

The next day, we made another long, bumpy ride back to Accra because we had a meeting arranged with one of our artisan partners, Charles Acquah, whose family of weavers produced stunning handmade textiles with Ethnotek. Charles was a father of seven children from Somanya. He made textiles at his family's workshop, alongside the train tracks outside Accra with his daughter Priscilla and sons Nathaniel and Abraham. The Acquah family's primary design influence came from the *Adinkra* book of symbols, which contains a mesmerizing array of visual icons representing a fascinating intersection of history, culture, and spirituality woven into the fabric of Ghanaian life.

The story of *Adinkra* symbols began in the early 19th century with the Gyaman kingdom, which spanned parts of present-day Ghana and Côte d'Ivoire. Legend has it that these symbols were the brainchild of Gyaman King Nana Kwadwo Agyemang Adinkra. Initially, they were exclusive to royalty and used for important ceremonies, celebrations and funerals. The *Adinkra* symbols were a regal expression of philosophical thoughts and social values. The Ashanti, a prominent Akan subgroup, adopted the symbols after their encounters and conflicts with the Gyaman. This cultural exchange led to the proliferation of *Adinkra* symbols across the Akan territories, turning them into a widespread form of expression. Traditionally stamped onto fabrics with carved calabash stamps* and natural dyes, these symbols transformed everyday garments into tapestries of wisdom and storytelling.

Each *Adinkra* symbol is a galaxy of meaning, representing rich proverbs, life lessons, and philosophical ideas. Take *Gye Nyame*, for example, symbolizing God's omnipotence, a testament to the deep spirituality and reverence of the Akan people, or the *Sankofa*, which depicts a bird looking back, embodying the mantra, "Learn from the past to build the future."

These symbols are more than decoration; they are a language spoken through art and guiding principles for life, relationships, and community living. They illustrate the Akan's deep connection with the natural world, their understanding of human nature, and their quest for cosmic harmony. In Ghana, they continue to be a proud emblem of cultural identity, adorning everything from clothing and pottery to modern digital art.

Adinkra symbols joyfully celebrate Ghanaian heritage, vividly reminding us of the richness of African wisdom and the enduring power of visual storytelling. They are a bridge from the past dancing into the future, carrying with them the timeless stories and spirits of the Akan people.

Throughout Ethnotek's journey, we've launched several limited edition collections featuring *Adinkra* symbols — 24 different styles to be exact. All are sold out and now only exist with the lucky few who swooped them up when they were available years ago. Embedding these incredible motifs into fabrics is a *batik* process.

The history of *batik* in Ghana is relatively recent compared to its ancient origins in Indonesia. *Batik* was introduced to West Africa, including Ghana, in the mid-19th century, primarily through trade and interaction with the Dutch and other Europeans who brought Indonesian *batik* fabrics to the region. Ghanaians, known for their rich textile traditions, adapted and integrated these techniques, giving birth to the distinct Ghanaian *batik* style we know today.

The process of creating *batik* in Ghana is an intricate art form. It begins with the wax-resist dyeing technique, where artisans apply wax patterns onto the fabric. The waxed areas resist the dye, allowing artists to create complex, multicolored designs. Typically, a wood or foam block or a brush is used to apply the wax, enabling a variety of patterns, from traditional motifs to contemporary designs. After waxing, the fabric is then dyed using vibrant colors. Next, the wax is removed by boiling the fabric in water, revealing the resisted pattern beneath. This process can be repeated multiple times for layering colors per the artisan's preferred palette.

At the Acquah family workshop, two small wooden buildings with tin roofs border a courtyard where dyed fabrics are hung to dry in the blistering heat. Long wood tables are used for the textile stamping process. Inside the workshop, a large metal vat perpetually bubbles and boils with hot wax, and several metal drums are filled with various dye colors and water for rinsing. The workshop is always a hive of activity, as the family of artisans carry out their magical *batik*-making process.

In addition to hand-stamped *batik*, Charles and his family have also created a process called "marbling," where a sheet of raw cotton fabric is submerged in water and then scrunched up, creating a random wavy pattern. Next, multiple dye colors are squirted onto the fabric in single rows before it is finally stretched out to dry in the sun. The end result is a fabric with a funky tie-dyed look (see Appendix for photos).

After making another textile order with Charles and his family, our textile-sourcing journey continued. Next, Reiss drove us a few miles across Accra, where we arrived at a small tin-roofed wooden workshop near a highway overpass. We met George Ameyaw and his team of Nana Ameyaw, Felix Boakye, James Atagbolo, and Willliam Agbo, who were all busy weaving *kente* textiles.

Kente cloth originates from the Ashanti Kingdom and is a symbol of African heritage known for its dazzling, multicolored patterns and intricate designs. The word "*kente*" comes from "*kenten*", which means basket in the Akan language, reflecting the cloth's basket-like pattern. *Kente* was first developed in the 17th century and was traditionally made from the natural fibers of raffia. It evolved with the introduction of silk and cotton, woven into intricate patterns of bright colors and bold designs. In Ashanti folklore, the inspiration for *kente* cloth is traced back to two brothers, Kurugu and Ameyaw, from Bonwire, Ghana. While hunting, they encountered a spider skillfully weaving its web. Captivated, they observed its techniques for two days. After returning to their village, they applied what they had learned, using raffia fibers to create a unique, intricate fabric. With its detailed patterns, this new fabric was presented to the Ashanti king, who, impressed by its beauty, declared it a royal cloth. This marked the birth of *kente*, a blend of nature-inspired artistry and cultural significance deeply rooted in Ghanaian heritage. Each color in *kente* cloth has a symbolic meaning. For example, black represents Africa, gold stands for wealth and royalty, green symbolizes renewal, blue signifies peacefulness, and red reflects political and spiritual moods. The creation of *kente* cloth is an elaborate process that involves several steps. The weaver uses a specialized loom, a combination of a warp beam* and heddle rods*, to control lifting the warp threads. Strips of cloth four to five inches wide are then woven. The weaving process is intricate and time-consuming, demanding both skill and patience. The finished *kente* strips are commonly sewn together to make large sheets used to cut into garments or various other products. At Ethnotek, we honor the *kente* original strip form and purchase them just as they are, giving our *Kente* Collection a distinctive minimalist stripe aesthetic.

Kente patterns are more than just art; they tell stories and convey messages. The names of the various patterns often reflect historical events, moral values, social codes, and religious beliefs. For instance, the *Oyokoman* pattern is named after the Oyoko clan, the royal clan of the Ashantis, while other patterns are reserved for specific events like funerals, weddings, or festivals.

In contemporary Ghana, *kente* cloth is not just a historical artifact; it's a living part of the culture, even today. It has also gained international fame in the fashion and home decor industries and recently featured in Hollywood movie costumes. Reiss told us that when he went to see the Marvel movie *Black Panther* in Accra, there was a scene when the main character, T'Challa walked into a scene wearing a *kente* cloth scarf. When he did, the whole movie theater erupted in applause. That's how important *kente* is to the people of Ghana.

Now that we have some background about Ethnotek's Ghanaian artisan partners and their work, it's time to explore the meaning woven into the many symbols and motifs that adorn the country's beautiful textiles.

Meaningful Motifs - Ghana

GYE NYAME

One of Ghana's most popular *Adinkra* symbols representing God's omnipotence, and featured on Ghana's largest denomination banknote (200 cedis).

SANKOFA

This backward-facing bird connotes wisdom of learning from the past to build a better future.

AYA

This beautiful symbol means endurance, independence, defiance, hardiness, perseverance, resourcefulness.

ADWENE ASA

Translates to "the mind is finished." The individual who invented this motif tried to impress the king by using all *kente* motifs in one design.

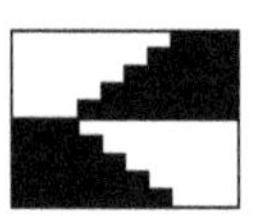

TIKRON ENKO EGYINA

Promotes collaboration, and translates to "you won't go far if you travel alone."

ADWENE SI ADWENE SO

Translates to "you need to think," which is apt because this is a complicated motif to weave.

Ghana

Photos from left to right: Cori, Jake & George in Accra; Charles Acquah; Nathaniel batik stamping; Obed Davor; Reiss Niih Boafo; Sekena Koby; Full Ethnotek Kente Collection.

Guatemala

We head across the Atlantic Ocean to Guatemala for the next stop on our journey through Ethnotek's artisan countries. This country of endless tropical beauty is home to steaming volcanoes, lush rainforests, and ancient Mayan sites.

Nestled in Central America, Guatemala is a captivating blend of ancient Mayan heritage, Spanish colonial influence, and a breathtaking natural landscape. Among the diverse Mayan groups are the Achi', Akatek, Awakatek, Ch'orti', Chalchitek, Chuj, Itza', Ixil, Jakaltek (Popti'), K'iche', Ka'qchikel, Mam, Mopan, Poqomam, Poqomchi', Q'anjob'al, Q'eqchi', Sakapultek, Sipakapense, Tektitek, Tz'utujil, and Uspantek, each contributing to the nation's vibrant cultural tapestry. The Spanish colonial era, beginning in the early 16th century, left an indelible mark on Guatemala's architecture and language. The colonial city of Antigua, a UNESCO World Heritage site, is a testament to this period, with colorful Spanish Baroque-influenced buildings echoing a bygone era. Spanish missionaries, instrumental in spreading Catholicism, influenced religious practices that endure in Guatemalan culture today.

Amidst this rich historical context, Guatemala's natural landscape unfolds like a living canvas. Serene lakes, misty mountains, and ancient ruins like Tikal depict unparalleled beauty and deep history. The country's biodiversity is equally impressive, with lush rainforests sheltering a plethora of plant and animal species, making it a haven for nature enthusiasts.

Guatemala's culinary scene celebrates diverse flavors, a testament to indigenous Mayan traditions and the fusion of European and Latin influences. Traditional dishes like *pepián de pollo*, *jocón*, and *kak'ik* coexist with modern culinary creations reflecting the nation's dynamic evolution.

The traditional dress of indigenous Mayan groups (referred to as tipica or *traje*) serves as a vibrant expression of identity against this natural backdrop. Each community showcases its own textile designs and color palettes unique to its region, reflecting distinctive cultural heritage. To the trained eye, you can go to many of Guatemala's bustling markets and identify whether a woman is Kaqchikel, K'iche', or Tz'utujil based on what she's wearing. The dress codes have loosened up a bit these days, and while locals like to honor their traditional dress, they also wear what they think is stylish and beautiful. It's common for women to own up to three different *tipica* outfits. These handmade masterpieces are quite expensive and make up a sizable investment of the family budget, further proof of the cultural value textiles hold in Guatemala.

Guatemala's weaving history is deeply intertwined with its indigenous communities, with each region offering unique patterns, colors, and techniques. The vibrant world of Guatemalan textile art, particularly the treadle loom*, which we use the most, is a spectacular display of cultural richness and artistic ingenuity. The Spanish introduced the treadle loom in the 1530s, revolutionizing traditional weaving methods by allowing for greater complexity and larger textile production. This loom uses foot pedals (treadles) to lift and lower the warp threads, creating a space (shed) through which the weft thread can be passed. This method enables weavers to create intricate designs like those made on traditional backstrap looms* faster and more efficiently. The introduction of the treadle loom expanded the possibilities of textile design and production, leading to a flourishing of creative expression in Guatemalan fabrics.

Two notable Guatemalan weaving techniques feature on Ethnotek bags: *Falseria* and *Jaspe*. *Falseria,* or "false embroidery," is an intricate weaving technique that looks remarkably like embroidery. It produces beautifully detailed patterns that look like they have been meticulously stitched by hand.

Falseria's English translation, "false embroidery," undermines the complexity that goes into this weaving technique. Although it is not brocade*, which is distinct from traditional backstrap weaving, its genius comes when the artisan translates the motif they see in their mind's eye to how they set up the loom. Instead of creating the shape by hand directly on the fabric, the artisan has to arrange various combs, shedders, ropes, counterweights, foot pedals, shuttles, and bobbins to create the shape they want when the loom is at full speed. They essentially have to think hundreds of steps ahead to get their desired result in a consistent and aesthetically pleasing way. If the loom isn't set up correctly, they can only find out after hours and sometimes days of weaving, and then they have to redo the entire setup all over again. This is why only the most skilled artisan can set up the loom, which usually takes one to two weeks.

Jaspe, also known as *Ikat in Indonesia*, is a resist-dyeing technique. In *Jaspe* weaving, the magic is in the tying and dying of yarn before the weaving happens in two processes called *cordeles* and *labores*.

Cordeles refers to the threads or cords prepared for dyeing in the *Jaspe* process. Multiple threads are tightly bound with string in specific patterns before dying. The areas of the threads that are bound resist the dye, creating undyed, patterned sections. This stage is crucial as the binding pattern directly determines the final design of the woven fabric. The skill and precision in binding these *cordeles* create the intricate and varied patterns characteristic of *Jaspe* textiles.

The term *labores* refers to the actual designs or patterns produced on the fabric through the *Jaspe* technique. These patterns are revealed once the weaving process is complete. The term can encompass the range of motifs, designs, and visual effects achieved through the strategic dyeing and weaving of the *cordeles*. *Labores* are the artistic expressions of the *Jaspe* process, showcasing the weaver's creativity and the cultural significance of the designs.

When we officially launched Ethnotek, we had textile designs from five countries where we still work today, and the Guatemalan styles quickly became our flagship products—people loved them! The bright, vibrant colors really resonated with our diehard fans. However, while textiles have always been popular, Guatemala has been a challenging country in which to work. One of the reasons was finding artisan partners who could weave the quantities we needed in the timeframe we needed.

Let me explain by taking a trip back in time to how our work in Guatemala began with the Sic Tzunun family of weavers, led by Manuel. For the first five years of Ethnotek, we worked with an artisan textile import intermediary due to the challenging nature of making direct relationships with artisans in Guatemala. But eventually (despite developing a great working relationship), bottlenecks developed. Also, as you will hear in the next chapter, we prefer to work directly with our artisan partners. Eventually, in 2016, the import company introduced us online to the Sic Tzunun family. And so, a few weeks later, I was on a plane to Guatemala. My contact who made the introduction warned me that communication with Manuel and his group of weavers was tricky as there was a language barrier — and they didn't use the internet much. This would be testing, but I was determined to give it a go. I spoke what residual Spanish was left in the deep recess of my mental archive from middle school Spanish class, which meant none! I remember arriving in-country on my first in-person sourcing trip, feeling exhilarated and stressed. But that quickly dissolved into childlike wonder the moment I stepped out of my hostel's front door and onto the cobblestone streets of Antigua. I scoured markets and spoke to whoever would listen in an attempt to explain the Ethnotek story, our intentions, and how I was there to make long-term relationships with weaving communities to order their textiles in large amounts every three months.

It wasn't easy. I wasn't greeted with the same enthusiasm as the other countries I visited, and I later learned this had to do with unhealed wounds from Guatemala's colonial past and the U.S.-backed civil war from 1960-1996. After educating myself about this appalling epoch, it's completely understandable why artisans keep things close to the chest.

After repeatedly hitting roadblocks and walking markets with a business colleague Hannah, she explained that Guatemala is a country of connections. If I hoped to work with real artisans, I needed to earn trust through people their community had already worked with for years. Ideally, that person should be Mayan, or local Ladino (is an exonym initially used during the colonial era to refer to those Spanish speakers who were not Peninsulares, Criollos, or indigenous peoples.)

I kept reaching out to Manuel on Facebook Messenger, WhatsApp, text messages, and phone calls, but with no answer. With my tail between my legs, I caught a *camioneta de pollo* (chicken bus) to Pana. Chicken buses are the most affordable transportation throughout Guatemala. They are colorful decommissioned school buses imported from the U.S. that the owners pimp out with their colors and decorations, and sound systems. It's quite the experience!

After a long, bumpy, and slightly nauseating journey over the mountains from Antigua to Pana, I arrived with renewed optimism that I'd find suppliers. I checked into my hostel, and after logging in to their Wi-Fi, I saw several missed messages from Manuel—woohoo, finally! He was delighted that I was there, and he could meet the guy behind all the orders he had been receiving through the importer we had been using up until that point.

The next morning, a rusty maroon Honda Civic pulled up as I stood waiting outside my hostel. I knew what Manuel looked like, and I could tell it was him sitting in the passenger seat. We exchanged basic greetings and shook hands. Manuel was with his business partner Daniel and cousin Claudia, who had come along to act as translator. Thank God! I didn't sleep much the night before because I was petrified by the fact that I'd have to do this complicated discussion using Google Translate on questionable cell service. Claudia to the rescue! She was dressed in K'iche *tipica* and, while shy, was also very friendly.

We took a two-hour ride to their village in Paxtoca, just thirty minutes northeast of Quetzaltenango. At first, it was a little awkward, but the atmosphere quickly warmed up. Manuel was jazzed to meet me and started our conversation by thanking Ethnotek for all the orders his community had received so far through our importer.

Manuel, Claudia, and I talked the whole way. I explained how we had a similar operation in four other countries, as with his community. I explained their handmade textile techniques, talked about their cultures, and regaled them with stories of our team sourcing adventures. The entire vibe in the car quickly went from stuffy to friendly. It felt really good; I felt accepted. I could stop nervously biting my fingernails as we headed further along dusty highways.

After arriving in Paxtoca, parking the car in front of Manuel's house, unloading, and walking over an arrangement of pine needles on the ground in front of the doorway to their family home (a common gesture for receiving respected guests), I received a warm welcome. They served me a steaming mug of bitter cacao and a plate of sweet bread.

I learned everyone's names and patiently waited while they explained my story and what we talked about in the car to everyone else, and then they gave me a tour of their village to visit various treadle loom weaving workshops and plantations. After a full day together and explaining our business's pains, risks, and needs, we agreed to commit to good communication, improved textile quality, and on-time deliveries. We spent two incredible days together. They taught me about their process, challenges, and needs as well. I learned more in those two days than I did in the five years of working through an intermediary importer.

I left Paxtoca to a ten-person entourage of the Sic Tzunun family, and Manuel's wife Louisa hugged me with her baby in her arms — what a vibrant soul. I really enjoyed getting to know her better, and after our meeting, we stayed in touch through social media. I often needed her to nudge Manuel when he wasn't responding, which began to happen often.

Although the trip was highly productive, and we all shared high spirits and good intentions, the dynamic of managing the supply chain between just Manuel and I only lasted one order cycle (6-months) before I had to enlist help from our Guatemala in-country sourcing director Averie (we'll catch up more with her in a moment) to help with communications and orders with Manuel. After Averie got involved, our output tripled, and quality improved dramatically. We collaborated with the Sic Tzunun family on many new styles that brought work to the community in Paxtoca and led to a flourishing relationship between us. The only downside was the communication, which, as we will find out later, became a problem we couldn't envisage at this time.

Fast-forward a few years to 2022. I was back in Guatemala on another sourcing trip. This one should give you more context for our deep dive into the world of textiles and working relationships in-country.

Fresh off the plane, my first call of business was to reunite with our textile facilitator, Averie, to embark on a journey from Antigua to Quetzaltenango, Paxtoca, and San Marcos Departamento together. We had some important (and fun) work to do on this trip. As some of our longtime customers might remember, Ethnotek switched weaving communities three times to try and keep the Mayan Star in our collection to feature in our bags. On this trip, we made a journey to visit the new weaving community Ethnotek was partnering with to create these beautiful textiles. Previously, we had produced two variations of The Mayan Star textile with Guatemalan artisans, with the star placed on a rich maroon or deep indigo color base. Over the years, customers have loved these limited edition styles so much that we have always struggled to keep them in stock. Weaving the Mayan Star textile is an incredibly time-intensive and detail-oriented style known as *pepinado*. For many years, we worked with Alida and Blanca in Comalapa, community leaders who kept the Mayan Star weaving tradition alive. Sadly, we lost contact with them during the pandemic as the community decided to move away from weaving the Mayan Star. However, in 2022, with the help of Averie, we found a new weaving community that wanted to keep the Mayan Star weaving tradition alive. This was the purpose of our 2022 trip to Guatemala: To travel deep into the foothills of San Marcos Departamento to meet with our new artisan partners, Alirio, his father Felipe, and sisters Rosa and Etelvina.

We bid farewell to Antigua on another blisteringly hot morning crammed into our driver, Heriberto's, shiny blue compact sedan. Averie and I rode in the backseat as we wound our way through the majestic landscape on a three-hour drive to Quetzaltenango, or Xela, as it's called locally. Pronounced "*shay-la*," it's an abbreviation of the original Quiché Maya name, Xelajú.

About halfway through the journey, we stopped off at our yarn supplier, El Rendidor Mish, in Salcaja. There, Averie bantered and bartered with her usual peeps while picking up a few bundles of yarn before we ventured onward.

With our new stash of thread in tow, adding to our already maxed-out carload of fabric samples and Ethnotek bags, we pressed on to Xela, where we met Flory, our textile sourcing project director in Guatemala. Flory is an indigenous Mayan from the Kaqchikel ethnic group who has worked with Averie for over eight years. Flory was wearing brightly-colored *tipica* (traditional handmade Mayan clothing) she designed that glowed with an energy of grace and joy. After a quick meet and greet, we all bundled in the car for another three-hour drive from Xela to San Marcos. While I struggled to keep up with the Spanish conversation flowing between the two women in the backseat, it's clear that Flory found Averie hilarious. The two of them giggled for hours, with Averie frequently labeling herself "*gringa*," which made Flory laugh even more and helped pass the time on our long, winding journey as magnificent vistas slipped by the window as we ascended into the verdant highlands outside Xela. At some point, the conversation changed to English, and I asked Flory about the textile trade in Guatemala, which she was more than happy to talk about. Our lengthy conversation led to some interesting insights. We discussed the positive and negative impacts of foreigners collaborating with Mayan weaving communities in Guatemala.

"It's mostly the foreign communities that took notice and action to help her people as opposed to the government," Flory explained.

"One of the many positive sides of working with foreign businesses is that it brings a wider global marketplace to our work that is otherwise slow to grow. It also informs us of color combinations that inspire us to adopt to increase orders and attract other foreign customers."

As we drove higher into the hills, our conversation took many twists and turns, eventually leading to Flory's opinions about the future of the weaving industry.

"I asked the weavers I currently work with within various communities if they're interested in learning new technologies such as web design or accounting to take the sale of their textiles online, but there's no interest. Life for these women revolves around weaving. It defines who they are. It's culturally ingrained. The younger generations, however, are keen to learn new skills in tech and are quite excited about these opportunities; they just need training. Most of them learn the craft while working in other industries or studying. Our youth could be excited to learn how to run an eCommerce store and do basic accounting and digital marketing to elevate their family enterprise. Suppose the younger generation takes on this responsibility. In that case, it will help keep the older weavers employed as they can teach the craft to the younger generation while taking the business online to expand export."

"And do you think that model (older generation's expertise and youth tech-savvy skills) would provide sustainable income from selling textiles domestically to make this a long-term option for the weaving industry here?" I asked.

"No, it'd need to be combined with supplying foreign brands as well."

Flory and Averie explained that most of the "awareness for weaving in

Guatemala comes from foreign interest," either from the tourism industry, international brands, or NGOs. Flory added that although the artisans' work with NGOs was Direct Trade (like Ethnotek), the charities also provided social programs and donations.

"Most NGOs in Guatemala are foreign-owned, and while they start well-intentioned and with great social programs, they often fall apart over time. Often, they have their own agenda and are influenced by their donors or other interests or policies abroad, which may not be in the best interest of the people they serve. They try to do too many things at the same time, which can lead to mediocrity across all programs."

Flory and Averie mentioned a few NGOs that promised the artisans donations, supplies, and mentorship. The artisans planned their lives and worked around these promises, but the NGOs never delivered.

"We've also witnessed some NGOs' founders spend more time advertising how good they are than taking leadership from the people they aim to help."

Within the artisan space, this is a common criticism directed at NGOs. Despite best intentions, efforts and resources can often be misdirected, leading to quality control issues and, as a result, diminished profits for artisans. The debate between Flory and Averie over NGOs continued for some time. Both agreed that NGOs are needed but would do better if they focused on one issue and did it effectively.

"For example, if an NGO focused solely on women's health, we would send all our weavers to that NGO," Flory said.

However, both women were still adamant that trade instead of charity was always the preferred way of working.

"Direct trade is a more sustainable method of supporting and continuing craft instead of charity. Jobs are always better than donations."

As I sat in the front seat listening intently, the scenery streaked by the window, and Flory's words washed over me. Her perspective on this issue of charity versus trade further validated Ethnotek's business and sourcing model.

Not long after, the road funneled through thick maize fields that swayed in the afternoon breeze — finally, the road dead-ended at our final destination: Alirio's home workshop. But instead of finding a busy workshop and a team of weavers, we found the place empty and deserted. *Was no one home? Did they forget we were coming?* It was strange to arrive at a workshop in the daytime and find empty looms. In the other artisan countries where Ethnotek works (Ghana, India, Indonesia, Vietnam), the looms clacking and banging ring out from dusk until dawn each day. They are intentionally kept busy fulfilling customer orders and maximizing output. But here, at Arilio's place, the scene was a picture of stillness other than a loitering dog, a sleeping cow, and a few rouge roosters running around the dusty courtyard.

A few moments later, a door swung open on the far side of the courtyard, and we were greeted by Alirio and his sister, Rosa. His jolly belly protruded through his black t-shirt, and smiling eyes shone through thick black-rimmed glasses while she wore a red flannel shirt, which she told us was her favorite color. "Because it's warm and strong like me," she said with a smile and a wink. After a couple of hours of exchanging pleasantries and touring their workshop, Averie, Flory, and I sat around a long table with Alirio and his family at their favorite local restaurant, sipping *atol de elote* (warm corn milk with sugar, cinnamon, and vanilla) sharing stories. Rosa told us about her four kids and how she had been teaching her eldest daughter (12) how to hand weave despite the physical demands of working the treadle loom and the fact that, culturally, this was mainly left to men in Guatemala. Yet Rosa and her sister, Etelvina, worked these looms and were intent on getting the younger generation (including their kids) involved to carry on the tradition.

Arilio then educated us all about his team's weaving process — and why the workshop was so silent. The reason was a simple one, he explained. Alirio and his team of weavers work unorthodoxly because their majestic textile requires a unique way of working to create the centerpiece of their work and intricate motif: The Mayan Star. The technique demands pure focus and very few strikes of the beater* and hand tree* (the big crossbar at the front of the loom near the weaver). The Mayan Star textile is woven on the back surface; essentially, the weaver is working without seeing what the finished surface of the fabric will look like from where they're standing. They hand trim sections of yarn and feed them through a precise number of warp threads to establish the motif, line by line. After a delicious lunch of *Kak'ik* (fragrant turkey stew), we spent the afternoon watching Alirio and his team of weavers get to work on the Mayan Star textile. It was a quiet, patient process, and we were delighted to see the level of craftsmanship and care they put into every single line of yarn. This was a huge relief for us because the future of carrying on the popular Mayan Star textile design was uncertain. Watching Rosa, Etelvina, and their father Felipe flow through the weaving process in the tranquility of their workshop quickly dissolved any doubt and concern we had about the continuation of this incredible textile. Not only was it being masterfully created right before our eyes, but the quality and detail were far better than those of the previous community we had collaborated with.

Finding Alirio had been a long journey of scouring markets, tapping Averie and Flory's networks, and long, dizzying drives through the mountains, but we're so glad we did it. What he and his family were creating was truly stunning, and I'm proud that these textiles are now featured on Ethnotek bags and worn by our customers today. It had been another worthwhile and meaningful sourcing trip! Fast-forward to today, and our Guatemalan designs are forecasted to occupy 60% of global sales.

Meaningful Motifs - Guatemala

QUETZAL

The quetzal is Guatemala's national bird, symbolizing Mayan heritage and resistance, reflected in its red chest—a reminder of their struggle during the Spanish conquest.

DIAMOND

The diamond is a very important motif that symbolizes the arms of a weaver, with her body at the bottom, and textiles at the top.

CORN

Corn symbolizes human creation in Mayan mythology, where different colors represent body parts and functions. It transcends its role as food, integrating into ancestral ceremonies.

VOLCANO

This zig-zag motif represents the sacred volcanoes across Guatemala.
It also represents the ups and downs of life.

BOCADILLOS

Elongated diagonal shapes represent the traditional candy sold at annual town festivals.

MAYAN STAR

Mayan culture deeply integrates astrology and cosmology, guiding its calendars and rituals, and shaping its societal and religious views.

Guatemala

Photos from left to right: Etelvina; Alirio; Rosa; Felipe; Averie & Flory; Manuel-Francisco; Kiana with GT14 Bagus Bag; Marina with GT11 Cyclo Sling; Jake with GT1 Raja Pack 30L.

India

Now it's time to follow the thread of our textile sourcing journey to a country we know and love well — India. Specifically, we're heading to the arid landscape of Kutch district and the city of Bhuj in the northwestern state of Gujarat, a place I've traveled to many times to meet our artisan partners.

Bhuj is a fascinating city nestled near the Kutch desert. It's a melting pot of culture, history, and natural beauty characterized by arid landscapes, seasonal wetlands, and the remarkable biodiversity of the Banni grasslands. This vast crescent-shaped region belongs to India's second-largest district, Gujarat, bordered by the Arabian Sea to the west and Pakistan to the north. Archeological records suggest that prehistoric humans appeared in Kutch 30,000 years ago. The city was established in 1510. The British had a significant influence during their colonial rule, and more recently, the 2001 earthquake reshaped much of the city's infrastructure and architecture. The natural landscape around Bhuj is a stark yet beautiful canvas, with the Great Rann of Kutch, a vast salt marsh to the north, and the grassy, marshy lands of the Little Rann of Kutch to the south. Kutch (pronounced *katchh*) comes from Kachwa and means "a turtle that has come out of the sea." One of the city's leading festivals, The Rann Utsav, showcases the region's cultural and natural splendor, attracting tourists worldwide. Bhuj is also famous for its food, boasting Gujarati flavors with a distinctive Kutchi flair. The food here is predominantly vegetarian, with delicious dishes such as *kutchi dabeli*, a local version of a burger; *bajra na rotla*, a millet-based flatbread typically served with buttermilk and jaggery; and *kutchi kadak*, a spicy tea.

Present-day Kutch is home to twenty-five different ethnic groups spread across more than a hundred villages. Two ethnic groups, the Vankars and Rabaris, are closely woven into the Ethnotek story. The region's cultural diversity is reflected in its ethnic mosaic. The various ethnic groups in and around Bhuj include the Rabaris, known for their nomadic lifestyle and intricate embroidery; the Ahirs, renowned for their cattle rearing and vibrant clothing; and the Jats, distinguished by their unique beaded jewelry. Each group adds to the region's cultural richness with its distinct customs, festivals, and art forms. Each community in the Kutch district also has its distinct embroidery style, such as the *Rabari*, *Mutwa*, *Suf*, and *Khaarek*. These styles vary in stitch patterns, motifs, and applications, ranging from mirror work to intricate thread work depicting local folklore and symbols of nature.

Ajrakh is a form of block printing using natural dyes and is another specialty of Kutch. Practiced predominantly in the village of Ajrakhpur, this craft involves a complex process that can take up to two weeks to complete, resulting in beautifully patterned fabrics with deep indigo, red, and black hues.

Rogan art is practiced in the village of Nirona and uses a thick, brightly colored paste to paint intricate motifs on fabric, often used for bridal trousseaus. This art form is rare, with only a few families in the village possessing the knowledge and skill to carry it on today.

Weaving is also prevalent, with communities producing shawls, blankets, and rugs. The art of weaving in Kutch is spearheaded by the Vankar (which loosely translates to master weaver) community. This is why I was initially drawn to Bhuj and its surrounding villages.

Historically, the Vankars belonged to a scheduled caste, traditionally engaged in the occupation of weaving. Over generations, they have honed their weaving skills and are known for their proficiency in creating woolen shawls and blankets, known locally as *dhabdas*. These textiles are highly valued for their quality, warmth, and distinctive patterns. The Vankars typically use wool from local Kutchi sheep, *pashmina* from the Ladakh region, or cotton grown in Saurashtra and dyed in Ahmedabad. They also use a series of natural dye techniques in the village of Bhujodi, where Ethnotek works with artisan partners.

The Vankar weaving techniques combine traditional patterns passed down through generations and more contemporary designs that have evolved with changing times and market demands. Conventional designs often feature geometric patterns with earthy, muted tones. However, modern designs display more vibrant colors as times change. The weavers' craft is not just a means of livelihood but also a cultural expression that reflects their identity and heritage. The Vankars have managed to sustain and evolve their weaving practices despite threats posed by industrialization and changing market dynamics. Their longevity has been mainly due to their adaptability and willingness to innovate while preserving the essence of their traditional craft.

Getting to Bhuj requires a bumpy and crowded bus journey overnight from Ahmedabad. Every time I travel there, I arrive bleary-eyed and exhausted at the local bus terminal. Then, I stumble through the bustling morning bazaar, which is always a hive of activity with vendors hawking vegetables, textile merchants selling colorful fabrics, and restaurants serving fragrant teas. On this particular trip, I checked into my usual hotel, showered quickly, and then headed off to meet Ethnotek's project facilitators in the region, Pankaj Shah and Mina Raste, who liaise between Ethnotek and head artisan and master weaver, Shamji.

After meeting Pankaj and Mina outside my hotel, we headed off in an auto rickshaw through the desert toward Shamji's village, Bhujodi. This little village is known for its weavers but also its extreme heat. Temperatures regularly top 40 degrees Celsius (+100 degrees Fahrenheit) and are often accompanied by strong dust storms that whip up face-stinging blasts of sand. En route to the village, we passed by groups of Rabari women walking on the side of the road wearing beautiful black and red Bandhani shawls to cover themselves from the relentless sun and wind.

Eventually, we arrived at Bhujodi and the Valji family compound, where the man himself walked out to greet us. My longtime friend and our India head artisan, Shamji! As is customary for him, he's barefoot and wearing a traditional cotton *kurta* shirt and pants (both hand-woven and dyed by himself, of course) that bear a beautiful color fade that can only be achieved by years of being worn in the unrelenting Kutch sun. Shamji and I embrace each other with hugs and smiles, as always. Every time we meet, it's like coming back to see an old friend, which is precisely how we feel about one another. It's been a long time since we last saw each other, and there was so much to catch up on.

Shamji is a local legend in his village. During the 1970s, his father, Vishram, took on the mission to build a weaving co-operative and travel far and wide to drum up awareness to bring a sustainable livelihood to Bhujodi for their handloom artisans. He participated in exhibitions and attended university lectures in Ahmedabad, Mumbai, and Delhi to promote the importance of the Vankar weavers' culture. These efforts brought a great deal of attention back to their village, leading to increased orders that piqued designers' curiosity across India and internationally.

Vishram received the National Award from the Indian government for his unique and complex style of weaving and for rallying a community behind a single cause — reviving the weaving industry in Kutch. Many years later, his son, Shamji, won the same award and has brought a modern spin and entrepreneurial spirit to the family weaving business.

They are true champions of craft, which is one reason Ethnotek has been so proud to work with this profoundly passionate and dedicated group of artisans.

The Vankar Weavers, which Shamji leads, primarily use pit loom* weaving, the main form of weaving adopted by Kutchi-based artisans over time. Pit looms consist of a concrete pit nested into the ground where the weaver sits so that he's level with the loom. The pit also houses the treadles* and the weft paddles* that the artisan operates with his feet. Pit looms are easier to set up inside the home because they don't consume as much space as a treadle loom and are also a way to escape the scorching desert heat while working. The pit looms used in Kutch use a manual throw shuttle and hand-warping, requiring great skill, attention to detail, and patience. The result is stunning works of art with dancing geometric patterns that leap off the fabric, a look and feel nearly impossible to recreate by a power loom*.

While it is mostly the men who weave in Kutch, the process is a collective effort involving the whole family. Women of the community prepare the yarn for dying and make bobbins* from yarn hanks, which they then set up into the loom's warp in preparation for the weaving process to begin.

On this sourcing trip, my goal was to reconnect with Shamji to understand any issues he and the artisans may be facing with Ethnotek orders and discuss the future of our work together. As I was about to find out, on this particular trip, Shamji was about to open my eyes to a new understanding of the Vankar Weavers' work and livelihoods. Refer back to Chapter 2: Take Leadership From Those You Seek To Benefit for the full story.

Meaningful Motifs - India

KUNGRI

Three stacked triangles symbolize the tops of temples: *Kalasha* (peak), *Amalak* (peak ornament), and the *Sikhara* (central tower).

VANKIYO

Vankars and Rabaris are pastoralists and patrons of livestock. The zig-zag *vankiyo* pattern represents the patterns cows and goats make as they urinate while walking.

HUDADHI

An 'H' shaped motif that represents the wooden frame used in the yarn spooling process.

FIVE FACES

This motif represents Shiva's five faces, and the cardinal directions, initially featured in *tangaliya* shawls of the *Dangasia* community.

DAMARU

This motif represents the *damaru* instrument attached to Shiva's trident. It's often played in ceremonies and is believed to make the sound that created the universe.

PEACOCK

India's national bird symbolizes beauty, joy, grace and love. Indian tradition often references the peacock in popular stories, songs, poems, and paintings.

India

Photos from left to right: The Valji family + Pankaj & Mina in Bhujodi; Shamji; Custom colors; Premji; VCA Raja Pack 30L; Sanjay, Suresh & their father Arjun Ramji; India 11 Premji Pack.

Indonesia

Next on our textile travels, we head to another of Ethnotek's second homes: Indonesia. This magnificent archipelago of 17,000 islands is a country of endless wonder, adventure, and diversity, with approximately 700 dialects spoken. Our destination is the island of Java, home to Indonesia's political and economic epicenter, the capital, Jakarta, and roughly half the country's population. Java's history is a tapestry of Hindu-Buddhist kingdoms, Islamic sultanates, and European colonial influences.

Whenever I travel to Java, my end destination is always Surakarta (known locally as Solo), home to a vibrant textile trade and where our Ethnotek artisan partners call home. The city was founded in 1745 and became the heart of Javanese culture and arts, mainly known for its royal palaces, Keraton Surakarta Hadiningrat and Puro Mangkunegaran. The food in Java, particularly Solo, is a feast for the senses. Traditional dishes like *nasi liwet* (coconut rice cooked with chicken, egg, and tempeh) and *gudeg* (jackfruit stew) are firm favorites among locals and visitors and reflect the island's rich culinary heritage. Street food markets burst with flavors, offering treats like *sate kambing* (lamb skewers) and *serabi* (Javanese pancakes). The best food is found at late-night streetside *warung* food stalls, where food is served as you sit alongside other diners on reed mats on the ground. If it's crowded, that's a good sign the food is sumptuous. Solo is a night owl, so be prepared for an evening of eating, drinking tea and coffee with lashings of sugar (local style), and chit-chatting with strangers until the early morning. But don't expect any bars; it's a Muslim country, and abstaining from alcohol is respectful.

Javanese culture is a beautiful blend of spiritual beliefs and traditions. The predominant religion in Java is Islam (90-95% of the population is Muslim). Hindu-Buddhist philosophies and animistic beliefs also played a significant role in the past and can still be seen as a creative influence on Javanese art today. This syncretism is evident in the Wayang Kulit shadow puppet shows, which often depict stories from the Hindu epics like the Mahabharata and Ramayna, and in the Slametan communal feasts that blend Islamic and Javanese customs.

When it comes to textiles, *batik* is a method of fabric decoration that uses wax-resistant dyeing and is Java's most famous cultural export. Recognized by UNESCO as a Masterpiece of the Oral and Intangible Heritage of Humanity, *batik* is not just a cloth but a representation of the Javanese soul. Based on the contents of the Sundanese Manuscript, *batik* has been practiced in Indonesia since the 12th century. Each region throughout the archipelago has distinct *batik* patterns, often influenced by local cultures, customs, and history.

There are two main batik-making techniques: *Batik tulis* and *batik cap*. *Batik tulis* is hand-drawn using a canting (pronounced "chanting"), a small, thin-spouted tool used to apply hot wax onto the fabric (similar to pen and paper). This method is thorough and can take weeks or even months to complete. On the other hand, the *batik cap* (pronounced "chop" and sometimes also called *ceblok*) uses a copper stamp to apply the wax — a quicker method but with less artistic freedom than *batik tulis*.

The *batik* process starts with hand drawing the motif design on paper and then laying the raw white cotton fabric on top of the drawing to trace the design onto the cotton by pencil. This guides artisans to hand draw the same designs onto the fabric with the canting tool. The stamping process does not use this step because the stamp is applied directly to the fabric after being dipped in heated wax.

Batik wax is made using a special recipe of palm wax, paraffin wax, pine gum resin, cat's eye tree resin, micro wax, recycled wax from past productions and damar tree sap. This carefully crafted concoction can only be made by master wax makers and has to be just right to create the perfect viscosity required for *batik* making. It must be liquid enough to penetrate the base fabric fully but gummy enough to not pool or bleed and keep the sharp resolution and edging of the copper stamps design. And it smells incredible, like incense, which makes for a pleasant sensory experience in the workshop. Traditionally, wood from the mango tree (and other fruit trees or trembesi lumber) is used for the fires kindled under the water vats that boil off the wax in the dying process. This wood is used because of its low smoke content, which is a consideration for keeping cleaner air in the *batik* workshop. These days, vat fires are gas or electric-powered to eliminate carcinogens. The wax resists dye in areas where the artisans don't want specific colors to go. Then, the fabric is boiled and dried, and the wax application process begins again. It will be repeated numerous times depending on how many colors the finished design requires. After each color is dyed, fixation is applied, where the fabric is soaked in a mineral solution to embed the colors permanently.

To create the colors, powdered dye pigments are combined in specific amounts to create the desired color. This is noted in a spreadsheet so it can be replicated perfectly over time and then added to water.

Surakarta, especially the Laweyan district (also known as Batik Village district of Solo), is synonymous with *batik* and is a confluence of Javanese, European, Chinese, and Islamic influences. The district has been the center of *batik* production since the 1800s. Surakarta's *batik* is distinguished by its classic motifs, often inspired by the royal courts, with intricate patterns and a predominantly blue and brown color scheme.

Their dedication to preserving traditional methods and motifs sets Surakarta and Laweyan apart in the *batik* world. While modernization has influenced production, artisans in Solo and Laweyan continue to champion *batik tulis*, ensuring the continuation of these intricate, handcrafted designs. Moreover, the *batik* from this region often tells a story, reflecting Java's local history, myths, and philosophies. For sourcing trip notes in Indonesia, see chapter 4 and Conclusion.

Meaningful Motifs - Indonesia

PARANG

A Javanese royal pattern symbolizing power with blade-like and wave-like designs, representing resilience and persistence.

KERTU

Represents a Javanese card game, featuring patterns like stacked cards, reflecting Indonesia's cultural blend through trade.

GARUDA

The sun bird, Garuda, Vishnu's divine steed in Hinduism, symbolizes life and maturity, bringing honesty, steadfastness, and strength to its wearer.

TRUNTUM

Typically worn by the bride and groom's parents on the wedding day, it signifies their duty to guide and oversee the couple as they start their new life together.

KAWUNG

A classic style that used to be worn only by royal families but is now worn by all. Some stories say the motifs were inspired by aren fruit, while others say traditional coins.

MEMANEN

This very detailed motif combines raindrops, rice, coins, and house tiles. It symbolizes rain, which helps rice grow, and the income and home that agriculture provides for families.

Indonesia

Photos from left to right: Yatmi applying dye; Iwan showing a copper stamp; Sri applying dye; Harjono stamping the Kertu motif; Boiling off wax; Teddy looking good; ID6 Satu Pack & the stamp that made it; ID11 Raja Pack; ID12 Bagn Bag.

Vietnam

Now for our shortest flights of the trip, from Indonesia due north to the country where it all began for Ethnotek, Vietnam! For this part of the journey, strap on your helmet and jump onto the back of my motorbike because we're going to zip through the bustling streets of Ho Chi Minh City, a densely populated metropolis with a vibrant mix of modernity and tradition, where skyscrapers stand alongside ancient temples. The food is a reflection of this blend, with traditional Vietnamese dishes like *Cơm Tấm*, *Bún Thịt Nướng*, *Hủ Tiếu*, *Bánh Xèo,* and *Gỏi Cuốn* sold alongside a plethora of flavorsome international fare.

Ho Chi Minh City (formerly Saigon) has origins that trace back to the1600s, when it was a small Khmer village known as Prey Nokor. Before the Vietnamese annexation, the area was sparsely inhabited, mainly by the Khmer people. The city's development accelerated in the 1800s under French colonial rule, becoming the capital of Cochinchina, a French colony. During this period, Saigon underwent a significant transformation, with the construction of grand boulevards, elegant architecture, and the establishment of the Saigon Notre-Dame Basilica and the Saigon Opera House. The city quickly emerged as a major port and commercial center, often called the Paris of the East. Following the tumultuous years of World War II and the First Indochina War, Saigon became the capital of the Republic of Vietnam in 1954. The city played a pivotal role during the Vietnam War, serving as the headquarters of the U.S. military and witnessing significant events leading up to the fall of Saigon in 1975. This marked the end of the war and the beginning of a unified, communist Vietnam.

In 1976, Saigon was officially renamed Ho Chi Minh City in honor of the revolutionary leader. Despite the name change, many locals still affectionately refer to the city as Saigon. Today, Ho Chi Minh City is

Vietnam's largest city, home to more than 8.9 million at the time of writing and is the economic heartbeat of the country.

For this next portion of the journey, we will ride by train through Vietnam's picturesque and sleepy countryside. The vibrancy of Ho Chi Minh City fades into the background as we head deeper into the heartlands of Vietnam's textile heritage, meeting the artisans who weave the threads of culture and customs into beautiful fabrics.

In central Vietnam, near Phan Rang, the Cham community has long captivated us all at Ethnotek with its rich history and spiritual depth. The Cham people, descendants of the ancient Champa kingdom (which formerly comprised all of Cambodia and the Southern Vietnamese landmass), practice a unique blend of spiritual practices, predominantly Hindu Shaivism, interspersed with elements of Islam. Like the iconic Tháp Pô Klông-Garai, their temples are architectural marvels and living embodiments of their enduring faith, dedicated to Shiva. This spirituality influences their intricate art, especially their textiles. The kingdom shrank considerably due to Chinese Communist pressure, French colonialism, and modern Viet influence, but the soul remains with its people, spiritual devotion, and artistic expression.

On this sourcing adventure, we travelled to the Cham Village. It's like stepping into a world where time moves to the rhythm of the loom. Their meticulous weaving technique is an art form passed down through generations. The Cham textiles are renowned for their geometric precision and vibrant colors, each piece a testament to the weaver's skill and deep spiritual connection.

The Cham weavers' process begins with preparing the cotton, often home-grown and spun. Traditionally, the dyes are sourced from natural ingredients: indigo for blues, bark for reds, and turmeric for yellows creating a palette that reflects the natural beauty of their land. Today, synthetic dyes are used due to customer demands for color fastness, stability, and consistency. You can see Cham textiles on the inside of most Ethnotek bags featuring their dog paw and cucumber motifs.

Our Vietnam sourcing adventure from the Cham Village heads to the northern highlands via overnight train. It's my favorite way to make this trip, but don't expect to sleep if you take this route (unless you book a VIP ticket). You will spend the night accompanied by crying babies, clucking chickens, laughing old ladies, beer-swilling young men, and a general party-like atmosphere. It's all worth it, though — the Vietnamese train experience is one I highly recommend. After a quick rest stop in Hanoi, I caught a connecting train further north into the highlands to the end of the line at Lào Cai. Arriving, tired but excited, my go-to submersion into the city is to let my belly lead the way. Moments after stepping off the train, my first port of call is whatever noodle soup stall is open and ready to serve a weary traveler a hearty bowl of *Phở* piled high with fresh herbs and sprouts and a steaming black cup of *Càphê* Đen. If there's a better breakfast on earth, I've yet to find it!

After refueling, I headed to the Ethnology Museum, one of my favorite destinations in the city. The museum's cornucopia of artifacts contained within the walls of this stilted wooden building partly inspired Ethnotek's inception. The first time I visited, I spent hours reading and examining the exhibits and learning about the 54 ethnic groups in Vietnam, their dialects, customs, arts, and crafts. And today, whenever I return to the city, I stop by and rekindle my relationship with the roots of the rich indigenous cultural history — and the origin story of Ethnotek. After another day at the museum, learning about history, it's time to head out into the Hmong heartlands, where communities have lived and worked for centuries.

Vietnam's Hmong tribes live throughout Sapa, Lào Cai, Lai Châu, and Hai Giang. They have a rich history of migration, resilience, and a profound connection with nature, reflected in their animistic beliefs. They see spirits in everything — the rivers, the mountains, the wind. Their textile work expresses this connection with nature, notably in their intricate embroidery and *batik* techniques. The Hmong communities emigrated from the Yunnan Province, China, to northern Vietnam, Laos, and Thailand. They are known for their rich cultural traditions, colorful clothing, and intricate handicrafts. The Hmong embroidery, *paj ntaub* (flower cloth), is a canvas of their culture. Each stitch is a part of a larger narrative, telling tales of their daily lives, dreams, and the natural world. The process is labor-intensive and requires immense skill and patience. First, the cloth is dyed using indigo, creating a deep blue canvas. Then, using a needle and thread, the Hmong artisans embroider intricate patterns, often improvising designs. The motifs are symbolic, each pattern carrying specific meanings: snail shells for protection, mountains for their homeland, and birds for freedom. Hmong *batik* is another fascinating aspect of their textile artistry. This technique involves drawing designs with beeswax onto hemp fabric and then dyeing it, with the waxed areas resisting the dye. After several dyeing and waxing cycles, the wax is removed, revealing intricate patterns. This art form is a slow dance of precision and creativity, each piece unique to the artist's vision. Hmong animism centers on a rich spirit world that influences daily life. This includes ancestral spirits, revered and honored through rituals and offerings for protection and guidance. Shamanism plays a crucial role, with shamans (*txiv neeb*) acting as spiritual leaders and healers. They perform "soul calling" rituals to restore health by retrieving lost souls.

Life events, including births and marriages, are marked by specific rituals reflecting the connection between the physical and spiritual realms. Nature is revered, with spirits believed to inhabit natural elements like rivers and mountains. Communal festivals, like the Hmong New Year, are significant for both cultural celebration and spiritual significance, maintaining harmony within the community. The Hmong community is divided into various subgroups. While sharing a common ancestry and cultural heritage, customs, dress, and language can vary significantly between the different tribes in the region.

At Ethnotek, we primarily partner with two communities: the Black Hmong and the Red Hmong. The Black Hmong mainly reside in Sapa and Lao Cai and are recognized for their dark indigo-dyed hemp clothing, which often appears black. Their attire typically includes a combination of beautifully embroidered fabrics with intricate designs. The indigo dye, a staple in their textile work, characterizes their traditional clothing. This community creates the Ethnotek Vietnam 5 textile.

The Red Hmong are revered for their vibrant clothing accented with bright red and orange embroidered sections. These colors are emblematic of their culture, symbolizing energy and festivity. The community that we work with resides in the Lai Châu and Sơn La Provinces. This community lovingly makes the Ethnotek Vietnam 6 textile.

Hmong clothing carries significant cultural meanings, reflecting aspects like marital status, age, and the specific subgroups within the Hmong community based on the color and motifs displayed. For women, certain styles and patterns in their clothing can indicate their marital status. Unmarried girls often wear more colorful and elaborately embroidered outfits, while married women's attire tends to be more subdued. Additionally, older community members might wear less ornate clothes, signifying their age and status. The clothing varies distinctly between genders. Hmong men typically wear simpler, less embroidered clothing, often black or blue jackets and trousers, occasionally with some embroidery at the cuffs or collar.

In contrast, women's attire is much more elaborate and vibrant, featuring intricate embroidery, pleated skirts, and a variety of accessories like silver jewelry, sashes, and headpieces. Hmong people are mostly agriculturalists who create handmade textiles in their free time. Only women embroider textiles; it's a chosen pastime as a form of creative expression and an avenue for financial independence. On average, one woman can hand-make two tribal skirts per year. They sell their skirts for a high price due to their incredible quality and high local and international demand. Because these handmade creations fetch a high price, they elevate women's status in their community. The Hmong (and Ethnotek) see these as luxury goods, so we are proud to include them in our Special Edition Collection.

In an average year, we purchase 550 to 600 skirts, which equates to 275 to 300 women per year sharing their handmade masterpieces with Ethnotek customers. Every single Hmong embroidered piece featured in our bags is unique because so many incredible women across a 55-mile radius are creating them in their unique way. This means no one else will have the same Vietnam 5 or 6 bag as you. Pretty cool, right?

So after another adventure north to meet the Hmong tribes we work with at Ethnotek and another year of purchase orders made, it's time to head back South. After a flight from Hanoi to Ho Chi Minh City, I arrive at yet another second home — our production facility. It's time to meet the family — and magic makers — who create our bags.

The Ethnotek workshop is powered by over 90 awesome and highly skilled humans. We do all design, prototyping, material management, molding, stamping, cutting, sewing, and fulfillment under one roof.

We work hard together and play hard together! Often, weekends and holiday time off are spent together, goofing around, exploring the outdoors, sharing food and drinks, and getting into all sorts of mischief.

One significant person behind all of this is my friend, Ái Phạm. Ethnotek wouldn't have been possible without this man. He has a vast knowledge of soft goods manufacturing and has an incredible eye for detail. In the early days, Ai convinced his team and suppliers to accept orders from Ethnotek with no minimum order quantities, which no other factory we had spoken with at the time would agree to. This was because Ai believed in our mission and loved Ethnotek's concept. Still, Ai refers to Ethnotek as his "special bag company." He has been incredibly patient and flexible and has treated us exceptionally well. In the beginning, Ai and our production director (and factory co-owner) Tú produced bags from a small villa. They had eight sewing workers and four admin staff, including themselves. Their factory, Kim Ta, is loosely translated to "our needle," a perfect name that captures their values of community effort. Throughout Kim Ta's early expansion, Ethnotek was their main customer. We're proud to say that thanks to our orders and the support of other like-minded brands that produce at Kim Ta, they have grown their team and just received Amfori BSCI certification for quality working standards and open and sustainable trade (see Chapter 10 and Appendix for details). This is a huge milestone, and I'm incredibly grateful to have been along the ride with Ái, Tú, and the team from the beginning. I'm also proud to say that Ethnotek is no longer Kim Ta's biggest customer. We still produce and grow slowly and steadily, and they now have customers who produce three to five times more volume than us, which is great. They're big dogs now! Congrats to all the Kim Ta team. I'm so proud to have seen you grow your business to what it is today!

Meaningful Motifs - Vietnam

FENCE

This print embodies the quintessential village boundary. Each "fence" is unique, whether its made from bamboo, wood, or lush plants.

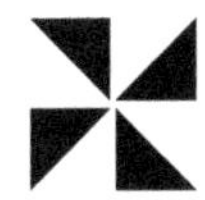

TRIANGLES

Known either as "triangles" or "windmills", this design is a testament to versatility. It symbolizes balance and adaptability, embodying the spirit of change.

FLOWER CLOTH

The "flower cloth", or paj ntaub, represents a rich tapestry of Hmong culture. Woven with protective symbols and ethnic identifiers, it's a symbol of maternal heritage.

MOUNTAIN

Echoing the resilience of the highlands and born from landscapes where hemp thrives, it stands for strength and heritage.

DOG PAW

Crafted by our Cham weavers, the "dog paw" motif captures the everyday charm of unpaved village paths dotted with canine footprints—a playful nod to our furry friends.

CUCUMBER

This motif celebrates a key ingredient in Cham cuisine. Inspired by the beloved vegetable, it's a staple design in our textile repertoire, as flavorful and essential as the veggie itself.

Vietnam

Photos from left to right: Our incredible production family in Ho Chi Minh City; Hmong artisans in Lai Châu; Cham village weaver; Hani & Inrasara; Chiburi Wallet in VN6; Aya Pack in VN6; Premji Pack in VN6.

That was some journey! I hope that's opened the door into the Ethnotek world of textile sourcing—how it works, who's involved, and why handmade artisan textiles are integral to our communities worldwide. In all the destinations we travel and work in, art is woven into the fabric of culture. It's a symbol of pride for the artisans, and that's why at Ethnotek, we work so hard to Celebrate Craft and Culture.

As we near the end of this chapter, I'd like to share some thoughts about what happens if we don't continue to Celebrate Craft & Culture. What happens if we don't value our diverse cultural arts heritage worldwide? This outcome is easier to imagine than you may think. Look at what's happened in the USA over the last half-century. While globalization has brought much prosperity to our country, it's also exported a world-cultural view of fast consumerism. It's celebrated the McDonaldization of the world, where fast food and fast fashion have extended hands across oceans to every corner of the globe (except Antarctica, thankfully!). I can't help but think whenever I wander the streets of Ho Chi Minh City, Hanoi, Mumbai, Guatemala City, or Solo and see a Mcdonalds or Starbucks about how globalized our consumer culture is becoming, how it's changing the nature of the streets and cultures: burger by burger, latte by latte. In many ways, our globalized economies allow for gradual homogenization, where the line between cultures begins to blur, and everything looks the same. Consumerism fuels these trends, so it's no small choice when we decide what to buy — and what not to.

The handmade artisan textile sector is a beacon of hope to fight against the tide of cultural homogenization and where consumers can consciously choose to Celebrate Craft & Culture, as well as global diversity.

> *"The role of globalization is to homogenize all cultures, turn them into commodified markets, and therefore, make them*

easier for global corporations to control. Global corporations are even now trying to commodify all remaining aspects of national cultures, not to mention indigenous cultures."

— Jerry Mander

Culture is humanity's unique fingerprint and something to be studied, cherished, celebrated, and shared. As a result, commerce can be an effective vehicle for change, and more social entrepreneurs are needed in this space than ever before. So, we leave this chapter with a simple truth: How we spend our money reflects who we are. Spending money directly with artisans helps celebrate the art they make, or as Anna Lappe puts it: "Every time you spend money, you're casting a vote for the kind of world you want."

That's why at Ethnotek, we Celebrate Craft and Culture as one of our core values. It shows that we (and our community) believe the world shines brighter when we express ourselves through art. This belief was planted in me all those years ago on that hike in the Bắc Hà highlands in 2007. Holding those beautiful Hmong textiles in my hands, I felt like I was peering back through many generations of craft and culture. I knew then I would work with textiles and artisans and share my love for their art — and that's what Ethnotek proudly continues to do today.

4

Go There

"Personal relationships are the fertile soil from which all advancement, all success, all achievement in real life grows."

— Ben Stein

Java, Indonesia
2012

The thick, humid air flooded in around me as I sat staring out at the beautiful view from the open door of a cargo train. The verdant flatlands of Javanese countryside streaked by as I hurtled toward Surakarta City, AKA Solo, Indonesia. I had traveled here with the goal of finding new artisan textile partners and *had to* make this journey in person. After all, it was my very first sourcing trip to meet one of our weaving partners — and I was about to learn another important lesson of my Ethnotek journey. To build trade relationships, the first thing you must do is **Go There.**

It was a few months after our first trade show in good old Salt Lake City. By this time, our Ghanaian batik thread designs had become a firm favorite of our Ethnotek fans and distributors. Of course, it was no surprise to us. The bright colors and kaleidoscopic geometric patterns were mesmerizing and hypnotic; people simply loved them!

With sales booming, it soon became apparent that the Ghanaian artisan community we worked with in the first year couldn't handle the order scale, so I had no choice but to find an alternative. And so, with eager distributors and customers, I began sourcing more threads internationally to add to the Ethnotek collection. Now that we had drummed up all of this demand and had a handful of big customers who trusted our ability to deliver, I had to get busy sourcing new threads. I had previously traveled to Indonesia and knew it was a hotbed for traditional batik textiles. Due to its healthy local demand, locating new artisan partners in an already thriving craft sector *should* be relatively easy.

Meanwhile, I was transparent with our distributors about the company goals of establishing new artisan relations to complete their orders (which had already been made). Still, they didn't know that I had no idea where to begin. I did as much research as possible on which areas of Indonesia would be best to start my sourcing quest, and then I didn't waste any time, booked the tickets, and dropped in.

I always travel on a budget, so after flying into the capital city of Jakarta, I took the nine-hour train ride to Solo because it was cheaper. Not long after, I watched towns, villages, and then long barren stretches of countryside whiz by the train's open cargo door. My legs dangled over the edge, and I drank in the scene. Now I was in it! There was no barrier between me and the world — exactly how I liked to travel. I spent the entire train ride there, taking photos and videos, grinning ear to ear, and writing about the experience in my journal.

After arriving in Solo, I flagged down a pedicab (a foot-pedaled rickshaw). I savored the early evening ride as we weaved in and out of thousands of motorbikes, soaking in the sights and smells. Clove cigarette smoke, spices, and steaming sweet and sour flavors drifted from nearby *warungs* (local food stalls) as a tangerine sun dipped lower over the city skyline. Arriving at my homestay after a long day on the road, I was about to call it a night when I heard the distinctive sound of *gamelan* music beating and clanging into the night from the family home behind the homestay. Wandering to investigate, I found the family's cement compound vibrating with melodic tones of bells, gongs, and drums. It turned out that this was the community room where the local *gamelan* troupe practiced. *Gamelan* is the traditional ensemble music of Javanese, Sundanese, and Balinese peoples, made predominantly of percussive instruments, the most common of which are metallophones and hand-played drums called *kendang*.

I sat at the front door of the room, watching the group play, all dressed in ornate traditional Javanese ceremonial attire. An hour later, after the music finished, I met the gong player, Dwi. He spoke excellent English and was extremely friendly. He lit a clove cigarette and asked what I had planned for Solo. I explained the concept of Ethnotek and showed him a selection of our bags I had brought with me. Looking up from the bags, smiling, he said, "You're in the right place; tomorrow, you come with me."

The following day, just after eight a.m., Dwi and I headed on foot to the neighborhoods surrounding the guesthouse on a sourcing adventure. At first, he took me to showrooms and souvenir shops. Still, after I explained that I wasn't a one-time buyer and was looking to develop relationships with artisans and make large orders every three to six months, he brought me to the biggest *batik* factories in the area, Danar Hadi and Batik Keris. These huge facilities teemed with workers, heavy machinery, and colorful *batik* threads, but it wasn't what I was looking for, either. They were great places to see the whole *batik* process but were too big. I explained to Dwi that I hoped to connect with a small workshop owner, preferably a family-run business that might be looking for a long-term business partner to work alongside. The point finally seemed to click with Dwi. "You need to meet my cousin Teddy," he said with a smile.

A short taxi ride later, I was shaking hands with the man of the moment, Teddy Priyanagroho, Dwi's cousin, and now the owner of his family's *batik* production business. From my first step inside his small shop, I knew I was in the right place. Immediately upon arrival, I could smell the tell-tale aroma of *batik* production, a heady blend of wax ingredients reminiscent of the sweet incense that burns at temples throughout this majestic archipelago of Indonesia.

Teddy was a shy, softly-spoken young man who seemed to smile with his eyes and possessed a deeply calming presence. I immediately felt connected to him, and it turned out we were similar in age — two young entrepreneurs from different sides of the world with a passion for design and trade.

As Teddy gave Dwi and me a tour of his workshop, he told us about growing up in Solo, attending school and university, and how, instead of following a career path away from his family's traditional business, he decided to stay and take on the responsibility of continuing his father and grandfather's craft of *batik*-making.

Teddy was exactly who I was looking for. He was deeply connected to his craft and culture and wanted to share his family's art with the world. It was clear from the first few minutes of our meeting that our values were perfectly aligned. We both wanted to elevate tradition, make high-quality authentic products, and ensure their future through innovation while respecting their origins.

Teddy's workshop was small but adorned with earth-colored threads, tools, and yarns and filled with workers handmaking *batik* textiles using the *ceplok* and *tjanting* methods (more on this later). Large vats sat atop hollow cement fire pits in the back of the workshop where a roaring woodfire boiled textiles in water to remove wax. Various dye baths filled with colorful liquid lined the side walls of the dimly lit space. A soft and fragrant haze of *batik* scents hung in the air as I drank in the whole scene. It was all perfect, exactly the traditional family-run *batik* workshop with which I had been seeking to form a relationship.

At the end of the tour, Teddy pulled back a curtain, revealing a large room with high ceilings and drying textiles. We ducked through a rusty metal door that creaked open and entered a dark space with pungent smells I couldn't quite place. It seemed like this was some sort of secret room in the workshop. Teddy sparked his lighter, and the flame illuminated the small space. After a few moments, my eyes adjusted to the darkness, and I couldn't believe what I saw. Every square inch of the walls was jam-packed with thousands of copper *batik* blocks.

"These are all my family's *batik* stamps," Teddy said, smiling, "Some of them are over 100 years old and were my great-great grandfather's tools."

This was his family's living museum of their craft, and it was an honor to be invited into this space. I was now sure this connection would lead to a great collaboration *if* he wanted to work with Ethnotek and me.

Teddy and I spent the rest of the afternoon searching through vast stacks of batik textiles that burst with color, intricate Indonesian designs, and traditional motifs. The level of detail and quality was impeccable, and it was almost impossible to believe it was all made by hand. But looking closer, there were just enough signs of imperfection, or "Signatures of Handmade," as we call them at Ethnotek.

Teddy and I talked for many hours. I explained who I was, what Ethnotek was all about, how we intended to order *batik* from him, and most importantly, that we cared about craft and culture. Then, I asked permission to share his family's *batik* and story through our company.

A few hours later, after getting to know one another, we shook hands and agreed to become partners. I bought three different *batik* thread designs from Teddy on that glorious day in Solo. In a matter of months, they would go on to be featured in Ethnotek's launch collection with REI (that small American retailer we mentioned earlier!). Within six months, we were buying hundreds of meters of Teddy's family textiles, and our business relationship was off to a flying start. The threads of a great partnership had been sewn, one that would bond us together for many years to come —all because I had decided to go on the sourcing trail to make this happen. And, of course, with help from a few new friends. Thanks must go to the incredible gong-playing good guy in this story, Mr. Dwi!

The day after that first meeting with Teddy, I took a pedicab for another day of sourcing in Solo. After securing an incredible partner, I was on a high and excited about who I might meet and what might happen next. My destination was the Laweyan neighborhood, synonymous with *batik* textiles in Solo. As I passed by houses and small businesses, it was clear I had come to the right place. Colorful *batik* textiles adorned every window, were draped over racks, hung from ceilings, and seemed to blanket the entire block — a *batik* paradise.

The pedicab dropped me off at no particular place, which was fine because I wanted to explore. I bounced between shops, gathering ideas, samples, and contacts. The neighborhood was so dense with small family-run *batik* businesses that it quickly became clear that finding contacts wasn't hard, but I needed to get clear on exactly what I was looking for.

I could literally close my eyes, wander into a shop, and make a partnership. I already had a solid connection to traditional motifs and earth tones with Teddy, so I wanted to know if there was something more modern that used traditional *batik* handmade methods but with brighter colors and geometric patterns.

After wandering around Laweyan in the sweltering sun all day and feeling the rollercoaster highs and lows from too many sugar-laden teas handed to me by friendly *batik* traders, I was about to call it a day. But then, just as I was about to hail down a pedicab, something caught my attention down the street. Next to a mosque was a shop with colorful *sarongs* (a long piece of cloth wrapped around the lower body worn by men and women across Indonesia) draped over racks that burst with so much color it was like they radiated glowing sunshine. I felt pulled to this place like a magnet, and upon entry, I was amazed to find the small shop festooned floor-to-ceiling with intensely colored textiles in wild patterns. Some almost looked like hand-painted contemporary art, starkly contrasting to the traditional neutral color ones or Earth tones, like I had sourced the previous day with Teddy. With no one in sight, I called out "*Monggo*," a Javanese greeting that can mean "please," "hello," or "go ahead." A few seconds later, a man wearing glasses, sporting a big smile, and holding a cigarette in his hand bounded out from behind a curtain. This was the first time I met Iwan, short for Setiawan, and we were about to form a friendship that would last years.

After brief introductions, Iwan and I were drinking sugary tea while he chain-smoked clove cigarettes and listened intently to this stranger's story about bags and artisan threads. Iwan then told me about his family's history with *batik*, which went back five generations. He and his father owned a factory outside Jakarta that produced polyester goods. While that's where they made their money, *batik* was their passion. They worked hard to continue their craft, with a twist to keep their customers interested. Iwan used his *batik* as a canvas for his artistic expression. He constantly experimented with new patterns, designs, and colors to create unique *batiks* unlike anything else in the neighborhood and Solo. Much to my delight, Iwan also loved bright colors, and his *batiks* burst with energy. He also refrained from dip-dying, which can impact the environment if not managed and disposed of correctly, which often happens, resulting in water and air pollution. Instead, he used a handpainted method, which created exceptionally beautiful results. He was the type of partner I was looking for and a perfect contrasting complement to Teddy and his *batiks*.

Iwan was also interested in working on custom designs and experimenting even more with his artistic expression. I had naively thought we only had to work with traditional designs regarding *batik*, but Iwan didn't think this way. For him, *batik* was the cultural canvas he was free to experiment with. I loved this attitude, and Iwan's approach also aligned with Ethnotek's Interfusing approach (Chapter 1) of blending traditional arts with modern techniques to textiles.

Iwan was also fascinating to speak with and learn about his thoughts on the evolution of cultural craft. For example, one of our early slogans at Ethnotek was "Keeping Culture Alive," which I must admit, today, I realize was a poor choice made by my younger self. But Iwan eschewed any views that he was "keeping culture alive."

"Look at me," he said as we sat on the floor of his shop, and he held out his arms, one hand with a permanent cigarette clasped between his fingers.

"I'm wearing a baseball cap, polo shirt, and jeans, not a *sarong* and *blangkon* (traditional headwear worn by men)."

"Culture is in here," he said, pointing to his heart, "and here," moving his hand to his head, "It will continue through the things we create and pass on to the next generation."

That was the moment when our relationship and working collaboration was decided. I deeply respected who he was and his philosophy on where craft and culture co-exist. This was also the start of a new friendship, and I remember clearly the thought drifting through my mind, "*I have the best job on the planet.*"

I lay in bed that night, reflecting on the past two days, and wrote in my journal.

"*I'm glad I made the trip. Reminder to self: I must* ***Go There*** *in person to find great artisans.*"

While it may sound like a simple idea, the importance of Ethnotek's **Go There** philosophy, which took root in Solo, has guided us well through many areas of our company life and longevity. After all, I place the success of our business firmly on the shoulders of the strength of our relationships. In an ever-increasingly digital world, our company and community are all about face time (real, not social media). By physically meeting and spending time with those you seek to do business with, you empower them by cutting out the middleman and developing a relationship founded on trust, transparency, fun, and co-creation.

So, let's break down in tangible terms what this approach can translate to in business. **Direct Trade** is the first point we can cover in our **Go There** philosophy. At its core, Direct Trade is a sourcing model that revolves around authenticity and connection. Picture a coffee farmer in a lush, sun-kissed field in Guatemala, shaking hands with a coffee roaster who has journeyed thousands of miles from his coffee shop in Chicago to the very origin of those flavorful beans. It's a relationship built on trust, communication, and a shared commitment to quality.

Unlike conventional supply chains, Direct Trade forges a direct and intimate link between producers and buyers. Whether it's the rich aroma of coffee beans or the vibrant hues of artisanal textiles, Direct Trade champions the beauty of one-on-one connections in our busy and complicated world of commerce.

There are many values of Direct Trade, but to cover the most relevant ones for working with artisans for our case study of Ethnotek as a business, we must begin with **Be Human**. As in the case of the Solo artisans, that first meeting was pivotal for the strength of our relationship, which is still going strong all these years later. I have been back five times to visit Teddy, Iwan, and their teams over the years, and with each visit, our business relationship has grown stronger. More face time has meant more human interaction and deeper relationships, whereas a natural positive effect is that we have become increasingly more open in our communication. We express fears, hopes, and desires for our relationship, and there are no secrets. This cannot be underestimated. As we heard in Chapter 2, this is only possible if the effort is made to seek out the artisans in person, show face, and turn up willing to listen as a human, not just as a business partner. Artisan-based business relationships are special in this regard. We're not in the business of faceless products. Quite the opposite, as every product has a person and culture behind it that needs representation and empathy, and that is only possible by being in the same space as each other. Not once, but many times.

Another benefit of Direct Trade is that magical D-word. By going **directly** to the source, you **Cut Out The Middleman**. In today's globalized marketplace, where product buyers and sellers may be on the other side of the world, it's rare for a company to send one or more people from their product development team to visit all suppliers in their supply chain because it's a substantial drain on time and finances. Therefore, it's common to work with agents and marketplaces to do most of the sourcing on the company's behalf. As you can imagine, this comes at a cost, but it also affects something much more important: transparency between buyers and sellers. The extra gatekeeper can add a gray layer of communication whereby it can become unclear how much profit goes into the artisan or product creator's pockets and how much commission goes to the middleman. Also, working with middlemen or agents can create opacity in the brand story and the supply chain and inhibit the community engagement of customers with the products they buy. Increasingly, customers want to know who is making the products they purchase and bring them into the brand's story, and this has always been a value we embody at Ethnotek.

It's essential to **Validate Working Conditions** when working with partners worldwide. Direct Trade puts in-person, face-to-face interactions at the center of the relationship, where the buyers can see that workers are producing products and art in safe, fair, and equitable conditions for all involved. Not only that, but it is also where people can work and thrive. This is such an essential issue for a social entrepreneur to invest time in to ensure the environments in which their international partners live up to the company's (and human) values and empower the people doing the work. It's a responsibility we have always taken to heart at Ethnotek. Without in-person visits to potential new suppliers, it's difficult to understand the quality of the working conditions, and taking a third party's word for this can be a dangerous, costly decision that can backfire in many detrimental ways. It can cost your business and reputation, and worse, support inadequate or unsafe working conditions that can lead to suffering and, in extreme cases, even death.

Going to the source and putting Direct Trade at the heart of your business is the only way I advise you to work with artisans. These days, just about anything can be faked on a website. Go there and meet the partners in their workshops — it's the only way to know. Visiting artisans and product creators directly is also really fun. Over the years, I've gained so much creative good vibes from our in-person collaborations that these interactions end up being a springboard for a new product, idea, or direction for our company that I couldn't have known if I hadn't made the journey.

This is why at Ethnotek I keep a mantra close to my thoughts of **Inspiration & Adaptation**. During artisan visits, sometimes I see a piece of cloth nearby, an accidental dye drip on the floor, or a dusty antique *batik* stamp discarded in a corner and get ideas for new designs that never would have occurred to me had I not been there. These ideas grow a life of their own when shared in the moment with the artisans. With their specialist skills and knowledge, they can nurture the seedling of a creative musing into something real, tangible, and achievable. The excitement and joy between both parties while co-creating locally in this way is the real magic spark that keeps the Ethnotek show on the road.

I can think of two examples of this point, which happened during a visit with Iwan in Solo while we were discussing the traditional *kertu* motif and custom colors. Because I had sourced some traditional floral and organic shaped designs from Teddy across town, I was now on the hunt for some geometric designs from Iwan. While he had a few options, the motifs I liked blended with many other shapes and didn't have the bold, colorful impact I was looking for. Knowing that Iwan was open to co-creating, I asked if it was okay to isolate the specific motif from the background patterns. I asked if this was okay culturally and even possible in his process. I asked because I knew from experience that our male customers had shown a preference for minimalistic designs. Iwan told me the whole story behind the *kertu* motif, which consisted of overlapping rectangular shapes with small symbols inside them. Iwan explained that *kertu* means "cards" and is inspired by the card games Chinese traders introduced to Java upon their visits in the eighth and ninth centuries. After learning this, it became clear that those overlapping shapes are cards —very clever! It was also an interesting snapshot that captured the Javanese's openness to accepting other nationalities into their trade and cultural identity.

Iwan said it wasn't just possible to adapt the motif but that it would be a fun, creative challenge, and he tasked his head artisan, Harjono, with building a new batik stamp, especially to print the custom design. Indonesian batik stamps are a work of art in their own right, so this was a huge honor. They are constructed by piecing hundreds of little strips of copper soldered together to create various shapes and patterns in the motif. When the front face of the block is sanded and finished, a handle is added, and it's ready to be used. Copper is used as the stamping component because it retains heat and cools quickly, which is essential because it is constantly dipped into the hot wax reservoir and then pressed onto the fabric. To create a stamp that can be used repeatedly and form one larger geometric pattern without causing any drips is truly a masterpiece of craftsmanship. It can take a lifetime to learn the technique, and Harjono, who was Iwan's father's close friend, had been creating batik fabrics for over 50 years.

Soon after, with a newly-crafted *kertu* stamp, it was time to select the base fabric for this new Ethnotek custom-made thread lovingly crafted by Iwan and Harjano. At first, we chose a fabric with a subtle striped effect (due to its combination of greige color and bleached cotton weaving) to give it more depth. We felt the plain white background looked too flat. These subtle decisions were made between all three of us as we brainstormed back and forth about what would work best with the particular motif. It was a fluid, joyful process of experimentation that, just a few months later, would become a core part of our Ethnotek product line, a steady seller, and a firm favorite worldwide with our community. What took two weeks of in-person co-creation, ideation, and experimentation led to years of constant demand for handmade fabric. This one example is further proof of the importance of going there to meet artisans in person. But there's one more I want to tell you about.

It was sometime in 2014 when sales of our Indonesian fabrics began to slow. We still had a responsibility to keep our word of bringing continual fabric orders to artisan communities, so I had the idea to freshen up the collection with bright new spring colors. I asked Iwan if he'd ever worked with Pantone colors. Luckily, he had and proactively purchased a new Pantone book for our new spring project together. Though dye pigments are very different from creating colors for hard goods or printed materials, which Pantone is primarily used for, we felt confident we could create color formulas to match almost perfectly to any colors our customers wanted. Iwan imports his pigments from Dystar, a German-Swedish joint venture because they are of the highest quality and reliable pigments with the lowest environmental impact. I chose some interesting new motifs with flowers and birds and specified new colorways from our Pantone books, for which Iwan made custom pigment formulas. Watching him create these formulas was like watching a chemist. He'd scoop out various powder-form colors, weigh them on a scale, blend them with water, paint them onto white cotton fabric, let them dry, and then cross-check them with the Pantone swatch. This process often took days to get a perfect match, and when we finally got the right result, Iwan would make note of the exact formula and step-by-step process. This was critical because it was the base recipe for the color of our mass production, and achieving a perfect color match from one cup of dye to ten gallons of dye requires perfect calculations. This process is rarely seen and appreciated by the end customers, but we designers and artisans must think long and hard about getting it right.

The new color palette we created for Iwan's *batik* sported a rich golden yellow style, a vivid turquoise colorway, a dark magenta style, and a fresh white and blue combo. The collection became the best seller that year and restored demand for fabric orders with our Indonesian partners — mission accomplished! It also caught the eye of a new distributor named Gustavo Trading at the ISPO Tradeshow in Munich, Germany, when we launched the new collection in 2015. That customer eventually became Ethnotek's biggest B2B buyer and now co-owns the company.

These two lessons with Iwan and the product micro-adjustments we made together through the creative process had significant results for our business. This is why taking the time to meet the makers, learn their process, and earn their trust helps in the process of co-creation.

Another benefit of forming a direct relationship with artisans through in-person visits is storytelling. With dwindling attention spans and a rise in misinformation in our digital world, **Seeing Is Believing.** This is why the simple act of filming a video of an artisan process and sharing it online is far more impactful, trustworthy, and entertaining than writing about it and hoping people will take your word for it. In our digital age, video is king. This point is closely coupled with the above note about the importance of in-person product development. If you're already there building relationships and creating things together, you might as well get the cameras out and document it. Afterall, it's usually unclear how long it will be until you return. Get over the shyness and document as much as you can. Simply ask for permission if you want to photograph someone; if they don't want that, shooting the hands or other parts of the process can be just as powerful.

But it is important to avoid prematurely bringing out the camera. I only start shooting videos and photos after a couple of days of meeting people and spending time with them. It's essential to bank smiles, laughs, shared meals, and a common commercial understanding before trust has been earned. And when someone feels comfortable with you, it shows. Good vibes shine a lot brighter when everyone in the room is familiar. So I say, take the time, and after trust is earned and permission granted, shoot everything you can, take lots of notes in the moment for later blog articles, social media posts, video narration, or even for a book (like this one). The content you capture doesn't have to be cinematic National Geographic quality — in fact, it shouldn't be. People will connect with and relate more to imagery that feels user-generated and authentic. Knowing that it's the founder fumbling with the camera and mediocre audio is much more exciting than a hired film crew. At least, that's what our customers and team tell me.

Let's pause for a moment to address the difference between Direct Trade and **Fair Trade**, which can cause some confusion. Fair Trade is an intermediary that uses a standard living wage model to ensure producers (artisans, coffee farmers, etc.) receive more pay, while Direct Trade cuts out intermediaries for a more hands-on approach to ensure producers receive more money upfront and have the opportunity to collaborate closer. At Ethnotek, we prefer for-profit Direct Trade as the most sustainable method. This is because Direct Trade isn't just about products; it's a story with fairness as its main character. By sidestepping intermediaries, this approach ensures that artisans and creators agree on fair prices for their exceptional work without the oversight of a third party who isn't intimately involved in their businesses or personal lives. The magic happens when skilled hands are recognized and compensated for the true value of their craft. Financial transparency is so important to us at Ethnotek, and it has always been. We are ardent ambassadors of Direct Trade and artisans getting their fair share free from any outside influence whatsoever. This is why I have visited all of our artisan partners in person to establish a relationship and make this fact possible. By getting to know each other personally, sharing meals and laughter, and earning trust, we deeply understand one another's long-term vision, hopes, dreams, and struggles.

There is also cause for optimism with the growing appreciation of Direct Trade from consumers and conscious brands. Two examples that spring to mind within the ethical fashion sector are People Tree and Everlane. Their commitment to Direct Trade ensures fair wages for artisans and factory workers and creates amazing products. Everlane even coined the phrase "**Radical Transparency**," which we fully support. It has created ripples throughout the fashion market and is fast becoming a new industry standard to aim for.

A more subtle benefit of Direct Trade is that there's a gradual **Compounding Of Quality** over time. When brands or buyers have a direct line to the source producer or artisan, collaboration leads to a shared passion for the products. This matters when things are going well, but especially when problems inevitably arise with orders or quality issues. When buyers and sellers have direct communication and a well-established bond based on trust, they both go above and beyond to produce excellence. When the end goal for the creator is to sell as much of their great product as possible so that it funnels more orders to the producer, both have a shared drive for quality and consistency. A bad customer experience, defective return, and inconsistent quality hurts both parties equally. Therefore, this well-understood and shared risk makes hard conversations easy when nitpicking details to improve things. Eventually, one side will make a mistake and need the other side to be flexible. That's why it's important to have a personal relationship to fall back on. You never know when you'll need to cash in a favor or need one yourself. Another small point about quality standards is that they can be subjective. Therefore, the brand's designer needs to have direct contact with the artisan or product producer to ensure clear, consistent communication of ideas and details. In my experience, I've always found that imagery transcends boundaries and language barriers when working internationally. I've always leaned on Photoshop and Illustrator to show precisely what I mean when discussing motif size, color variation, straight lines, stripe spacing, etc. Even hand-drawn sketches can be much more effective than trying to explain them verbally.

It's also essential to define your level of tolerance over quality control. For Ethnotek, we aim for perfection but always accept a 10% variance. If a color is 90% matching the original reference sample and previous production run, we accept it. Although we have very high standards, we empathize that rejecting things burdens the artisans, especially if a large quantity has already been produced. This is why it's crucial to establish these quality control guideline rules at the beginning of a Direct Trade relationship.

I've also found it's helpful when working on new designs with artisans to print a multipage document with yarn trimmings and anything visual that helps convey the expected final output. Then, I put everything into a folder and mail it to the artisan team, so they have it on hand. We do most of our business through WhatsApp, which is great for communication but limited in the visual realm. Holding a one-to-one scale printed pattern, Pantone swatch, or yarn trimming next to the fabric on the loom often leads to way more accuracy than a phone screen can communicate.

In the garden of Direct Trade, sustainability takes root. By fostering long-term relationships, this sourcing model nurtures environmental stewardship. From ethical production practices to reduced environmental impact, sustainability becomes integral to the narrative. For example, most mass-produced textiles for garments and accessories are made on a Jacquard electric power loom*. These hulking and expensive computerized machines suck a tremendous amount of electricity leading to a sizable carbon footprint. In contrast, an artisan-powered hand loom uses zero electricity and a miniscule carbon footprint. Backstrap*, treadle*, and pit looms* are cheap to build and can be constructed locally. They are often built with natural materials such as wood, rattan, hemp, cotton, reeds, metal, coral, and stone. Most importantly, they can employ far more people than their mechanized successors.

It's also essential to remember that handmade textiles are deeply rooted in many cultures worldwide, and moving away from traditional weaving methods shouldn't be just a decision based on the quantity of goods that can be produced. Larger, mass-produced methods can replace culturally-significant artisanal ones and also be detrimental to the environment.

An interesting and related topic to this point is the *Swadeshi* Movement in India, that swelled in 1903 after the British introduced power looms, which took many jobs away from those in the handmade textile industry. *Swadeshi* was a nationalist protest to protect localized handmade production. To this day, you can see many famous images of Gandhi spinning yarn on a *charkha* (a wheel that feeds raw yarn into a spool for weaving). This movement gained so much traction that the *charkha* adorns India's national flag. Similar stories of weavers protesting against mass-production methods abound across the globe, and I encourage fellow curious, conscious consumers to seek them out.

Check out Maiwa Handprints for a great example of a Direct Trade relationship with handmade textile artisans. They're based out of Canada and sell threads from the Kutch region of India. They embody a spirit of transparency we've long admired at Ethnotek, and they blazed a trail for the work that we do today. Founder Charlotte is also a champion, so I tip my hat to her team and their mission and encourage you to visit their website.

Before we depart our learnings from Direct Trade, I want to highlight that Ethnotek is just one player in the cultural neighborhood living this example. We hope that our approach can be an inspiration to larger brands that have a much larger imprint in the world and could consider moving to a Direct Trade method of sourcing in the future. After all, a more fair, equitable world is one where buyers and sellers are equals, and we end the practice of sweatshops and overworked artisans in the developing world straining to make a living wage to supply Western mega-brands huge orders and indirect, unfair sourcing approaches. Direct Trade is ethical and a way of being in the world that's good for everyone.

There's much room for positivity, too. In a time when consumers are taking to social media to demand ethical sourcing on a mass scale, two beacons shine brightly, embodying the essence of Direct Trade principles in their work: Nest and Powered By People. These organizations are not merely platforms but architects of positive change who are redefining B2B and co-creation to leverage ethical supply chains and artisan empowerment. Please, go check them out!

We opened this chapter with our **Go There** philosophy, which has been the source of so many good vibes for our business. We've seen examples of Direct Trade in action and learned why Ethnotek always chooses this sourcing method.

While that first-sourcing trip to Solo seems like a lifetime ago, the lessons I learned have endured to this day. It's funny, I recently found a video from that day on the train as I sped across Java en route to Solo. The video makes me laugh — not only because of the shaky video and quirky edits. I see my fresh-faced self, and I look like a bundle of nerves and excitement. I had no idea what to expect. We can only know in retrospect the importance of relationships that we begin, grow, and nurture. And as I look back now, and at all the thousands of bags we've now made, sold, and shipped worldwide that carry those Solo artisans' work and threads, I'm filled with joy. And I know in my bones that it all started because I was willing to Go There and find them.

Our company's success has been because of our relationships. It's just that simple. And so I say, whether starting your own business or working for one, if you want to find success in your social enterprise, then you have to put people at the center of your world. Show up in person, ready to listen and with empathy in your heart, and you'll do well. Turn up ready to trade but also ready to make a new friend.

5

Build A Community, Not A Brand

"Never doubt that a small group of thoughtful, committed citizens can change the world; indeed, it's the only thing that ever has."

— Margaret Mead

Kanderai Village, Gujarat, India
2015

It had been a long drive through the Kacchi Desert in Bhuj, northwest India, near the border of Pakistan. I had set out with Shamji and our local facilitator Pankaj as we sped through the arid plains, leaving plumes of dust in our wake, the sun beat down all around. This was India's largest salt desert. The scorched landscape stretched as far as the eye could see, with no trees, wildlife, or people in sight for miles. This lonely and hostile environment covers 10,800 square miles, transforms from salt marshlands in summer to a parched desert in winter, and draws travelers worldwide to witness its natural wonders. But I wasn't here for the desert; I was just passing through on a special mission for Ethnotek. By the time our dust-covered sedan rolled into Kanderai Village, I was exhausted from the road but excited for the rendezvous we had planned. After all, I had traveled to meet a pair of weavers who were a rarity in today's textile industry. Not only were they twins, but the 18 year olds actually wanted to carry on the family business. As you can probably guess, in an era of social media, technology, and migration to megacities, a growing challenge weaving families face is to inspire the next generation to carry on the craft. This is why I came to pay homage to these two special brothers: Sanjay and Suresh. After hearing about the brothers, I became excited to meet them and do whatever I could through Ethnotek to fan the flames of inspiration. At the time of our arrival, the brothers had been training with our head artisan, Shamji, and their father, Arjan Ramji, for a few weeks now — learning from the masters.

There wasn't a soul in sight as our car rolled into Kanderai, a rural village with tight-knit rows of terracotta, mud and stucco homes, and slid to a stop. It was clear the reason why as soon as I stepped out of the car — the heat. It was so hot that it was difficult to breathe. Bhuj temperatures can regularly top 104°F. As Shamji, Pankaj, and I wandered through the village, a few locals came into view, some taking shelter in the shade under trees while others lounged on the porches of their homes. Shamji began shouting "*Ram Ram*" in a sing-song way that echoed along the lonely village streets. The term is a local greeting in homage to Lord Rama and triggers friendly banter. Moments later, a throng of villagers emerged from their homes, happy to see their old friends (and their blonde-sunburnt foreign sidekick). Women in colorful *sarees* surrounded us and touched the top of Shamji and Pankaj's heads as they bowed, a custom greeting for well-respected community members and elders. Shamji is a local legend in the village for his tireless efforts to promote the weaving trade of the region, including the Kandherai weavers.

It had been a couple of years since I had traveled here in person, and so Shamji and Pankaj took time to introduce me to the villagers, who smiled and looked at me with curiosity and warmth. Kids merrily jumped up and down around me, yelling, "Hello, hello," as the adult villagers nodded and smiled with their signature warmth and welcoming nature.

Shamji then led us on a village tour, stopping off along the way to embrace more old friends as he went. Seeing how people gravitate toward him (and his father) is a joy. It's not just his magnetic personality; it's because of his selflessness to ensure everyone is cared for and receives their fair share of profits within the weaving community. He's known throughout the greater Bhuj area as a pioneer of the weaving trade and championing community involvement in arts. As a leader of the wider weaving community, Shamji sees it as his duty to pay respect to all the villagers, trying to check in on as many artisans and their families each time he visits. Witnessing a genuinely inspirational model for community and purpose-driven business is beautiful. I could see a clear and cohesive thread running through everyone's hearts here. The community spirit was palpable, with long-lasting bonds of trust and respect woven into the fabric of the village over many years. I'm incredibly grateful to have witnessed such community spirit in the villages, towns, and cities where our Ethnotek artisan partners have lived and worked worldwide since our inception. I treasure them allowing me – and the company — to be a part of their lives, and it fills me with joy each time I get to visit and be welcomed into the communities as a partner with a shared love for textiles.

Toward the end of our village tour, Shamji introduced me to Sanjay and Suresh, who, entirely unbeknownst to me, had been walking with our little posse the whole time. I felt silly and rude for not saying hello until just now, but the young brothers brushed this aside, and we immediately set about getting to know one another. Taking a rest under the shade of a nearby home, soon after, we were all drinking *masala* tea and getting to know one another. I felt an immediate connection with the young brothers. They were humble, curious, hilarious, spoke English well, and, for some reason, loved my sunglasses. We kept taking turns wearing them and striking poses. After a while, the conversation moved to Ethnotek customers, and I pulled out my phone to show the brothers some photos on our social media channels. As they scrolled through the pictures on my phone, their puzzled looks grew into huge grins and excited chatter in Kutchi as they saw Ethnotek customers in many different parts of the world wearing their family's textiles on our bags. Their eyes lit up as they realized the far-reaching scope of their family's work. Shamji and Pankaj then explained the Ethnotek mission of working with handmade artisans worldwide and how, if they wanted to continue to weave, this was one destination where their family's textiles would eventually be distributed to a global customer base. Over the next five minutes, Shamji explained the Ethnotek business model and how the boys could fit into the project — if they wanted to. I listened intently and smiled as the brothers got more excited as Shamji finished his story. After a few moments of silence, the brothers looked at each other, smiled, and said, "We want to keep weaving!"

Right then, by the look on their faces, I knew that this was an important moment for them and Ethnotek. The brothers explained that they found pride in seeing their work as part of an international network of artisans worldwide. They loved seeing the textiles from the other countries where we work (Ghana, Guatemala, Indonesia, and Vietnam) and understanding how their work fits into the bigger picture. I knew this gratification and validation of their work was a big deal, and I made a mental note to continue this simple gesture of showing new artisan partners their work out in the world and to make this a crucial part of our **Build A Community, Not A Brand** philosophy. The simple act of showing, not telling artisans how their work impacts other people's lives, is powerful. Especially for the younger generation thinking about a career in weaving, showing them what's possible — and where their work will find a home — weaves threads of understanding and inspiration. They will see that their great-grandparents' craft can take on new life in the modern world and be cool and relevant. While their family's textiles were woven into rugs in the past, today, seeing their weaving take on new life as backpacks on urban commuters in the busy streets around the world, from Berlin to Bangkok, California to Canberra, Tokyo to Toronto, opens their horizons and connects them to the wider world. This is a generation connected to the internet, after all. That longing for interconnectedness is an undeniable generational shift occurring worldwide, including in the villages of the Kacchi Desert.

This is a simple but important point for social entrepreneurs working in the artisan space: Share the love. Show the artisans their work in the world. While this sounds obvious, this is not the norm in our globalized world of soft goods and fast fashion. Quite the opposite, most artisans or garment workers are hidden (often intentionally) from the end product of their work. We at Ethnotek stand firmly against this shameful and outdated practice. The collaboration shouldn't stop after the textile order ships and the balance is paid.

Meanwhile, later that night in Bhuj, the young brothers, Shamji, Pankaj, and I, sat around the dinner table sharing stories and plans for our future working relationship; they kept asking to see more photos of Ethnotek customers. Each time they did, it sparked a series of creative conversations about what they would like to create with their textiles. As we shared a memorable night, discussing endless possibilities and our working relationship for the future, I realized that in business, sharing is caring, as corny as that may sound. Sharing the love — and connecting artisans, or any kind of worker — with the end effect of their work is always a great way to Build A Community, Not A Brand.

Because Ethnotek is a people company, we focus on relationships and community-building. I realize these words can be thrown around a lot these days (not all companies honor their importance), but for us, this was our primary concern early on.

By focusing on creating meaningful relationships and internal culture instead of brand image, our rock-solid team and unique artisan supply chain have overcome consistent challenges while growing our business and base of superfan customers. In this chapter, I'd like to take you on a joyful journey into the village of community building.

The first marker along the trail in this philosophy is the simple truth that we at Ethnotek embody: **People Invest In People**. Putting a human face on your brand's products is a surefire way to create a visceral human connection between customer and producer, artisan, designer, or creator. So many brands today create faceless products, but for all you social entrepreneurs out there, going the extra mile to humanize your products and those who make them is the only way to go. At Ethnotek, customers frequently say, "I just bought a Raja Pack with Maria's fabric!" or "Hey, Shamji's new textiles look awesome on the new Cyclo Sling!" These personalized messages of feedback make me smile every time, and I always try to pass along the good vibes to the artisans. Most new customers learn about the artisans who made their bags from the hangtags and booklets we provide with each bag with detailed descriptions of the textiles featured on the product they just bought. Over the years, many customers have given us feedback that the "emotional connection" to the artisans inspired them to buy the bag. While they love the colors and textile designs, the human story gives the bag a soul. Hearing this kind of feedback is mission success from our viewpoint.

The same is true for the artisans, too. When I interviewed Shamji for this book over a Zoom call, he told me a heartwarming story with a customer.

A bit of context: Shamji is a sought-after speaker internationally because of his dedication to the weaving craft and his social entrepreneurship in his homeland. As such, he travels regularly across Asia, Europe, and the USA. Shamji uses these international talks and workshops to raise awareness for his community by teaching his craft to excited entrepreneurs and enthusiasts.

On a recent trip to Zurich, Switzerland, he had an experience he was eager to share with me—and now with you all.

"After my seminar, I decided to walk to a lookout point overlooking the Limmat River. While taking in the beautiful view, something colorful caught my eye by the river. It was a woman wearing ***my bag***! She was probably a hundred meters away, but I knew exactly what it was the second I saw it."

Pause here for a second to note that Shamji said, "***My bag.***" He didn't say an Ethnotek bag or a backpack with my fabric. He said, "***My bag***". When he said that, I've never been so proud. The fact that he takes such pride in his work and our collaboration together that he takes personal ownership tells me that we have built a community of artisans and creators who take pride in each other's work — not just a brand. I built Ethnotek as a bridge to connect customers to artisans. You won't see us bragging about how good we are or reciting diatribes about our company manifesto in our marketing. We lift up our artisan partners and customers. After all, they're the magic makers in this whole show. Ethnotek is the glue that binds the two halves together to make a whole. That's it! Now, back to Shamji's story.

"After seeing ***my bag***, I took off running! I ran through alleyways and streets down to the riverside, hoping to catch up with the woman so I could talk to her. Thankfully, she was still there, wandering along the river. I was breathless when I tapped her shoulder and introduced myself. 'I am the artist who made the textile on your bag. I just wanted to say thank you'. The woman was so surprised and told me that she had many Ethnotek bags already, mostly from India! I explained all about my community of weavers who made her bag, and she told me how she loved our textiles so much and that she was so happy I had come to introduce myself."

At this point in Shamji's story, over the Zoom call, he paused and took a deep breath as if reminded of something.

"You know, hearing that stranger's words reminded me of my father," he said, his voice cracking with emotion.

"My father (Vishram Valji) passed on our family's weaving business to me many years ago. He was a pioneering figure for the artisans of the Kutch region and almost single-handedly revived the weaving craft from the brink of extinction in the 1970s. Seeing that stranger with the bag by the riverside in Zurich made me think of him and how far our art has come."

Side note: Shamji's father's work is backed up with stats, too. In her book *Shifting Sands*, Archana Shah notes: *The Gazette* in India recorded in 1945 that there were 4,800 looms in the Vankar society. By 2011, that number had reduced by 81% to 900 looms. Its steepest decline happened between the 1950s and '60s. The demand reduction was attributed to the introduction of mechanized jacquard weaving, which appealed to business owners because of its low cost and production speed compared to its slower and more expensive traditional counterparts.

"When my father handed me the family weaving business, he told me that the only way for our craft to survive and grow was for it to change and innovate," Shamji continued.

"'Never lose our people's craft, but you must breathe new spirit into it,' my father told me. You can experiment with changing techniques, motifs, and colors, as this will open our art to more people."

Shamji paused momentarily, and I could see his eyes welling up with tears as he told his story. Despite sitting half the world away—me in the USA, he in India—I had never felt closer to my friend as he told his father's story. After a long pause, Shamji wiped his eyes, and his signature smile returned.

"It made me so happy to meet that stranger in Zurich and to hear her appreciate our art. We are building upon my family's legacy, which continues to grow. That encounter made me feel very proud about our work together."

Wow! I'm not going to lie; hearing Shamji's story brought a tear to my eye. I felt so proud that we could feel safe and vulnerable to share his family story with me and all of you. He's a true legend of the craft, and I'm beyond grateful for his service to his community. He continues to inspire Ethnotek, our community, and our customers. Shamji's Zurich encounter and his family story perfectly encapsulate the point I'm trying to make about building a community, not a brand. When there's a clear thread between the artisan (Shamji & his father), customer (stranger by the river), and purpose (promoting handmade artisans' work), an unbreakable community bond is woven together. Also, shout out to the wonderful woman in Zurich. If you read this book, we'd love to hear from you!

Early in the Ethnotek journey, we adopted our **Positive Social Power** approach to marketing. We leveraged social media as our go-to channel to create conversations and bridge the gap between end customers and our artisan partners.

We invited customers to join us on sourcing trips when we could afford it. We occasionally connected our community members with the artisans for in-person visits even if we couldn't be there—anything to bridge the gap between artisans and customers.

The first time we invited customers to join us on a sourcing trip was after our first Kickstarter campaign in 2016. Justin and Kirk, both from the USA, met us in India. The campaign was to launch a new backpack design called the Premji Pack, named after one of our longest-standing weavers in India. We thought it'd be nice for Premji backers to meet the man himself and, of course, meet the rest of the team on the ground to enjoy the local food and intimately mingle with the handmade process. It was a blast! We did this again a couple of years later for our camera bag collection launch when Kirk joined us again in Indonesia. Between these trips, we connected the Uchiyamas, a married couple from Japan with our weaving team in India, and a woman from Germany named Lias, who visited our facilitator Reiss and head *batik* artisan Charles in Ghana. Most recently, we hosted Marina and Laura from Germany, Kim and Kiana from the USA, and Otavio from Brazil in Guatemala. We had so much fun! Here's a quote from Kiana Sosa from that trip.

"Traveling to Guatemala, meeting some of the weavers, and gaining a better understanding of Ethnotek's values was the highlight of my year. Not only did I have a blast exploring a new country and meeting new people, I developed a new zest for adventure and connection. Before the trip, I knew Ethnotek as a company that did cool work and sold cool bags. After an inside look, I realized that Ethnotek doesn't just sell useful and aesthetic products; it drives impact for entrepreneurs and their families, thus having a ripple effect on communities and the preservation of the impressive skills deeply rooted in culture and tradition that are passed on from generation to generation. As an artist who cares deeply about impact, I am quite picky about the brands I give my loyalty to — Ethnotek is a brand that I wholeheartedly support."

These trips are expensive and difficult to quantify regarding return on investment, but that's not the point. It's all about living our mission, raising awareness for the cause, and connecting artisans with their end customers.

On a personal level, these trips fill me with immense pride. I take a back seat, adopt the observer role, and enjoy watching the interactions between customers and artisans without my influence shaping the relationship. From the beginning, it was a goal of mine to share my love for sourcing trips with others, especially die-hard fans and supporters. Sure, there are ways to do this on a much larger scale to involve more people, but we're at least getting started, and it's been rewarding so far. After all, we're a bag company, a manufacturer, not a tour agency!

Our guests often enthusiastically share their experiences on social media during and after their trips, which is fantastic for raising awareness and further authenticating brand credibility. These infrequent trips have a profound effect on sparking interest and engagement from our wider Ethnotek international community. Even for people who weren't on the sourcing trips, the feedback online is hugely supportive for the lucky ones who did go. It's rare for brands to go this extra mile for their fans. Walking the talk is essential, even if it doesn't necessarily lead to short-term financial gains.

One of the feel-good community-focused initiatives we supported early on (and still do to this day) at Ethnotek is the **I Made Your Bag Campaign**. So much globalized business is hidden. That's a huge problem in the fast fashion industry and something we are passionately against. We want our customers to know who made their products.

It's the whole reason for our being, so we wear the cultures and people who create our products with pride — we don't hide! And so I would advise (actually prompt) any other entrepreneurs to adopt this strategy. In today's consumer world, we need transparency between makers and buyers of products. One example of how we bridge this gap is in our marketing, which happens every April, when we join the Fashion Revolution movement online with the I Made Your Bag Campaign. Saying the word "campaign" feels big because it's actually a simple initiative to implement. The movement is for SMEs in consumer products and fashion to share photos and short introductions of the people who make their clothes, shoes, bags, fabric, pottery, etc. To meet the makers and validate working conditions. For our campaign, we meet with our production teams and have our various unsung heroes hold up a sign that says "I Made Your Bag" and snap a photo. We then share these photos online with a brief introduction to name them and explain what they do. These social media posts almost always drive the highest engagement, with our customers worldwide thanking the makers for their work. This campaign provides transparency about their fair working conditions. It's a simple yet powerful gesture connecting our community and values our people.

Creating Company Culture is something you hear a lot about, but often, it's an afterthought that brands try to reverse engineer into their DNA — and that simply doesn't work. Customers are smart, savvy, and switched on. They know the difference between brand speak and authentic communication. Creating a company culture is about open communication at every level. I worked hard on this from the start of Ethnotek and sought to educate all our staff, suppliers, and distributors about who we were and what we stood for. This was also a big part of our early success because we effectively communicated our mission, which won us great media attention (see Chapter 1) and got us off to a great start.

A close cousin to communication in the realm of community building is commitment. I'm a big fan of intrinsic motivation. **Commitment To The Mission** is a must-have criteria for anyone we bring into the Ethnotek family. We've been fortunate enough to attract incredible people organically from all over the world throughout the years who are inspired by our artisan focus and genuinely want to be a part of what we do. They're also usually fellow bag nerds, textile enthusiasts, or world travelers.

When I believe in a cause bigger than myself and helps people worldwide, I will likely work hard for it. I also have to love the things I'm making or selling. It doesn't feel like work when these tenets are intertwined with a team of like-minded people who share the same motivation. It feels like play. That's why I always vet new recruits to ensure their "why" aligns with ours. There's a story I like that punctuates this point nicely. In 1961, President John F. Kennedy visited NASA headquarters for the first time. While touring the facility, he introduced himself to a janitor who was mopping the floor and asked him what he did at NASA. The janitor replied, "I'm helping put a man on the moon." Absolutely right, good sir, and a contender for the best comeback of all time!

Little is written about **Empathy & Transparency** in business, which is unfortunate and a missed opportunity for community good vibes and creating a culture of trust. Within Ethnotek, we think it's important to walk around in someone else's shoes. We ask ourselves what their life is like and their struggles, inspirations, and motivations. This helps us relate and provide a better experience for one another. After all, empathy is at the core of creating products and services that benefit the lives of others. While I like to hire people with strong emotional intelligence, not everyone has this skill set, so I try to maintain an internal culture and safe inner circle where participation can teach it.

Eventually, people emerge from their shells and feel secure enough to express themselves fully. The closer we get to one another as a team, the higher overall performance and loyalty toward a shared goal becomes. Vulnerability is strength, in my opinion. Truly making an effort to see things from another person's perspective is what breaks down the social boundaries that separate us. Creating a space for this is where great creative work can abound. Empathy also manifests itself everywhere in our process at Ethnotek. It guides the development of new relationships and maintains them with artisans, suppliers, and vendors over time. For example, I empathize with the end customer when I design a new bag. I have to imagine what they're carrying daily and foresee their pain points. I have to envisage the comfort or discomfort of wearing and using something as a large or petite person. I have to become a different gender and think about breasts when designing shoulder straps. I picture customers in various settings, including the office, airport, beach, and forest, running in the rain, trekking through snow, or walking in the midday sun. I also have to consider their interests, hobbies, color, and pattern preferences. I have to become them to improve my design solution's likelihood of improving their lives through ease of use and self-expression.

Empathy also plays a part in other roles. A good customer service person feels the customer's frustration and a sense of urgency to solve their problem and make them happy. Meanwhile, the production manager needs to consider their international distributor and retail partners, who depend on them to palletize a shipment correctly and load it onto the container on time.

At the same time, the e-commerce manager needs to empathize with the person browsing the website to create an inspiring experience that reflects the brand values and design principles and, most importantly, make it seamless from the point of landing on a webpage to getting a bag on their back — and not to make people think. People on a website usually hate extra steps and too many options. We're simple creatures, and that simplicity can be surprisingly hard to design for people.

On the feelings front, I've had people tell me to leave emotion and my personal life out of business. I appreciate their words because they were trying to protect me, but I respectfully disagree with that advice. Of course, I try not to make emotional decisions, but to deny our internal community the opportunity to share their grievances, fears, struggles, hopes, dreams, excitement, frustrations, and wild ideas is to miss out on the chance to build a container of safety. When we feel safe to emote and try new things, real innovation comes into play. I prefer to lead with love, positivity, vulnerability, and praise/reward-based performance response instead of fear. The adage "you can catch more bees with honey than vinegar" resonates with me. Sadly, I've worked with managers at other companies who have adopted the opposite approach. One particular memory comes to mind. I was struggling with a team member under my watch and running out of ideas to get them to step it up. My manager then told me to embarrass that person in front of the other designers for how badly they were performing. This made me feel deeply uncomfortable, so I asked if it was okay if I tried something else before going that route. He confirmed, and instead of making a spectacle of that person in front of our peers, I pulled them aside and explained my situation, how it made me feel, and how I needed their help.

"Hey, can I share something personal with you?" I asked.

"Of course," they replied.

We already had a very positive and friendly working relationship.

"I'm feeling stressed at the moment," I explained, "I'm losing sleep, and

I have a pit in my stomach right now just talking about it. We have a deadline approaching, and even though we're all doing a great job, I need your help to speed up and bring our project back into focus. I'm worried but confident we can crush it and nail this deadline together. Can you please help me with this? I'll stay with you after hours to help if needed."

She happily obliged and moved into a higher gear. We smashed our deadline, and the designs became hot sellers. I later found out from my coach that this was authentic relating 101. Instead of pointing a finger at her and projecting blame and fear of consequence, I made it about me and asked for her help. Very rarely do we want to disappoint or harm someone else. I found through numerous examples like this throughout my career that people will usually fall all over themselves to help you when you ask them to. In this specific example, I found out she was simply excited and distracted because she loved her job so much and had difficulty prioritizing which tasks to finish before the other things she was more excited about. We were both young and learning then, and I'm quite sure handling things the way my brute of a boss suggested wouldn't have been fun or fruitful for anyone. Sure, we probably would have finished the project on time just the same, but I would have made an enemy instead of an ally. Teams can't afford this type of latent toxicity floating around the group. Here are a few words from one of our team members on this matter:

"As a freelancer who has worked with dozens of e-commerce companies I can say with 100% certainty that Ethnotek is my favorite one to work with by far. Even though I'm a contractor, I feel like I am part of the team. Most companies limit you to your area of expertise; you do what you were hired for, and that's it. You don't have a say on strategy or other topics, or at least you're not incentivized to do so. With Ethnotek, we (contractors) were always in the loop regarding the company goals and what products would be launched months or years ahead. That gave us the feeling that we were part of the company because we actually were. The bottom line is that what I find unique about Ethnotek is that we build a strong team, even being contractors there. That was done through weekly one-on-one meetings (also monthly team meetings), and each team member had great energy. But again, most important is that our meetings always had a personal vibe that strengthened the bonds between the team."

— João Paulo Paim

Curiosity & Originality is another thread in the fabric that ties our community together. Ethnotek was built on defying the status quo. We're change-makers willing to break the mold of previous jobs to keep our business innovative and different. We are ready to take on new projects, step outside our comfort zone, and be open to ever-changing responsibilities. We're a merry band of curious experimenters. Our only constant is change; our culture is about facing the moving times with flexibility, excitement, and open minds. We're hungry to find unique creative solutions to the problems we encounter every week and pride ourselves in looking at things differently. I know that might fall into the trough of usual entrepreneurial rhetoric, but for us, it's true because we have no other choice. Our supply chain and product design differ from everyone else on the market, which comes with no shortage of unique problems to solve. Believe me, it would have been much easier to follow industry standards and use common mass-producible materials in our products, but we're not interested in being like everyone else. We are radically different, and with that understanding, we threw the rule book out the window years ago and approached every new challenge with a beginner's mindset. We apply this ethos to everything. When looking at digital marketing data, we're curious to find anomalies and creative ways to amplify surprising positive trends through new content creation, UI/UX, or product design. The key characteristic of the curious worker is being proactive. This should not distract away from your top priority work, but occasionally carving out time to go after these hidden areas for the benefit of the whole ecosystem will almost always be rewarded. This is a unique kind of person, but the kind I like to look for when recruiting. It's less about what you already know and more about what we can teach each other and learn together through collaboration. We thrive on self-development and making valuable mistakes. Failing shows we're trying and that we're courageous enough to expose ourselves. Meanwhile, stubborn people rarely find their way into our inner circle, but when they do, they don't last long. Curious people always find the best solutions because it's usually a patient approach of asking, "Yeah, but why?" enough times until you come away with a positive result that even the person you're debating didn't know was possible.

A good example to illustrate this point happened during a team meeting in 2020. We were looking over our usual performance reports for each channel: Meta Ads, Google Ads, Newsletter, Social Media, etc. We were having low performance and needed to figure out why. Then our Meta ads manager, João, asked what products were selling well for which we weren't running paid ads. It was a smart question that none of us had thought of for some reason. After digging through Shopify reports, we found that the Chiburi Accordion Wallet was selling well on its own, more so than any other product for which we weren't running targeted ads. It was a product that we didn't have many lifestyle photos of — no videos and very few product reviews; but despite that, customers loved it. Immediately, we decided to record a new video to show the wallet in different colors, walk through its various features, and see what types of items can fit inside. It was the pandemic, so my partner, Cori, and I shot an amateur video at home and uploaded it to the team folder in various formats. That same day, Joao built Meta ads, Ruben crafted Google ads, Marissa wrote a newsletter, and I scheduled some social media posts with the new content. Sales started going gangbusters for that product, and we sold out within two months. We re-ordered heaps of those and kept the evergreen ads running for three years before changing anything. That was a 48-hour effort from a curious insight during the team call, which led to a passive six-figure income. There were no discounts or special promos; we just raised awareness for something people already loved.

Through the same discovery process, we found that our Cyclo Sling was a best-seller hiding in plain sight and applied the same turnaround with nearly identical explosive long-term results. These two bags were slated to be discontinued, but after this little exercise, they have been top sellers ever since and won't leave our core product line any time soon.

This simple line of inquiry had a cascading effect. After the success of the Chiburi Wallet and Cyclo Sling, we could see a trend toward shoulder bags and products under US$100. The shoulder bag and accessory category were never that big for us. We were a backpack company — until now. Due to this recent swell of newly discovered and tapped customer demand, we brought back the Bagan Bag (a satchel-style bag) from retirement (which had been discontinued two years before) as a test. We made a basic video and blasted it on all channels just like we did for Chiburi and Cyclo. It sold out in one month. We then re-ordered more Bagans and designed and launched a new 13" laptop bag to round out the collection and ride the shoulder bag + user-generated video wave. That also sold out right away! Thanks for the curiosity, João!

Uncertainty and confusion are thieves of joy in the workplace. That's why we've always been big on **Clarity & Empowerment**. Anyone in a leadership position owes it to the team to provide a clear plan of objectives, priorities, and timeline to ensure everyone in the boat is clear on what we're all sailing toward. It's also impossible for one leader to be an expert in all areas of business or have time to manage them. That's why it's important to delegate to the team. It empowers them with your trust. I like to give people full autonomy to own their area of the business through self-management, goal setting, reporting, and sharing results with the rest of the team. This type of full-trust approach (when given to curious and proactive people) leads to them wanting to do their very best and go the extra mile even if they weren't asked to. If you want part-time contractors to behave like full-time managers, this is how you do it.

"A word that comes to mind is responsibility, which is linked to trust. Since the beginning, Jake has always given people full responsibility for their roles within the team. That shows trust and gives an amazing feeling of autonomy, energizing the person to go the extra mile. Because of this, I've grown a lot, and it made me want to step up for the team, for the family, and for the brand.

— Ruben Vrinzen

"Jake has the unique gift of getting the whole team excited and motivated to put in their best work, no matter the challenge or level of complexity. He inspires the team with enthusiasm and has a clear vision with long-term goals. I know Jake as someone who highly values human relationships. In my years working with him, he has never referred to the team as 'them' or 'the freelancers.' Instead, he always talks about 'the team'. Or even better: buddy or friend. And guess what: who doesn't want to work long-term with a good friend? What I love the most about working with Ethnotek is the fun and healthy (remote) company culture. Jake has put a lot of effort into building a business where people thrive and love to be part of it. For me, the real magic is in the way we work and communicate with each other: open, respectful, honest, and fun. Example: A meeting is often called a 'jam session,' which sounds less formal and more open (and there's a cool guitar emoji we use for it in Slack)."

— Niels Janszen

As the organization's leader, I feel a duty to provide as much clarity and inspiration as possible. I'm also aware of my flaws and parts of the business I'm not an expert in, so when I create strategies, I set them very high-level, detailed in my specific area of expertise, and ask everyone else in the team to set their own goals and timelines. We build the quarterly and annual plans together. And as usual, it doesn't matter what your role or rank is; you get a say. When we co-create the company plans as a group, it galvanizes us and makes the work more exciting because we're all clear on the direction we're running in as individuals and as a collective. It's unity in the form of collaboration.

The **Pursuit of Excellence** can help and hinder your business. In the beginning, I did absolutely everything for the company, mainly because I couldn't afford to hire anyone but also because I was eager to learn new things. If you want to learn how business works, start your own. It's an accelerated crash course and sink-or-swim experience that will teach you more about how companies operate in a year than you would get in 10 years working for someone else. Being in this everything-everywhere-all-at-once role also allowed me to make sure everything the customer interacted with was done at the highest quality and had a special branded touch to it. From the smallest stitching to the internal labels, hang tags, invoice branding, website font, studio photo look, customer service tone, trade show booth design, social media post style, sales pitch strategy, catalog layout, or newsletter formatting; I wanted all of it to look as "pro" as possible.

I felt that Ethnotek always deserved a seat at the same table as big well-known brands like Patagonia, The North Face, and LuLuLemon.

Even though we were a one-person show in the beginning (we're still a small team today), the quality of our products, online presence, and customer experience should feel no different than those of big-name brands. I'm thankful to say we've achieved this feat, and many times over the years, I've had enjoyable encounters when shocked retailers and distributors find out how small our team is and that I designed every product.

"We thought you'd be much older and your team would be bigger," one distributor responded. In my eyes, that's mission accomplished. It means we're playing at the same level as the big dogs. Because I'm a product designer, my highest level of scrutiny goes into our products. If a first-time customer has a bad experience with their product, it's very hard to win them back. That's why I moved back to Vietnam the first year we launched — to be close to our production facility — and it worked. We received that early attention from REI and Urban Outfitters because of my commitment to quality. I knew it was our chance to shine — to underpromise and over-deliver. The core value of excellence has always been where I walk a very fine line.

"Hi, my name is Jake, and I'm a recovering perfectionist."

Phew, that feels good to say out loud. I joke, but while this trait in the workplace can lead to incredible results, beware: It can lead to burnout and bottlenecks that get in the way of growth!

Of course, I know perfect is not always possible, but I always try to make every product near-perfect within reason and without causing undue stress to the team. As mentioned in Chapter 4, we allow a 10% margin for imperfection from our artisan partners' textiles.

When it comes to products, packaging, online channels, anything visual, and our customer service, I expect the same level of attentiveness and Pursuit of Excellence. I want people to feel like they're not only talking to a human with a heartbeat, but a close friend. It should feel casual and familial, and it's always good to share personal stories and take an interest in the customer's life, as we do in our internal jam sessions. This has always worked well, but it can be a struggle when new people jump into the customer support tickets when they worked for a previous company where an efficient robotic response sufficed. This is not us at all, so it can take some time for our new customer service recruits to loosen up and shake off the corporate cultures they have broken free from.

This is a good time to mention Cori in more depth. She was Ethnotek's co-owner, administrative, and community manager (and my wife). She was with the company from the beginning and was the heart and soul of this customer culture. She often introduced herself as co-owner and the founder's wife and let her personality shine through. I think she's a genius at this. It came naturally to her, and she enjoyed it immensely. We'd often be out for dinner or on vacation, and she'd be tapping away on her phone with a smile, and I'd ask, "What are you doing?" She would respond, "Just chatting with a customer."

"Oh no, what happened?" I'd ask.

Nine times out of 10, she'd say, "Nothing, Anthony (our operations manager in California) and I solved their problem ages ago; now we're just chatting."

A little puzzled, I'd say, "Chatting about what?"

It was always something different and personal. She'd often say something like, "I'm talking to Julie about her pregnancy and the anxiety of being a mom for the first time," or "I'm talking to Robert, who's buying a bag for his son who's going off to college and how bittersweet that experience feels."

The examples are endless. She just genuinely cared. Anthony, too, and I'd say those are our second most common reviews of people mentioning or thanking Anthony and Cori for how helpful and kind they were. Now that's what I'm talking about! An excellent customer experience by making it personal and human. In our case, we didn't have to design that experience or write a script; we already had the exact right people who this naturally comes to. Thanks, Cori and Anthony, you guys are amazing! While the expectation of excellence can lead to positive results, it also has its shadow side.

"With every gift also comes a dark side. And if you've ever carried an Ethnotek bag, you know what gift I'm referring to. Or joined one of Jake's photoshoots or have seen a social media post produced by the company. It's the gift of producing the highest quality products and content. It's a bliss having Jake as a leader with such high standards. But as you can imagine, it can also be challenging if you're swimming in his lane. Jake might spread himself very thin as he wants to control the output, simply to be sure it offers the most exceptional user experience."

— Niels Janszen

Feedback well received. I'm working on it, and perhaps this can be a word of caution to those perfectionists and, dare I say, "micro-managers" out there.

We take our job seriously, but not ourselves. That's why we love to come together to laugh, joke, and play—it keeps us creative and energized! **Celebration & Play** is a huge part of who we are as a business, and I believe it has immeasurable benefits across our community. We allow time in every meeting to ask about each other's personal lives, banter, and celebrate the wins. When we see a team member do something awesome like land a sale, finish a complex project, or impress a customer, we acknowledge them and celebrate together. We embrace silliness by sending each other funny gifs and sharing pics of ourselves out in the world, adventuring with our Ethnotek bags, with family and friends in our #fun channel in the company Slack account.

We also encourage each other to rest. We are an anti-hustle culture. There's so much entrepreneurial hustle-porn out there. It's kinda gross and leads to burnout; that's not us. We see the value in not making decisions when you're tired. No worries if it takes you longer to hit your deadline simply because you have low energy today and need to take the day off to chill. I'm almost always okay with not pushing because I know when that person returns fully recharged, the quality of their work will be way higher. I'm about quality over speed any day of the week!

We're also a results-not-labor-focused team. We don't count hours or care about how you work, where, when, or who you work with as long as you get the work done. In fact, we hope you work unconventionally in the best way for you. We've never had an office and love co-working spaces for the sense of community. That's how we met most of our team actually, at Hubud in Bali. What a magical place that was!

There's a philosophical viewpoint I've long admired: *Ubuntu*.

In the Xhosa culture *Ubuntu* means, "I am because we are."

There's a legend about this beautiful worldview. So it goes that long ago, an anthropologist proposed a game to the kids of the Efe tribe in Zaire. He put a basket full of fruit near a tree and told the kids that whoever got there first won the sweet fruits. When he told them to run, they all took each other's hands and ran together, then sat together, enjoying their treats. He asked them why they had run like that, as one could have had all the fruits for himself.

"Because of *Ubuntu*!" they replied.

"How can one of us be happy if all the others are sad?

I've long admired this proverb, which embodies community spirit so well. I've tried to take this lesson to heart in my work and life endeavors, including Ethnotek.

There are also business benefits to putting the community first. It can turn a small group of individuals into a superpowered community. Ethnotek has achieved so much with such a small team that it almost defies belief. For a global social enterprise with such a complicated supply chain and unique products sold in so many places, people usually expect me to say we have a 50-person team. When I tell them it's just three full-time people for design, accounting, customer service, admin, and operations and five contractors for marketing and IT, the perplexed look on their faces always makes me laugh. However, we can only achieve this seemingly superhuman feat because of our company culture. We'd go to war for each other, but we'd rather have fun selling bags and solving interesting problems together instead.

Another signpost along the trail on our community-building quest is remembering to stop, take a breather, and **Ask The Audience**. In the co-creative landscape of the community, there's simply no better way to find out what's happening in the minds of your customers and network rather than to simply ask them. I've tried hard on my Ethnotek journey to ask questions, test my ideas at every step, and ask our audience for their input! I'd highly advise taking heed of this in your work or business. Do not presume that knowing what's happening in the minds of your community and customers is a good way to operate and maximize your chances for constant learning while at the same time building trust and loyalty through inclusiveness. People love to be asked their thoughts and opinions, especially about things they're into, like fashion or bags!

One of the easiest tools for outreach is the humble survey, which we've leaned a lot on over the years at Ethnotek and learned a lot from. Most customers consistently say they view us as an adventure travel brand. We occasionally (every two to three years) send surveys to our community to make sure we're still on point with our products and relevant in our messaging and overall vibe. We also do this if we are about to make an important company decision or we hit a bottleneck on a decision and want to springboard some ideas with our wider community. One example of using surveys (and their benefits) happened in 2018. At the time, we wanted to understand better what our customers valued the most about us and why. Why did they purchase things, and more importantly, why didn't they? We did the same in 2023. The results were consistent and unsurprising despite so many years in between surveys, which is what we wanted to know. The most common response to the question, "Why do you like Ethnotek?" was, "I like the artisan fabric and knowing that my money gives back." Similarly, we asked what types of marketing content and stories they'd prefer to get more from us, and the majority said, "Stories about the artisan process and their culture."

These are encouraging signs that most of our community supports us because of our artisan mission. Another interesting result that surprised us in the 2023 survey was when we asked: What type of bag would you most prefer we launch next? The top responses were "Large adventure pack over 45 liters" and "duffel bags." While there is some internal debate about whether these two types of products would be wise for us to work on, the feedback helped us learn that our customers view us as an adventure travel brand and want to see products to match. This was an important insight because, at the time of that particular survey, we had been focusing a lot of our design efforts on smaller and more inexpensive urban-style bags with mostly black minimalist exteriors and small discreet stripes of artisan fabrics instead of large colorful panels. These also sell really well, but the survey helped us to lean back heavily into our main outdoors and adventure product lines. At the core, our community loves supporting artisans and their cultural stories, colorful bags, and the spirit of adventure travel. This critical note from our community told us it's good to try new things but not lose sight of our original founding vision and brand vibe. This is such fantastic feedback after all of these years in business.

Let's circle back to India and say "hey" to the twins Sanjay and Suresh, whom we met on the sun-scorched streets of Kanderai Village way back at the start of the chapter that kickstarted our jaunt into our conversation about community building. After learning how to weave Ethnotek's most popular designs, the boys led a collaboration with the incredible NGO Viva Con Agua (VCA), which works worldwide. The twins diligently applied their weaving skills to create hundreds of meters of colorful textiles for VCA. On Sanjay's loom was a rich charcoal gray textile flecked with dancing geometric patterns featuring the *vankiyo*, *hudadhi*, *kungri,* and *dhulki** (also known as *damaru*) motifs in aqua blue, white, and black. Meanwhile, Suresh worked on the same textile design in the inverse colorway. They fulfilled this order with skill and dedication that fills me with happiness to recall that day all those years ago when they looked at photos on my phone of customers around the world wearing their family's textile and said that they wanted to carry on the craft. How far they have come! Well done guys!

A quick note on Viva Con Agua, which means "living with water" in Spanish. The NGO promotes access to clean drinking water, sanitation, and hygiene. They rely on activism and use the universal languages of music, sport, and art as vehicles for change in their national and international projects. They provide clean water wells, sanitation, infrastructure, and educational programs that teach and promote potentially life-saving hygiene practices. Their projects span India, Nepal, Ethiopia, Uganda, Kenya, Rwanda, Tanzania, Zambia, Malawi, Mozambique, and South Africa. Our team, led by our managing director, Jim, pitched Viva Con Agua with the idea that Ethnotek could weave our traditional textiles in their NGO brand colors to raise awareness for both our missions in a co-branded cross-promotion. They loved the idea and jumped on board. To take things one step further, we gave 10% of our gross revenue from selling Viva Con Agua products to their water and sanitation projects on the ground. To date, Ethnotek customers, through the power of their bag purchases, have raised well over US$100,000 for Viva Con Agua projects worldwide — we're all proud of that! This is yet another example of the power of community in action. Amazing things can happen when curious and creative problem solvers join forces for a common cause.

Before heading into the next adventure, let me explain how we plot a course internally at Ethnotek and keep us headed in the right direction regarding our community-building practices. It took me the first five years of Ethnotek to realize that something wasn't quite working with our team internally. Back then, we were a small team of C-level equity partners, and senior managers who ran their own business areas siloed independently. We didn't know any better at the time, but it led to opacity, ego clashes, and messiness that nearly sank the business. After realizing this wasn't working, we changed how we worked, and ever since, we've been a remote team of young, talented, and curious part-time contractors who we treat like family. The lifeblood of our organization is empathy, transparency, strong communication, and a collaborative culture centered around fun and mutual respect. When people ask about my management style, I usually respond, "We're all friends that happen to do business together."

If there's one takeaway from this chapter, it's this: People invest in people, and customers who buy art want to know who makes it. Connecting the dots between products and the people who make them is crucial to the end customer experience. Looking back through all our communications with our customers and community, I can see this is something we did (and continue to do) well at Ethnotek because, in every post, comment, article, and video, we kept front and center in our minds that community comes first. We're a people-first company — always have been, and I hope always will be. But to do that takes commitment to mission, empathy, transparency, curiosity, originality, the pursuit of excellence, clear communication, team empowerment, and good old-fashioned fun. So do the surveys, develop a company culture, speak to customers and artisans, and talk, talk, talk — it will help create dialogue, trust, and strong relationships. As I said in the beginning, we're a company that celebrates people and the things they create. Pretty simple. It's not about how fast you make something and hiding the people in the creation process. It's about slowing down to make an effort to build a community and show you care. To end with a quote...

"We cannot live for ourselves alone. Our lives are connected by a thousand invisible threads, and along these sympathetic fibers, our actions run as causes and return to us as results."

— Herman Melville

6

Slow Down

"Nature does not hurry, yet everything is accomplished."

— Lao Tzu

Đá Bàn, Vietnam
2014

A gentle breeze flowed through the jungle valley as the palm silhouettes swayed against a star-speckled night backdrop over Hon Ba Nature Reserve in Khánh Hòa province. The last embers of our campfire smoldered nearby as I lay on a warm rock looking up into the blanket of stars above. Around me, our team was sprawled out in sleeping bags on the massive rock we had decided to sleep on, located right in the middle of the surging Suối Dầu River. After cooking in the sun all day, the giant slab kept us cozy and warm as we fell asleep to the sounds of frothing water and singing cicadas. It was a magic night for our Ethnotek team, one of many excursions we would have over the years with the Vietnamese production crew.

Our group of merry pranksters was led by our production manager, Ái, his best friend and head of the factory that prints all of our hangtags and catalogs, Bảo, and our factory owner and head pattern maker, Tú.

On this occasion, a few of their friends had tagged along, too. Our guide for our mini-expedition into the jungle was Ai's friend Thọ, a pattern technician for the brand Quicksilver. Thọ grew up in Khánh Hòa and knew the forests and best camping spots well. Our weekend adventure was part getaway and part team bonding exercise, but it also served another purpose as a real-world test for our flagship backpack, the Raja Pack. In fact, that night, I used my bag as a pillow. For the whole journey, I had put this new bag, which was stuffed to the gills with gear, through its paces: hiking, climbing, wading, strapping firewood to the sides and then smearing it with mud, splashing it with water, suntan lotion — you name it, it happened. This was sample number 25, and I knew we had finally nailed the design. And while I couldn't wait to sign it off for production, first, we had to put the pack through its paces in the dense Vietnamese jungle. A mission we were all looking forward to.

Today, a decade later, Ethnotek is selling our Raja 46 liter generation five, and I'm so happy to report that it's still rocking steady and is our most beloved backpack. It now has three younger siblings: The Raja 30 Liter, Lite Ecopack, and Camera Pack, all based on this original design. The Raja Pack is the bag we launched the company with in 2011. It was the only bag we offered in the first year and has since become an underground icon with our community and fellow bag nerds. I remember when our Singaporean distributor attended a global sales meeting in 2013 for the legendary snowboard brand Burton, and he sent me a sneaky photo during their sales presentation. On the screen in one of their slides was our Raja Pack, which was being used to describe two growing trends Burton saw in the market: tribal and ethnic patterns and customizability. This was a big moment because I grew up obsessed with Burton as a knuckle-dragging snowboarder in frosty Minnesota. I dreamt of working for them as a designer someday and applied to a few job listings, but never got in. But as things turned out, I ended up on their radar eventually, even if only for a few moments during a sales presentation.

Around this time, I also remember having lunch with a friend who was the director of product development for the behemoth outdoor bag brand Osprey at their design headquarters in Saigon. He told me that they were going to develop a line of backpacks and bags with modular interchangeable front panels. But after doing some market research, their designers discovered our Raja Pack, and their team decided to pivot away from the whole project to not infringe upon the unique design feature we had become known for — our interchangeable front panels called Threads. Osprey is a giant in the industry; they could have charged forward with their collection of interchangeable bags and squashed us in the courts if we had put up a fight, but they didn't. This speaks to Osprey's integrity and is a welcome reminder to all of you would-be social entrepreneurs out there about the leverage you can benefit from if you embody the Be The Only philosophy we covered in Chapter 1. We're a small company, but our products speak for themselves, so the public market insulated us. Throughout Ethnotek's lifespan, there haven't been any copies or knockoffs. The more we became known for that special thing we made, the taller the wall became to prevent copycats from jumping over it. Some folks may have felt a competitive twinge toward the above-mentioned instances, but I felt flattery and reassurance. Two industry-leading giant brands confirmed things we already knew, and we had a three-year head start. Needless to say, it lit a fire under my ass to keep going and not stray too far away from that original design recipe and our Interfusing approach.

Knowing how wide of a footprint the Raja Pack has in the industry, we revisit its design every few seasons to ensure it's still the best it can be. We're also very cautious about changing something unless it's well justified. As the age-old saying goes, "If it ain't broke, don't fix it."

It might seem like a lot when people hear 25 samples and five generations of a bag, but that's normal and pretty light compared to other, more complicated products. Ask yourself what generation of iPhones we're on now. Then imagine how many prototypes Apple's fleet of designers tinkered with since the first generation launched in 2007 to where we are today—probably hundreds or even thousands.

The well-known Dyson vacuum cleaner has become a household name synonymous with quality through meticulous engineering. Hence, their high price points are justified. The founder, James Dyson, went through 5,127 prototypes over five years to arrive at the vacuum cleaner that most of us take for granted while it dutifully gobbles up the crumbs from our floors every week. I can't liken my creations to these legends of product design and mechanical engineering, but you get the point. A lot goes into product design before it graces your home, and I think it's a valuable exercise to put that process under the microscope in this chapter.

That trip into the jungle with our Vietnam team and our trusty Raja Pack was unforgettable. It brought us all closer together and had the added benefit of being a real-world testing ground for our most popular backpack. It may have taken a long time, but we needed it to get it right. As discussed previously, we're not a fast fashion brand and actively avoid chasing trends. Now in this chapter, I want to take our conversation one step further. I'll argue why it's in everyone's interest to go in the opposite direction and **Slow Down** at the most important step in the product development journey— the design stage.

As we take a relaxing stroll into Ethnotek's Slow Down design philosophy, I'd like to discuss how this leisurely approach to product development saves time and money. I know this sounds ironic, but it's true.

Slow Design goes against industry norms and avoids chasing trends. Our goal wasn't (and will never be) to be a trend-based company, so we always prioritize slow planning at the start of every project. This leaves lots of time for rapid iteration and real-world testing to avoid unintended social and environmental harm and to produce mediocre products. We aim for the best and highest-quality products possible, so we embrace this slo-mo approach.

My aim for this chapter is to leave you with a newfound appreciation for the many steps and hands involved in creating a new product before it lands on your doorstep. Also, I hope to inspire any managers, decision-makers, or social entrepreneurs to rethink your process next time you feel the urge to rush your design team or any production-related decisions.

First, let's dive in with one of my all-time favorite Slow Design principles: **Be Timeless.** As part of our commitment to cultural heritage, we're equally committed to not following trends. I like to use the analogy that our bags are an easel for the painting that is our artisan partners' handmade textiles. Our brand exists to elevate their art. Our bag designs are a functional vehicle to support the mission and be a helpful tool to benefit our customers' daily lives. To that end, we follow the traditional work of artisans whose designs reach far back in time, not what fashion blogs say is hot right now.

In the fast fashion world, new trends emerge monthly and sometimes weekly. These trends often influence other market segments, including the outdoor industry (which Ethnotek is a part of), which have slower quarterly seasonal trends. Designers and startup owners can have difficulty keeping up with what continually churns out of the runways of Berlin, LA, Milan, New York, Paris or Tokyo, and often have to rely on resources like WGSN, Fashion Snoops, and Edited to keep up with the latest market insights. This rampant pursuit of rapid change to feed the insatiable beast of "what's cool" is one of the root causes of our planet's ecological strain. It's part of the more, more, more, now, now, now mentality that we need to move away from to create a more sustainable, equitable international trade system that benefits people and the planet.

At Ethnotek, we like to take the opposite approach. Rather than making textile sourcing decisions based on color trends, I try to find our artisan partners' most traditional pieces in their showrooms. I work hard to create an even balance of cool, warm, neutral, and multi-colors. This enables us to offer a wide variety of style options to cater to a larger variety of customers and also provides balance to ensure that one country's fabric designs don't cannibalize another. The motifs, stories, and cultural identity embedded in each piece are more important than color, qualifying factors for us when we find ourselves nose-deep in stacks of fabrics at our artisan partner's showrooms.

There's also a practical reality we're up against regarding trends. Because handmade artisan fabric takes such a long time to make, we couldn't realistically follow trends even if we wanted to, simply because we can't keep up. It would also lead to waste because of the speed of change within the fast fashion industry; if we operated within that system, by the time we launched our trend-based collection, we would struggle to keep up given our handmade approach and end up with heaps of excess inventory. This would waste time, money, resources, and our artisan's hard work.

Side note: Our aversion to following trends is also another reason why the base color for our tech fabric on all our bags is black. This was a deliberate Slow Design decision I made early on. It's a way to reduce waste by using the same base material for our full product offering, and black is a neutral color. Black is timeless, will never compete with flashy color trends, and is a great base tone for making our artisan fabrics pop.

The same logic applies to bag shapes, silhouettes, sizing, and deciding which tech gear to scale the bags to fit. At the same time, we do pay attention to what other players in the bag space are doing when it comes to these design details but we rarely follow them because of our Be Timeless principle. I say rarely because we followed trends in the beginning, with unfortunate results that led to the formation of this principle and a whole lot of self-growth in the process.

Two bags that come to mind where we did follow trends are the Acaat Messenger and the Wayu Pack. While we loved those designs internally, they followed in the slipstream of trends at the time. The Acaat followed downwind from the messenger bag trend that had seen a surge in popularity led by brands like Timbuk2, Crumpler, and Chrome Bags. However, we entered the market at the wrong time and ended up with an oversupply of stock.

It was a similar story to the Wayu Pack. We thought we needed a classic school bag format backpack (which, to be fair, was a timeless trend, but a trend nonetheless) led by brands like Eastpak and Jansport, but we missed the mark. Because our artisan fabric is so expensive and we always strive for innovation and quality, our Wayu Pack was two to three times more costly and bulkier than our competitors. Sales on both these bags were slow and led to years of overstock and resource burn. Meanwhile, our timeless Raja Pack has never faced these issues, a clear indicator that our customers don't care if we follow trends; they care about the story and mission crafted into its creation. Even though we had only taken minimal influence from two trends in the marketplace, this was costly and a hard lesson to swallow in the early days of Ethnotek—and I wouldn't make it again. But the silver lining from our wayward wandering into chasing trends was the creation and adoption of our Be Timeless principle, which has served as a guiding light, keeping us on track and away from any time-wasting or hazardous forks in the road leading us deep into trend-rabbit-hole territory.

All mistakes are learning opportunities if you choose to see them that way. Our trend-chasing detour happened because we should have noticed the basic principle all start-up founders should build into the foundation of the business: KYC (Know Your Customer). In the first couple of years, we didn't have reliable data to know who our customers were. This only became clear later when we learned that our core customers were 35-45. No wonder the young and hip high school and college kids weren't buying our classic school bag backpacks when they were twice the price and more teched-out than other brands on the market. I mean, duh! But we knew what we knew then. We made a costly mistake, learned from it, and eventually established a robust set of demographic data to always refer to when embarking on a new product design endeavor.

Similarly, we steer clear of chasing trends in the smartphone, tablet, and laptop case segment because sizes change frequently. While some of our competitors go to great lengths to have a form-fitting case, and specifically timed marketing campaigns every time Apple or Samsung launch a new device, we're more interested in designing products that will fit most past, present, and future devices. In this way, we're proactively passive to trends in this segment. When we do infrequently play in this space, we err on scaling things up to fit various gadget sizes and reduce the risk of waste. Because our bags are designed as chameleons to blend into your personal and professional life seamlessly, our customers are usually happy if the laptop or tablet sleeve has a loose fit because they can also use it for notebooks, magazines, and papers. Being too snug of a fit or not fitting isn't a fun situation.

In short, when in doubt, do your own thing. Push your design team to do something original that's true to your brand's core values and your community's lifestyle. Avoid the rat race of fashion trends by thinking years into the future, not months or weeks.

One saying I like to use in our Slow Design philosophy is **Garbage In, Garbage Out**, which I'm borrowing from the legendary social entrepreneur Yvon Chouinard, the founder of Patagonia. It's all about the importance of being slow, mindful, and testing a lot of ideas at the planning, design, and decision-making stage to avoid unwanted adverse downstream effects on people and the planet.

For this point in our journey through our design approach, I'm looking directly at the managers and professionals in decision-making roles out there.

According to a study conducted by Shopify, Statista, and the NRF (National Retail Federation), consumers returned products worth a staggering US$817 billion in 2022-2023. The NRF estimates the cost of returns amounts to US$101 billion. The number one contributor to this is clothing, and the second is bags and accessories. According to Power Reviews, 81% of online shoppers reported their products as damaged or defective.

If you're like me, reading that made you feel nauseous. Those statistics are mind-bogglingly concerning but can be avoided, or at least significantly reduced, if major consumer product brands slow down during the design phase. Adopting careful planning, testing, and collaborative team strategizing instead of impulsive and reactive decision-making is imperative for a positive customer experience and a lower environmental footprint.

By the time a product is on the manufacturing line, it's already too late. The positive or negative impact that product will have on the world happens well before the production team gets the signoff and green light. It's during the initial ideation phase that these conversations need to happen. For example, when a manager and designer sit in person or on a video call, this is the time for ideas to flow and a rapid ideation phase.

At this point, the manager and designer must engage in open discussions about specific product details: Who's it for? What's the target price point? What materials will be used? Where will those materials be sourced from? Where will the products be shipped to? How many sell-through quantities will be needed? What percentage of them will be for B2B vs D2C (direct-to-consumer)? These are all careful considerations that shouldn't be rushed or shrugged off. In other words, garbage planning often leads to garbage end products and a poor customer experience!

To avoid this, and having learned the hard way in the past, we deliberately only launch new products and artisan textile designs once a year (as opposed to two to four times like most of our competitors) and heavily involve our best distributors during the design process, which has been hugely successful for our business.

A regional distributor that sells to thousands of people in their market has to have their finger on the pulse of their country to be good at their job. Because they represent such a large demographic, they're a precious source of knowledge. I involve our distributors in Europe and Asia-Pacific and on home turf in North America for collective brainstorming sessions over six months in the lead-up to our biggest spring order season. This is often conducted over monthly meetings after I have new samples and drawings to show and have gathered insights from the other markets to share. It's my job to absorb and filter each country's feedback on the latest designs and distill them into something we're aligned with that we all share based on opportunities we see in our respective markets. It's a delicate dance, and we don't always agree. Sometimes, I have to politely disregard some of the feedback and follow my intuition. However, this slow global brainstorming formula has worked well for us, and I highly recommend this approach. This collaborative design process is also backed up by evidence.

While the industry standard product return rate for e-commerce brands is between 20% and 30%, Ethnotek's average global return rate is 8.5% (5% in the USA and 12% in Europe and Asia-Pacific). These statistics, alongside our 2,000-plus five-star product reviews, are a feel-good testament that our slow and careful upstream planning has positive effects flowing downstream, where happy customers reap the benefits. While pleasing, these stats also show that we are not 100% perfect regarding returns. There's always room for improvement.

Let's dive into some nitty-gritty details of our Slow Design philosophy with what I like to call **Mindful Cuts**, a term I use to describe our bags' form factor and design details. Every seam, zipper, buckle, strap, and sewing line has a particular reason for being. We *like* to sweat the small stuff, which all has to do with reducing waste as much as possible, being as valuable and practical as possible, and doing what it takes to elevate the star of the show, the handmade artisan textiles.

I like to avoid organic, rounded, or ostentatious shapes and unnecessary style lines for our bags, mainly to reduce waste. Think about a cookie cutter and a sheet of delicious dough. Fabrics are cut in a production process called die-cutting, a similar method that a baker uses to cut out perfectly shaped cookies; waste is not wanted. The baker wants to use all the yummy dough to save resources; just like when making a bag, we want to use all the fabric. To do this, our production team stacks 20 to 30 sheets of fabric together and stamps various shapes under a hydraulic press that quickly stamps the die tools through all fabric layers like a hot knife through butter. Most bag designs have several of these die tools. It's how we construct a two-dimensional material like fabric into three dimensions. The various die-cut shapes are then sewn together to make a 3D form. The cutter is tessellated around the sheet to minimize waste. To make waste savings extra sweet, I make our bag shapes boxy. While it may not look or sound like the most palatable form factor, it's the most waste-efficient.

Our goal at Ethnotek since our inception has been to waste as little as possible, with a maximum of 10% scrap waste created from each product. Depending on the material, we usually sell the scraps we create to material re-grind suppliers, who then convert them into other products or raw materials. On the few occasions when we veer from our boxy shapes, it's usually a tapered trapezoid (a rectangle that's wider at the top and narrow at the bottom), like a funnel. This is both a functional decision (to make it easier to load a bag that's wider at the top and helps funnel the contents to the bottom) and a material conservation decision because the trapezoid shapes can be inverted and neatly stacked together to reduce waste.

We make an exception to this design rule because sometimes it's beneficial to have rounded corners, like when opening your laptop compartment at airport security, those rounded corners make the zipper movement faster and smoother. You're welcome! Every cut on our bags has a reason for being there, and my priorities behind every design detail are functionality first, material conservation second, and aesthetic last. You'll never see something superfluous in our bag designs; everything must serve a functional purpose; otherwise, it doesn't belong.

I like to design things from a back-casting approach, meaning I design the best possible bag with heaps of innovative features, details and the use of materials to make it as unique and useful as possible. Pricing considerations come last. After I'm pleased with a bag that I think will serve the needs of the particular customer in mind, then I start trimming away the excess. It's a subtractive process from that point on. We decide the most essential features that must stay and then get rid of the rest. This helps us achieve our price targets after we have the best possible design, not before. Eventually, we reach a point where we can't take anything else away without jeopardizing functionality, and then, it's complete. I'm of a similar mindset to Dieter Rams, who said, "Good design is as little design as possible." My other favorite quote from him aligns with why I started Ethnotek, "Good design is making something intelligible and memorable. Great design is making something memorable and meaningful."

The key word there is meaningful. Look at the sea of bags and backpacks out there. Very few have actual meaning. Perhaps look at the bag you're carrying right now and ask yourself, does it have a soul? Does it have a story? Our bags do, thanks to our artisan partners. Without them, it's just another bag.

Alongside my points about Slow Design and careful planning to reduce waste and returns, I spend a lot of time staring at bags when they're in pieces and flipped inside out, the way no one else can see them after they're assembled into a finished product. I'm always looking for weak points, where the heaviest loads will occur on the bag, and how we can reinforce those areas to double or triple strength without adding extra cost. Many of these micro-additions are invisible to the end customer but are what I think of as **Hidden Strengths** and are what make our bags tough, but clean-looking.

Bartacks are one example of hidden strengths, and are little computerized stitch lines that are essentially a hundred little overlapping zig-zag stitches that add tons of strength to whatever they're applied to. It's like adding welding to two pieces of metal that join together. Often, we bartack the areas internally or externally where shoulder straps attach to the bag body since that single seam is under the most stress when your bag is fully loaded with heavy things.

Great design is also about adding specific details that allow customers to freestyle and use those details in their own way according to their lifestyle. I also like to hide certain details for customers to discover well after they've been using their bag. These **Design Opportunities** are not only functional but also a lot of fun to dream and build into the final products. Nearly all our backpacks feature a distinctive woven label bearing our logo, elegantly wrapped around a loop crafted from recycled artisan fabric on the shoulder straps. As previously highlighted, the die-cutting process inevitably produces a modest amount of waste scraps. Utilizing these remnants to create our logo loops is one of our numerous methods of repurposing artisan fabric scraps. This approach ensures that each backpack strap logo loop is unique, showcasing a variety of colors, textures, and patterns. Moreover, the loop serves a practical purpose. It's designed to hold the temple of your sunglasses securely. This thoughtful detail provides a convenient spot for your sunglasses to rest on your chest, offering easy access and protection during your adventures.

Another example of functional design can be found on our Raja Pack, Aya Pack, Premji Pack, and Somanya Sling, which have two parallel webbing straps with side-release buckles. In the case of our backpacks, these straps have many functions. They can be tightened to compress the volume of the main compartment and to fasten a camera tripod, yoga mat, skateboard, jacket, or anything else you want for easy access on the outside of the bag. We've noticed that many customers like to add pins and patches to these straps to accessorize and express themselves. Extra style points for those folks!

Surprise And Delight is a little design game we like to experiment with and have fun with at Ethnotek. Some of my favorite personal items are jackets or pants with pockets lined with funky-colored or patterned material. No one else sees these things except me, but they delight me and make me appreciate the care and attention to detail that went into the design. Similarly, you'll almost always find a patch or lined section inside every bag made with artisan fabric. Especially on our all-black bags, even though they look minimalist and discrete from the outside, they get an extra special treatment of artisan fabric on the interior. We also like to screen print our mission tagline with clear silicone ink inside various panels of our accessories, like the Coyopa Zip Kits or on the backside of our sunglasses cases. Because it's clear ink on a black surface, it's very subtle, and you almost don't notice it, but when you do, it's usually smile-inducing. We also like to hide Easter eggs, and some bags will have a branded Ethnotek carabiner stashed inside a pocket or a special edition woven label that describes the artisan who made the textile. Take another look inside your bag; you might be surprised by what you find!

We can't talk about our Slow Design approach without mentioning materials, especially what we call **Common Materials.** Over the past decade, we have consistently used the same high-quality materials across our product range, including 840-denier ballistic nylon, recycled PET for our main bag fabric, internal ripstop honeycomb lining, and durable components like zippers, buckles, snaps, webbing, and binding. As a startup, navigating minimum order quantities (MOQs) can be challenging, even with knowledge of surcharge loopholes.

This is why we've maintained a consistent and limited selection of core-line technical materials. This consistency helps us meet MOQs by spreading them across our entire line and simplifies inventory and quality control for our materials manager, Huong, and QC director, Man. Moreover, the repeated use of these materials across all products has fostered a cohesive visual identity and offers the added benefits of streamlined production and cost savings. If we didn't have artisan fabrics or make them the star of our show, we'd have to frequently change our tech fabric offering and colorways like other brands to stay relevant, which can be tricky to manage and risky as a startup. Thankfully, we don't have to worry about that.

Now, this may sound kinda funny, but I believe you have to **Embrace The Ugly**. While this overlaps with Mindful Cuts, it's a different point. Here's a truth bomb: I think our bags are kinda ugly — and I designed them! The form factors are very boxy, and some external features that serve practical functions take away from the beauty of the form factors or simplicity you might see from other brands. However, the ugly bag is intentional.

One of these ugly details that bag designers argue over endlessly is external water bottle pockets. Most designers hate adding them because they detract from a clean external aesthetic. Still, I'm in the camp of slapping those things on the side of every backpack regardless of how clunky they look because it satisfies our top priority: functionality. People just need 'em! We all gotta stay hydrated, so carrying a beverage that's easy to access without having to take your bag off or open and dig inside is just better because it's convenient. It becomes a part of the "tek" aesthetic of our brand's Interfusing approach (Chapter 1), so it's a double bonus.

The same can be said for external pockets and the straps. We mainly use coil-out zippers on laptop compartments because the zip glides smoother than reverse zippers. Zippers have many little teeth or coils that allow the zip puller to travel along them, which is the zipper tape's interface to open and close. Those who prioritize aesthetics prefer reverse zippers because it doesn't show the coil. It looks cleaner and smoother. Coil out looks bulkier and techier, but it just works better because there's less resistance between you and the thing you're trying to access when opening the bag. You'll thank us for that little detail next time you're rushing at airport security to get your laptop out before the people in line behind you start complaining. There are so many examples of this throughout our designs, but to save time, I'll leave you with a funny story and then move on.

We laugh every time we retell this story internally. It happened at Berlin Fashion Week (I can't remember the year). One morning, an exceptionally well-dressed fashion buyer was loitering around the Ethnotek booth, taking a long time to cast his eyes over our product range. One of our team members greeted this fashion-conscious gentleman and briefly explained our mission concept, various products, and their unique selling points. The man said nothing for a while and then confidently replied: "Hmmm, okay, I see, but does it come in cool?" Then he pivoted on his heels and strutted off into the crowd. At first, our team members stood their mouths agape before bursting into laughter. Mic drop! What a line! Of course, he was implying our bags weren't cool-looking, but we weren't offended in the slightest because we know who we are, and it's not to be in the service of cool. Have a nice day, sir! We'll be over here looking off-trend and serving a higher mission.

To be an effective designer and social entrepreneur, you need to **Live Your Mission**, which I believe means living in the countries of your supply chain and production. While I understand this is a bold statement and might not seem like an easy thing or even possible for you to do, for me, it was the most important decision for the company and for me personally to grow into the person I am today.

I learned how to design bags over three years when I lived with my then-wife Cori in Ho Chi Minh City, Vietnam. After continuing our careers in Switzerland and the USA, we returned to Vietnam for the first five years of Ethnotek. We then moved to Bali, Indonesia, for five years, all with the express goal of being close to the production team and artisans. Ethnotek wouldn't be what it is today and possibly would have failed within the first three years without making this commitment.

If you're interested in producing overseas and collaborating with artisans, living where your source materials are created will teach you a hundred times more than doing it hands-off from an isolated office far away. It's also an incredible quality of life. It's the best opportunity to immerse yourself in cultures other than your own, and the latter is the most important to become a world citizen.

On an average day in Ho Chi Minh City, I woke up around 6:30 to 7:00 am, got ready, and then hopped on my motorbike to drive through the heart of the bustling concrete jungle, zig-zagging through busy streets jammed with motorbikes, honking cars, food vendors, hawkers, loitering dogs, passersby, and the odd stunned tourists, all the while savoring the sights, smells, and sounds of one of Southeast Asia's most vibrant cities gearing up for another day. I loved my morning drive to our production workshop in Hóc Môn, and I'd often stop along the way to sip a strong *cà phê* đen ít đường (hot black coffee with a little sugar) and snack on a fresh Bánh mì ốp la (crispy fried egg and pickled vegetables baguette) or slurp a steaming bowl of *Hủ tiếu* (a Sino-Vietnamese-Cambodian dish eaten as breakfast).

Living close by enabled me to connect deeply with our factory owners,

Ái and Tú, and various production team members. I was practically a fixture in the sample room. Instead of the cumbersome process of assembling multi-page PDFs in Adobe Illustrator, sending emails, and enduring a two-to-four week wait before seeing a sample, I collaborated directly with Ai and our sample team in person. We hand-sketched new designs and created hundreds of test pieces and prototypes. This approach allowed for swift adjustments to individual components of the bags before assembly into a final product. Such immediate access facilitated rapid iterations often out of reach for brands separated by oceans, time zones, and cultural divides. Meanwhile, I was living and breathing the same air as our Vietnamese team and forming friendships that made our designs all the more collaborative and creative. Being there daily as part of the team, sharing meals, enjoying ice-cold Tiger beers, and engaging in spirited *karaoke* sessions after long work days nurtured a sense of intimacy, trust, and camaraderie crucial to our partnership. Despite hearing some travelers over the years describe Vietnamese people as distant or impersonal, my experience showed me that once their trust is earned and you're accepted into their circle, they are among the most loyal, joyful, and friendly people you could ever hope to know. Building this trust takes time, but it's an invaluable investment for a company like ours reliant on relationships. This Live Your Mission principle holds true throughout our supply chain, underscoring the importance of personal connections in business. But don't just take my word for it. Here's what Mr. Ái had to say when asked about the importance of designers and business owners living near the production team:

"I think it's very important that Jake lived in Vietnam. We faced numerous challenges at the beginning of our work together, from selecting suitable fabrics, trying different methods to ensure the artisan fabrics were strong enough for sewing, and working with weavers to achieve the right colors, patterns, and sizes to meet the requirements, and designing many product iterations. Without Jake in Vietnam, frequently visiting the production site for detailed discussions and adjustments, I might have given up on the Ethnotek project due to the time-consuming nature of these tasks and uncertain outcomes. Our relationship with Jake became closer through this long process of working together. We had disagreements and arguments, but after such incidents, we understood each other better and grew. Our good relationship and familial bond today stems from the time spent working and socializing together. Also, what kept me going was my strong belief in Jake's first design, the legendary Raja Pack, which we continue to produce a lot of. The feature of interchangeable front panels of the backpack was unique and promising. Moreover, exporting these products worldwide helps promote Vietnamese culture and other ethnic groups globally. I am very fond of Ethnotek products, inside and out."

— Phạm Hữu Ái

I frequently encounter queries from fellow entrepreneurs grappling with challenges like quality control or their projects needing to be prioritized in the sample room or production line. My advice is always to Go There (Chapter 4). It's not about asserting control or overseeing everyone to instigate fear for quality results and on-time delivery; it's fundamentally about building relationships. Living adjacent to the factory, I've witnessed numerous business owners, newly arrived from their international flights, enter the factory with an authoritative demeanor. It's disheartening to see, and although I feel compelled to offer advice to save them the strain, I remind myself that it's not my place. Most of those brands didn't stick around our workshop long anyway. They simply didn't get it — it's all about relationships!

As our earlier discussion on company culture highlighted (Chapter 5), individuals excel and deliver their utmost quality when they feel secure, empowered, and connected personally, rather than working for a faceless person behind an email address. When you live amongst your producers, you can Live Your Mission because empathy and understanding happen through osmosis. You become your work when there's no literal ocean or screen between you and your suppliers.

Throughout the Ethnotek journey, I've followed the thread to the end of the line. Across multiple continents, I've seen where our cotton is grown, where our ballistic nylon is extruded, spooled, woven, coated, and dyed, where our camera strap anchor points are injection molded, where our bags are sewn, and where the textiles are hand embroidered. These are details you can't unsee and unlearn. Faces you can't forget and production constraints you must know. They all become a part of your DNA and subconscious. These shared experiences become you, and then you become your designs. Only then can your designs truly reflect the people who made them. A bond and energy that your customer who buys the final product deserves to feel and support. So Go There, Live Your Mission, soak in life experience, and learn to celebrate the differences and commonalities of those you cohabitate with on this beautiful planet. Hit the road, get the wind in your hair and dirt under your fingernails, and be free. It's one hell of a ride you won't regret!

As we are deep into our Slow Design philosophy, it's about time I mentioned our logo, which has eluded us until now. Our logo design resonates so much with some people that one customer tattooed it on his arm — seriously!

At Ethnotek, our logo symbolizes our values. I like to think of the purpose as an intentional act we decide to make with a new product to **Wear Your Values,** like a seal of approval.

We wear our values and take them everywhere we go. I mean this quite literally. There's a reason why the handmade artisan fabric is displayed loud and proud on the outside of our bags. We could have put them on the inside and had the bag's exterior more neutral and minimalist, looking to have a more mass-market appeal, but we didn't. Sure, we make some black-only bags because a bag company has to have at least one all-black option for those lovely customers, but 90% of our product line bursts with bright colors and patterns that proudly shout the cultural identity of their makers. The effect I wanted to have was for people to get the mission, or at least a hint of it, enough to get curious to check it out more upon first glance and without having to say anything. And so show, don't tell is a guiding principle for many of our designs.

Instead of huge logos with our company name, we have little logo flags from the countries where each artisan's textiles are made. Usually, country of origin labels (which are often legally required for import) are hidden inside the bag or product. However, we take these mandatory labels (known as COOs) one step further by also proudly displaying the country's flag on the outside of our bags. Frequently, these flag labels are coupled with our hand logo. This design is an open hand with a spool of yarn in the palm. A strand of yarn weaves through the fingers. This logo, of course, is meant to symbolize handmade. When the country flag, combined with the hand logo (without any words), is sewn on top of the artisan fabric, it signals that this incredible textile is handmade in this country. The real-world testing for the brand identity was a fun and informal process but led to useful feedback that validated our mission. I simply held our bags in front of people and asked what they thought about the bag, its design, and what the brand was about. I'd say 75% of the time, people said, "Wow, that's beautiful. It looks like this fabric is handmade in the (insert country name depending on flag shown on the bag)?" After their correct assumption, I'd reply yes, absolutely correct. Excitement would immediately follow: "That's so cool!" most people would say. That's when I knew I had something, and it was enough for me to pursue the brand ID and logo concept.

After the bag is purchased, the logo becomes a badge of honor for the customer. It's essentially a flag you wave that says, "I support handmade." It displays the values that both brand and customer share: to Celebrate Culture (Chapter 3) and support artisans. Also, our customers aren't afraid of color. That's another reason bright artisan fabrics populate most of our bags' exteriors. Our customers are fun, funky and express themselves through their clothes, footwear, accessories, and lifestyle. If you want a plain-looking bag that helps you blend into society, there are a lot of great brands out there for that, but it's not us! We wear our values.

This point pairs well with Be The Only (Chapter 1). It significantly benefits social entrepreneurs when people quickly identify with your mission when they see your product in public. We get comments from customers weekly about how they always get asked about their bags. This is such great brand validation for a product designer and brand. I can't say this is an easy reaction to achieve from viewing a logo and product only once, but through several iterations and real-world testing, once the code is cracked, it's only needed once. This visual identity will be durable and stand the test of time.

Now, we've reached a point in our stroll through Slow Design where I'd like to take you on a little sideways adventure. Let's follow the journey of one of Ethnotek's bags in visual form!

Journey of a Bag

Ideation

This stage begins with market research before moving to design concept discussions with the internal Ethnotek team. Then comes the hand-drawing ideation phase, CAD (Computer-Aided Design) digital design spec drawings, sampling and prototyping, followed by a drawing and sampling loop, which can repeat five to 10 times on average. Around this time, we always remember to organize plenty of dinners and parties with the factory team to keep the good vibes flowing.

Feedback

Next, we share design progress and collaborate with B2B customers, followed by the B2B feedback loop, which can be repeated three to four times. The semi-final samples are then shipped to B2B customers, which is usually repeated twice. We then produce sales samples to ship to B2B trade shows and then move to renderings, line sheets, product specs, and product descriptions for B2B shows.

Orders

After the trade shows, we have a post-show feedback loop and then make final changes to our designs. Then comes the magical stage of production sign-off and we also reference and archive samples. We place seasonal purchase orders with the factory, place artisan fabric orders (five to nine individual orders), and finally place our tech material orders (40 to 50 individual orders in total).

Materials

Cotton fibers are grown, picked, washed, and separated in a process called ginning. Ginned cotton is then formed into a cotton ball in a process called carding. Carded yarn is spun into individual threads, dyed, and spooled (30 days)

Nylon Tech Fabric involves a chemical process of extracting diamine and adipic acids to create polyamide Nylon salt polymer crystals. These are then heated to produce pellets, which are then heated and extruded to form yarn. The yarn is then stretched to increase strength and elasticity.

The spooled yarn is fed onto a waterjet power loom to weave into raw tech fabric. Woven fabric is dip-dyed, coated with polyurethane for waterproofing, spooled onto the finished roll, and packaged for shipping. (30 days)

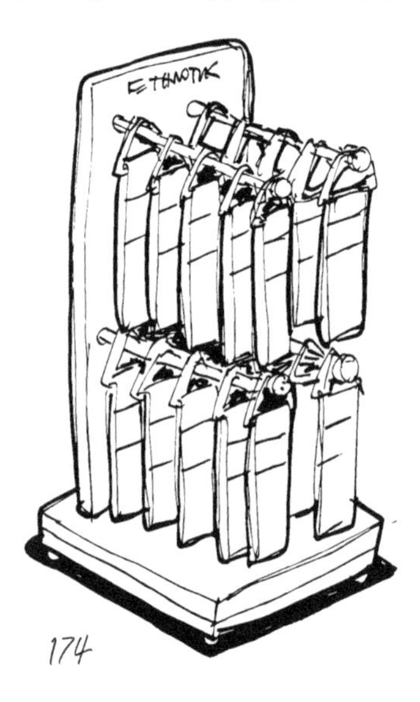

70%

of Ethnotek's supply chain is run by smart, strong and amazing women!

Recycled PET Tech Fabric is an amazing material. First, these bottles are made through a chemistry process to form polyethylene terephthalate (PET) crystals that are heated to form pellets. These pellets are then fed into a hopper, melted, and blow-molded into plastic bottles. The consumer buys, uses, and discards the finished plastic bottle. The discarded plastic bottles are gathered and transported to a recycling facility where they are washed and re-ground to make the clean bottles into pellets. These pellets are then heated and extruded into individual PET yarns before being spooled onto a waterjet powerloom to weave into raw tech fabric. This is then dip-dyed and coated with polyurethane for waterproofing before finally being spooled onto the finished roll to be packaged and shipped. (30 days)

Considering **Trims and Padding,** we use snap buttons, which are stamped. Plastic buckles are injection molded. Zipper tape is woven and dyed. Coils are molded, and both are combined. Zipper pullers and travelers are cast and assembled. We use Polyethylene, Polyurethane, and EVA foam, which is extruded and rolled. Piping is extruded. Labels are woven. Hangtags and packaging are printed and cut. Nylon and rayon sewing machine threads are extruded and spooled. (30 days)

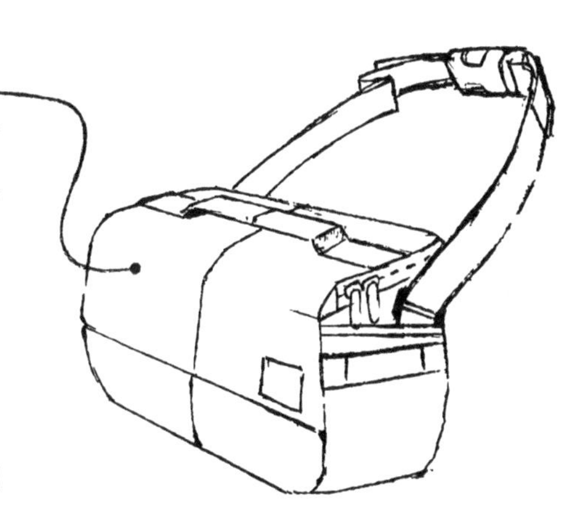

+150 steps go into making one Ethnotek Raja Pack. (Not all are listed here).

For our **Artisan Fabrics** (see Chapter 3 for a more in-depth description), raw cotton yarn and rolls of woven fabric arrive at artisan workshops worldwide. In Ghana, George and the team load yarn onto the looms and start weaving *kente* cloth— Charles and team *batik* wax-resist stamping and dying. In Guatemala, the artisans receive dyed yarns from Artexco, set the warp yarn, and spool bobbins for weft yarn. The process of weaving on the treadle loom begins. Meanwhile, in India, yarn arrives at the Bhuj weavers, where they separate spools, create the loom combs, and deliver them to each village team. They then begin weaving on the pit loom. Over in Indonesia, our Solo artisan partners begin applying *tjanting* hand-drawn wax application and block stamping to fabrics and dye, a process that needs to be repeated numerous times. Finally, in Vietnam, our team of Hmong highland artisans bring their hand-embroidered tribal skirts to project manager Lung Sapa. (90 days)

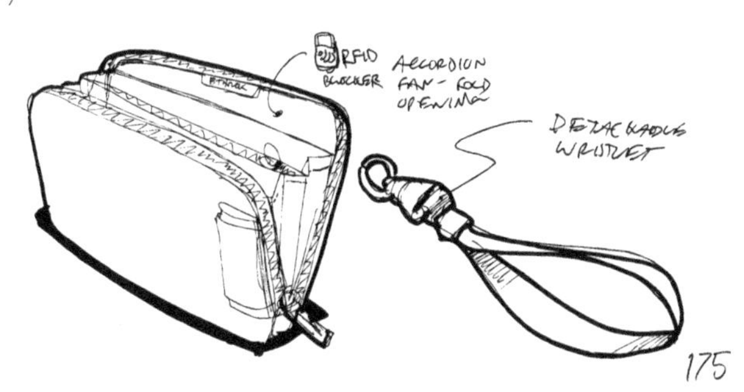

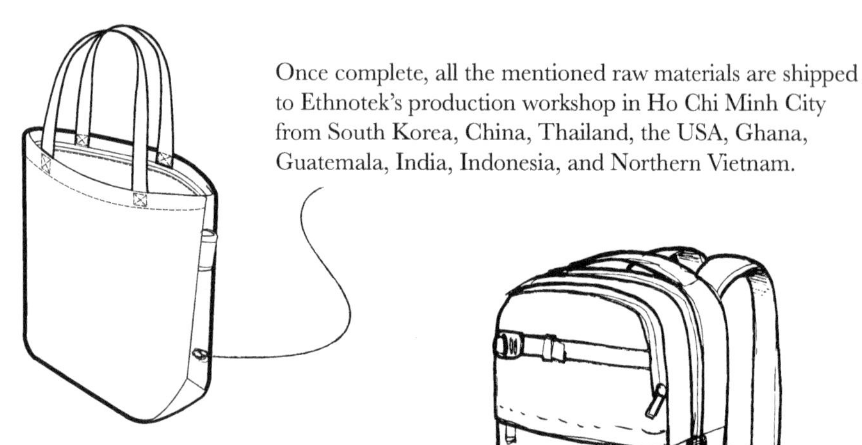

Once complete, all the mentioned raw materials are shipped to Ethnotek's production workshop in Ho Chi Minh City from South Korea, China, Thailand, the USA, Ghana, Guatemala, India, Indonesia, and Northern Vietnam.

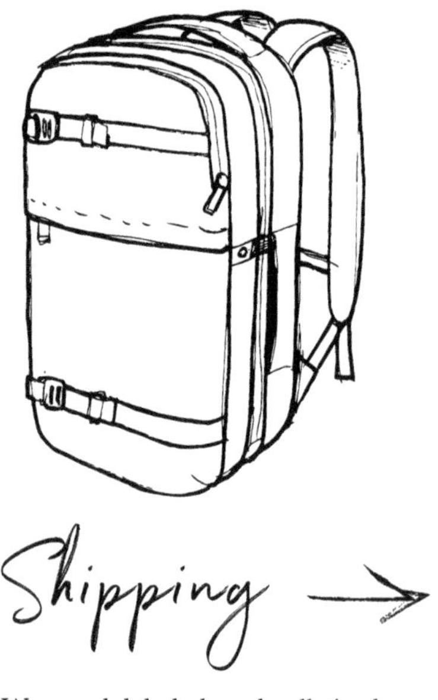

Production

When materials arrive at our Ho Chi Minh City workshop, Ms. Huong, our office manager, and her team count everything to ensure the correct quantities have arrived. All inventory is recorded in a spreadsheet. The tech and artisan fabrics are then die-cut, and the webbing strap rolls, binding webbing tape rolls, zipper tape rolls, and piping rolls are cut to length. Zipper pullers are added to zipper tape. Stacks and bundles or pre-cut materials are brought to the production sewing line. Production sewing begins (30-40 people). Finished bags are inspected, approved, or rejected by our production manager Man and her QC team. Hangtags are tied to QC-approved bags. Final bags are put into recyclable polybags and sealed for freshness. Sealed bags are combined into multi-bag carton boxes, added to a shipping pallet, shrink-wrapped, and finally labeled. (40 days)

Shipping →

Wrapped, labeled, and palletized goods are loaded onto a shipping container on the back of a truck at our factory before being sealed. The truck drivers transport the container to the port, where it is loaded and sails to the USA, Europe, Australia, and Japan. Containers unload at our warehouses in-country (20-40 days). We ship small bulk orders to local retailers. The customer then sees a fun image on our social media or newsletter and buys a bag from our website—and the bag ships from our warehouse to your doorstep. The customer does a happy dance — and **the journey is complete!** (5-10days).

Wow, what a journey! Now, when you see our little hourglass icon on our bags as part of our brand ID, you know what we mean by Slow Design and Slow Production. We consider all the details I explained and do it fairly and responsibly. But there's one element I left out of this chapter, and it's integral to making our whole approach work – and they are our customers. They are the most important part of this global process because we have no brand or business without them. When our loyal customers hit checkout on our site or buy one of our bags in-store, they're empowering our full supply chain of amazing humans, and casting a vote for the kind of world they want to live in.

We've covered a lot in this chapter. I hope you've seen how slowing down during the design process can greatly benefit the business. While Slow Design may go against industry norms, that's why it's the right thing to do. The truly unique brands and social enterprises all go against the grain, defy norms, and don't conform—that's how change and impact happen.

Avoiding trends at all costs to deliver timeless products to customers is always the best approach. Allowing yourself time to test ideas and products is guaranteed to help the business endure. Rapid ideation at the design stage allows for ideas to be fleshed out fully, leading to a better end product, less waste, and happier customers and staff due to more efficiency. When designing, remember to look for mindful cuts, as we discussed. Sometimes aesthetics should be sacrificed, and that's okay. As we saw in this chapter, the bag is not a make-and-sell process, far from it. There's a whole journey that needs to be considered, from an initial idea through the value chain of the product's life cycle. Every stage in the journey affects people's lives and has an environmental cost attached to it. Slow design is also about total immersion. Living and truly engaging with the countries you live in and work in creates a better designer and a holistic experience throughout the product journey. Also, the materials the products are made from really matter, so choose wisely.

Side note: The appendix contains more on materials specifics if you want to explore their pivotal role more deeply.

Also, wearing your impact proudly through your brand ID and shouting your values from the rooftops by how you express and carry yourself is a must for social entrepreneurs today and should be threaded into the entire manufacturing process.

Finally, we are all consumers, and by supporting social enterprises that embody the Slow Design and Slow Production philosophies, we cast a vote for the kind of businesses we value and want to see more of in the world.

When it comes to Slow Design, there are some simple truths I reflect upon. It may have taken me several years to nail one bag design (Raja Pack), but it was worth it. To date, we've had an unbelievably positive outpouring of customer support and a very low product defect rate. I'm not tempting fate, but that's a clear sign that the bags we took a long time to produce are well made, long-lasting, and have made for happy customers. In a world of fast fashion and ever-moving trends, I'm glad we actively went in the opposite direction and took a slow, mindful, and collaborative approach to what we conceive and put out into the world. Slo-mo truly is the way to go.

7

Collaborate Don't Appropriate

"To give real service you must add something, which cannot be bought or measured with money, and that is sincerity and integrity."

— Douglas Adams

Pasadena, California
2009

It was another scorching summer's day in Pasadena. I ducked into an outdoor retail store for some much-needed air conditioning and – if I'm honest — to snoop. For the past few months, I had been soaking up all the inspiration I could, spending many hours in stores like this one (that will remain nameless for this story). As I wandered deeper into the belly of the store basement, I made a beeline for the bag section, one of the largest I'd ever seen. There were multiple aisles and wall-to-wall racks with every permutation of backpack, sling, satchel, suitcase, bum bag, messenger bag, camera bag, dry bag — even tote bags; you name it. There was every type of bag you could imagine in enough colors and sizes to make your head spin. After about half an hour of wandering the aisles, something caught my attention. The colors and patterns sucked me in like a magnet. It wasn't only because I'm a color addict but because this bag had a specific pattern I was looking for.

Let me explain by backing up a bit. During the incubation days before Ethnotek had a name, legal registration, and a website, I did what every designer who loves their work should do — my homework. I spent endless hours studying the market online to see what bags were being made and sold across the USA. Mainly, I was trying to understand an important question we've already covered in this book in the Prologue: Why did the product need to exist? What was its reason for being? Did it have a story, a soul? I also spent many days like that sunny Pasadena morning doing real-life bag research. Scanning the market to see what was out there, what was trendy, what was unique and innovative, what materials were being used, what dominant color palettes were in play, and who were the brands leading the way.

Around this time, I also spent a lot of time at the Pasadena Public Library where I poured myself into research the old-school way. The library also served as a makeshift office in Ethnotek's early days, and I tried to surround myself with books that inspired and informed my decision-making at the time.

Meanwhile, in the store with no name, the colorful object that caught my eye was a bag with rainbow stripes that I recognized right away. It was a direct inspiration (maybe imitation) of a Mexican *sarape*. The *sarape* and poncho are Spanish for blankets woven as a vertical rectangle on the loom. *Sarapes* are closely associated with the Mexican state of Coahuila and the city of Saltillo where some of the most famous *sarapes* originate and are considered iconic symbols of Mexican culture. They embody national pride and are often used in celebrations and ceremonial occasions. Making a *sarape* involves skilled craftsmanship and a deep understanding of traditional weaving techniques. Complex weaving methods passed down through generations have intricate patterns and vibrant colors. This craftsmanship highlights Mexico's artistic talent, supports local economies, and preserves cultural practices.

Today, many of us might recognize this colorful rainbow pattern from blankets widely sold worldwide. Some of you may even have one in your car or home. They are often used as a beach blanket or sofa throw, and it's common for outdoor and fashion brands to convert this pattern into a sublimation-printed fabric that can be produced en masse for garments and accessories.

Meanwhile, in the store, the bag I was looking at bore the *sarape* colorway; but it was a cheap imitation. Looking closer, I studied the bag, turning it over and reading the labels closely. Looking at its cheap faux *sarape* print, I felt mixed emotions.

In the weeks before, I had been studying books on anthropology, ethnology, and traditional textiles. I was also planning to launch a company that supported artisans and their authentic handmade crafts. Yet, here in front of me was a product that did the opposite. In short, it was a rip-off. This faux *sarape* bag didn't mention anything about the person who made it, the *sarape* weaving technique, its place of origin in Coahuila, or the culture surrounding it. It simply had a brand name, a list of features, and a price tag. It made me feel hollow, sad, and slightly angry. I realized at that moment I was staring at a clear case of **Cultural Appropriation**. It was a bag without a soul because the brand had chosen to separate the product from its culture. It was just a trendy object priced at US$89.95. But I had come into the store looking for this all along. And for the past few months, I had been actively trying to find examples of Cultural Appropriation to see how prevalent this issue was in the market. Let's just say it didn't take me long. Examples were on sale everywhere I looked.

Yet the longer I stood staring at this faux *sarape* bag, the more questions flooded my mind. Why had this come into existence? How did it happen? What series of decisions made it possible? Who was the decision maker? Where was the responsibility? The more I thought about it, the more another feeling welled up in me: empathy. The designer who made this bag might not have known what they were doing was wrong. They may have followed the latest consumer trend guidance from a publication like WGSN, which said that tribal and ethnic prints were in fashion that season. Or, they could have simply pulled inspiration from Instagram, where Cultural Appropriation is rife and unmonitored. Unfortunately, this is the sad truth, but it's how many time-squeezed designers source for ideas. Because of fast-fashion demands and timelines rampant within the industry, there can be little time for due diligence or research. This can lead designers (and their managers) to make poor decisions, errors in judgment, or simply be ill-informed about the design "inspirations" their work is based upon.

Another thread of this conversation is the counterintuitive reality that more demand for traditional textiles, designs, and patterns (even ill-informed demand) can benefit handmade artisans because market forces drive business and economic growth in the communities where these textiles originate. Interest in the surge of textile demand can also inspire social entrepreneurs in-country or overseas to collaborate with artisans to sell textiles ethically.

As I stood looking at the bag, I felt inspired to funnel these emotions into Ethnotek's mission and create an ethical roadmap for business in this space. I knew this business model could be done better to be more inclusive and equitable. It was right there in the basement of that store that I decided to go all in on my path as a social entrepreneur and forge ethical relationships with artisans in business. I wanted to be a part of sharing the stories of the art, not hiding it. It was also when I decided to go in person to meet every artisan, which would later become an integral part of our company and the inception of our **Go There** (Chapter 4) company philosophy. To invest in flying to every region to collaborate and establish personal relationships with the artisans: Asking permission, earning trust, following their lead, helping only in ways they request, involving them financially, and helping spread awareness to promote cultural celebration and the importance of diversity. This ideology sounds good on paper, but it's difficult in practice. As a caucasian male, I knew that running such a company and creating a platform around this type of social commentary could be potentially problematic. I gave myself a pep-talk early on: To make a change and do something meaningful, I must take the risk and put myself out there. Believe me, I wanted to hide and create awesome bags with authentically made and ethically sourced textiles and remain anonymous. But I knew, and my family, friends, investors, and advisors all knew that it's important to humanize the brand —and to be an ethical business working in this space, it was essential to do so.

That said, even though you try to do everything as ethically and transparently as possible, skeptics and haters will always tell you you're doing the wrong thing. It's an exciting space to be in. I've discussed this with other social entrepreneurs, and nearly all have had similar experiences. The common sentiment is that the second you say you're doing a good thing, it's like an open invitation for people to flock in and challenge that. Needless to say, I went for it, took the leap, and here we are. Far from perfect, striving for improvement, open to learning new things, and listening to other people's perspectives.

Like any cross-culturally collaborative company, we've received our fair share of unsavory labels thrown at us like "modern slavery," "cultural appropriation," "white saviors," and the list goes on. I think it's important we address these points. So let's dig into it.

Collaborating between cultures in today's often highly charged online environment can be tricky, but if you trust your ethics, stay true to your core values, and honor your collaborators, you can interact with customers (and even critics) with generosity, openness, and willingness to learn.

In this chapter, I'll explore this problematic but hugely important issue of our time and how fashion and lifestyle brands fit into this complex cultural intersection.

So, let's dive into a sensitive topic I'm sure we're all familiar with: Cultural Appropriation. Far too often, traditional textile motifs are copied and reprinted in the sports and fashion industries without gaining permission from the original creators or including them financially. We firmly stand against this form of theft! We are in the business of elevating the artisan entrepreneurs who authentically create these traditional textiles and promote their cultural roots. This core value and the textiles give our bags a soul, meaning, purpose, and story. Combined with our exceptionally high standards for quality, functionality, simplicity, and beauty, we're proud to be a market leader in the ethical bag space. Even if you don't buy a bag from us, we encourage you to do your homework when searching for other brands to ensure they have built-in ethical and environmental benefits. As conscious consumers, we owe that to our beautiful planet and its incredible humans.

My intention for this chapter is to illuminate the unintended consequences of the heated discussion surrounding this topic, particularly its negative effect on social enterprises, their cross-cultural collaborators, and their supportive customers. To understand the issue as a whole and ultimately arrive at some proposed solutions, it's essential to break this topic into its constituent parts to know what we're even talking about in the first place.

Social enterprises and their entrepreneurs are under intense scrutiny today, especially those working in cross-cultural fields and advertising their work as "doing good." Much of the scrutiny is fuelled by liberal consumers who share the same values as the company they seek to hold accountable. That's a great thing, which, of course, we fully support at Ethnotek.

But there's a flip side. In recent years, scrutiny has turned to witch hunts, and cancel culture has become widespread, fueled by an online mob mentality. Often, this can be misdirected, but the damage can be done before a brand can defend itself or refute any accusations it may face.

Specifically, when it comes to cross-cultural collaboration, there's much to say on this matter. I believe culture, art, and ethnic diversity make this world such a rich and beautiful place, and we need more small businesses that embody those values, not less.

In my discussions with other social entrepreneurs, I have found that they increasingly feel a culture of fear surrounding their brand is becoming pervasive online. Fear of doing it wrong. Fear of getting called out. Fear of getting canceled. These good people want to support culture and artisan craft but often feel they have to shrink into the shadows or not participate because of all the noise and finger-pointing online. That's not what we want. The social entrepreneur, artisan economy, and conscious consumer are on the rise, and it's our time to fan those flames for a better world and consumer marketplace, not snuff them out.

This is not to excuse the bad actors, for whom there are many. Just type Cultural Appropriation into any search engine, and you'll receive a litany of blatant offenders, mainly from the fast-fashion sector.

On the contrary, our position at Ethnotek is that bad actors should and need to be called out by activists and everyday consumers online. We are not here to debate this issue but rather suggest that a little more nuance and research are needed to call out the *right* brands. I say this as the founder of a brand that has faced the online ire of trolls on many occasions for uncalled or unfactual reasons.

We have to call out Cultural Appropriation, but we also have to elevate the brands doing it right so that more entrepreneurs take up the challenge and create better businesses built on Direct Trade, **Cultural Collaboration**, and ethical trading partnerships.

Now, please don't assume that this means we got everything right at Ethnotek. We didn't. We've made mistakes in the stories we told about our brand and in how we communicated with our customers (I'll share more on these later). For now, I want to renew some optimism for all you social entrepreneurs and conscious consumers who want to celebrate culture and share it with the world in an ethical business manner.

Side note: Many people have told me to exclude this chapter entirely because it's too risky and could be taken out of context in a way that could sully the company's reputation. But I believe businesses like ours should be taking on this challenge to be part of the conversation and stand by our values and mission.

Talking About Cultural Appropriation

To gain an overview of ethical business practices while collaborating in cross-cultural business relationships, here are the key points our brand believes every social entrepreneur should ask themselves.

Definitions

- What is culture, and why is it important?
- What's the difference between Material Culture and Non-Material Culture?

- What's the difference between Cultural Appropriation, Cultural Appreciation, and Cultural Collaboration?

Discussion

- Who gets to wear what, and who decides that?
- How is Intellectual Property involved in the conversation?
- Why do words matter?

What's Ethnotek's Sourcing Route?

- We engage in Cultural Collaboration
- We share learnings and experiences with other social entrepreneurs to spread this message and inspire others to follow the same souring path

What's The Way Forward?

- Who are the good guys doing Cultural Collaboration?
- Is there any cause for optimism?

Talk about a broad topic! As you can see, these simple talking points open the door to worlds of conversation—far larger than I can ever hope to tackle in a single book. There are hundreds of books, papers, and articles on this subject. So, I'll explore these points with that in mind while focusing on these issues from our perspective and our own learnings.

Let's start with **Definitions.** What is culture, and why is it important? The University of Minnesota's Sociology Department and the Government of Ontario, Canada, published articles to help us break this nebulous topic into digestible parts. **Culture** in its Latin origin, "*colere*", means to "tend" or "cultivate." Culture can be defined as all the ways of life, including arts, beliefs, and institutions of a population that are passed down from generation to generation. Culture has been called "The way of life for an entire society," according to the research paper *What Is Culture* by Boston University. This includes all codes of manners, dress, language, religion, rituals, and art.

As this definition suggests, there are two basic components of culture: **Ideas** and **Symbols** on the one hand and **Artifacts** on the other. The first type, **Non-Material Culture**, includes the values, beliefs, symbols, and language defining a society. The second kind, **Material Culture**, contains all of society's physical objects, such as its tools and technology, clothing, architecture, transportation, eating utensils, or any other physical objects born of that particular culture.

Culture is the lifeblood of a vibrant society, expressed in the many ways we tell our stories, celebrate life events, share knowledge, remember the past, and imagine the future. Our creative expression helps define who we are and helps us see the world through the eyes of others.

Participating in culture can benefit individuals in many ways, some of which are deeply personal. They are a source of delight and wonder and can provide emotionally and intellectually moving experiences, whether pleasurable or unsettling, that encourage celebration or contemplation. Culture is also a means of expressing creativity, forging an individual identity, and enhancing or preserving a community's sense of place.

Participation in culture in children and youth helps build self-esteem and improves resilience, enhancing their overall education. For example, students from low-income families who participate in arts activities at school are three times more likely to get a degree than those who don't. In the USA, schools that integrate arts across the curriculum have shown consistently higher average reading and mathematics scores than similar schools that don't.

Diversity of culture and gender in education has also been proven to be beneficial. A study by Alison Sprecht and Kevin Crowston on PLOS ONE shows that ethnic and gender-diverse teams in science and academia perform better due to increased creativity, innovation, and the ability to tackle complex tasks effectively. Diverse teams can leverage various perspectives and expertise, leading to improved problem-solving capabilities and higher-quality outcomes.

Participation in culture contributes to healthy populations in several ways. Creativity and cultural engagement have been shown to improve mental and physical health. Culture is being integrated into healthcare systems, notably in the UK, according to research by Arts Council England, but also increasingly in other countries. A growing body of research also demonstrates that the arts can improve the health and well-being of older adults. Art participation can relieve isolation and promote identity formation and intercultural understanding. Culture helps build social capital, the glue that holds communities together. Cultural activities such as festivals, fairs, or classes create social solidarity by fostering social inclusion, community empowerment, capacity-building, and enhancing confidence, civic pride, and tolerance.

Now, let's circle back to the differences between Material and Non-Material Culture, as they are essential for our journey through Cultural Collaboration. This differentiation becomes relevant when assessing or holding to account those brands or businesses perceived to be engaging in Cultural Appropriation because these two elements have different shades of qualifying criteria within the wider debate. The latter is more challenging to pin down.

There are **Opposing Viewpoints of Cultural Appropriation**, and the waters can become murky quickly, with many misconceptions muddying the waters that lead to confusion and floods of online fights, trolls, and a bottomless vortex of vehement and online abuse. It can get really toxic and fast, so it's imperative to steer the ship in the right direction, ensure your business is involved in ethical practices, and communicate this responsibly and with the correct language. Many ethical companies have been hit by a rogue wave and canceled because of simple miscommunication. Don't let that happen to you or your business. If you're genuinely doing good work and engaging in Cultural Collaboration, communicate openly and transparently, you can expect smooth sailing.

Okay, so about opposing viewpoints, some people argue that Cultural Appropriation is a natural and positive part of cultural exchange. They believe that borrowing from and trading with other cultures can help foster understanding and appreciation between different groups. In contrast, others argue that Cultural Appropriation is a form of theft that perpetuates systems of oppression. They believe that dominant cultures have historically stolen and profited from marginalized cultures and that Cultural Appropriation is a way of continuing that trend. Furthermore, some people argue that Cultural Appropriation is a meaningless concept. They believe that cultural boundaries are fluid and constantly shifting and that it's impossible to draw a clear line between "appreciation" and "appropriation."

One **Common Misconception** about Cultural Appropriation is that it's always wrong. While it can be harmful in specific contexts, it's not always negative. For example, if a person from one culture adopts a practice from another with consent and in a respectful and informed way that benefits both parties, that can be a positive exchange. Another misconception is that Cultural Appropriation only applies to specific cultures. In reality, any culture can be appropriated, and any individual can appropriate from another culture.

Furthermore, to add to the confusion, some people believe Cultural Appropriation is the same as Cultural Appreciation. While it's possible to appreciate another culture without appropriating it, the two concepts are different. Many issues I've witnessed in the debate online stem from simple miscommunication issues around some of these complex ideas. While Cultural Appropriation takes elements of another culture disrespectfully, without consent or compensation, Cultural Appreciation respectfully acknowledges, learns from, and honors the culture's origins and significance.

Stemming from the branches of Cultural Appreciation is Cultural Collaboration, where our company sits alongside international artisans worldwide under the canopy of Material Culture. The products we produce together are the fruits of our collective efforts and trade. Cultural Collaboration merges culture through consent, respect, acknowledgment, shared financial gain, and co-creation that sprouts from this relationship.

Side note: It can be helpful to break the three categories down even further. Cultural Appropriation: Theft; Cultural Appreciation: Intention; Cultural Collaboration: Action.

We like collaboration because it's active. You can appreciate a culture other than your own from home by learning about it online, in books, and following relevant social media accounts and news feeds. If you decide to hit the streets to join a protest for that community, buy or co-create a product with that community, donate to that community's project, or go into business together, you are collaborating. You're taking action.

During a panel discussion a few years ago at USC Pacific Asia Museum in Pasadena, Viet Thanh Nguyen, a Pulitzer-winning author and professor, noted, "Cultural Appropriation often raises questions of ownership and power in various domains, including food, music, and clothing." Josh Kun, another panelist, highlighted the role of capitalism in these scenarios, where cultural elements become marketed or commodified, leading to financial gain through what could be termed as "racial capitalism." Aditi Mayer, a photographer and journalist, acknowledged during the panel discussion that social media has both positively and negatively impacted the issue: "It has become a platform where Cultural Appropriation is both highlighted and criticized." However, as Mayer points out, "The Internet often strips away important information, leading to misunderstandings or misrepresentations of cultural elements."

This leads us to our next question: **Who can wear what, and who decides that?** While researching this chapter, I found the article by Refinery29, *How "Cultural Appropriation" Fears Blur The Line Between Helping & Hurting Indigenous Creators.* It's an interview with the founder of the jewelry brand Oltem, Tatiana Toro. Her brand creates stunning hand-beaded jewelry with the Embera Chami indigenous group of women in Colombia. Tatiana is an indigenous woman born in Colombia who emigrated to New York City when she was 10. Despite her origin story, her customers have faced backlash over Cultural Appropriation claims. I should point out that these claims (to the best of my knowledge) were not directed at Tatiana herself but at her customers. Consequently, people said they wanted to buy her jewelry but were scared to.

In an example in the article, one of Tatiana's friends said she showed her brand's necklaces to a friend, who replied, "Wait, but isn't that Cultural Appropriation?" Tatiana replied, "These are their (the Embera Chami indigenous group of women) designs, and we are employing them. It's not appropriation."

This article further details the issues and dangers of misguided mob justice surrounding this topic. After reading the piece, I found the comments under the article fascinating, too. Aside from having really cool screen names, they made excellent points! Here's a snapshot.

PURPLEMELON, 28 June, 2021

"... Consumers are still concerned about being accused of cultural appropriation if they buy the item, even if they know it is ethically made. The problem is still whether or not you can comfortably wear it in this environment where people are quick to judge. Is it just a simple issue of educating people that you have to buy ethically made, or is it a wider issue about the literal who can and cannot wear things? For example, I would never wear a sari, even if I was given one by an Indian friend, because it is not my culture, and I would feel like I had to stand next to said Indian friend constantly to sort of justify wearing it. So what's the real answer to this question, how do you take part in ethical cultural sharing, without fear of accusations?"

NEON_WILLOW - 29 June, 2021

"I'm a white-passing Latina who was born in Mexico (long lineage and generation of Mexicans) and was constantly berated when wearing pieces of my OWN culture growing up and even worse now while out and about. So I get the fear of wearing these items and fear of being attacked/ berated while out in the streets. What people don't understand when they're gatekeeping in the end is... they're destroying and further hurting the businesses of the people they're trying to defend. People need to understand it's APPRECIATION when buying and wearing directly from the source. It's truly become a sad state of affairs."

KITTIESLOVEYOU - 30 June, 2021

"As much as I love fabrics and jewelry from certain other cultures, there is no way I will be buying or wearing any of it because I don't want the braying mob to come after me, cancel me, or get me fired from my job.

It's just not worth it to make a point."

NELLSPENCER - 1 July, 2021

"People need to stop judging others based on what they "think they see." I have a granddaughter whose paternal grandfather is 100% Native American, however, she has bright red hair & freckles with pale skin. She has been gifted family jewelry by Native Artisans and has encountered strangers screaming at her for wearing it. Of course, no one bothers her when she wears her shamrock earrings! I have also been gifted Native American jewelry and scarves, and been judged."

WILLOWBARK - 29 June, 2021

"Mob justice ends badly no matter how noble the intentions behind the original mob were. Remember, mobs are simple organisms. Complex points and distinctions tend to be immediately shot down because they drain off the raw emotional energy that feeds mob mentality. Celebrating the silencing of freedom of speech, thought, expression, and style is guaranteed to end in a place that hurts everyone."

After reading this article, I wanted to speak to someone in the know on the ground in Guatemala. I could think of no better person than Erin Semine Kokdil, the former director of Maya Traditions and now an award-winning documentary filmmaker and National Geographic Explorer. Here's what she had to say.

"Most of the accusations I've seen online are coming from uneducated, hateful people. Social enterprises are important because they help educate consumers and connect them with the makers of their goods in an increasingly globalized world. Blatant examples like Dior and similar fashion houses directly copying an indigenous sweater and selling it at a high price without acknowledging or financially compensating the artisans is wrong and should be scrutinized. The goal shouldn't be to attack small social enterprises trying to do direct trade correctly. The conversation is good, but if restorative justice is the goal, those being accused and criticized should be allowed to learn and make improvements to do better by their accusers, not canceled or publicly shamed."

How is Intellectual Property involved in the conversation?

Unfortunately, Cultural Appropriation is not a standalone legal violation that can be directly enforced in court. However, it often overlaps with intellectual property (IP) rights, where legal action can be taken. The enforcement and legal implications of cultural appropriation typically arise within the framework of intellectual property law such as Copyright Infringement, Trademark Infringement, False Advertising, Misrepresentation, Moral Rights and Right of Publicity, Cultural and Intellectual Property Rights of Indigenous Peoples, and International Treaties and Conventions.

While litigation proceedings and the inner legal framework of Intellectual Property rights aren't the sexiest subjects in the world and stay out of the public eye for the most part, they are essential protections for cultures, artisans, community groups, and indigenous peoples worldwide. There are thousands of unsung heroes working in this legal space to protect people's rights in the USA alone, but this is a global cause and a critical one.

A handful of these heroes come to mind: People such as Jacob Adams, who prosecuted Neiman Marcus on behalf of the Sealaska Heritage Institute for the copyright infringement upon native weavers' Ravenstail knitted coat design; Brian Lewis represented and won for the Navajo Nation in their case of trademark infringement and violation of the Indian Arts and Crafts Act, an unauthorized use of the "Navajo" name and motifs by Urban Outfitters. Beatriz Gutierrez, the wife of the president of Mexico, confronted Ralph Lauren for plagiarizing indigenous designs from the Contla and Saltillo peoples. Following the case, Ralph Lauren pledged that all new products using indigenous designs would be created under the "credit and collaboration model." They have taken corrective action supporting the Association for Indian Arts (SWAIA) and Creative Futures Collective (CFC). Indigenous Communities are increasingly taking legal action against Cultural Appropriation by Western brands — and winning — that's great to see. Although the legal process is complex, and not all cases result in clear victories for the plaintiffs, these efforts speak loudly and send out a ripple effect among Western brands and their customers to start paying better attention to what they're designing and consuming, to be more inclusive, and avoid Cultural Appropriation from happening in the first place.

These cases could have been avoided. It's a needless and senseless way of doing business. If the defendants purchased the art and Intellectual Property directly from the artisans who created it, or at the very least requested permission, there might have been very different outcomes. But as it too often plays out, Western brands creating their own "inspired-by" collections without collaborating, involving, or consenting with the cultures in which the art originated leads to only one unfavorable result: Cultural Appropriation.

When it comes to this discussion, **Words Matter**. If we want culture and diversity to be more prevalent in society, we mustn't be so quick to judge. We must do our own research and develop our own viewpoints, and not just parrot whoever is shouting the loudest on Facebook, Instagram, or X—because context matters.

The most fruitful conversations we've had with activists who have called us out for Cultural Appropriation came from the shared goal of common understanding first and corrective action second. This takes time and patience on both sides. It also takes courage and self-awareness to admit when you're wrong and take action to change if you are.

We often invite those challenging us to read the various materials we've published that explain our sourcing process, relationships with our artisan partners, and how our trade relationship works regarding permission, collaboration, and payment, as well as to watch the videos of our process. I'd say that nearly 100% of the time, this additional information turns doubt into trust and misunderstanding into understanding simply because the person interacting with our brand online didn't have that information on hand when they saw our ad in their social media feed. They made an assumption and reacted accordingly.

Meanwhile, I fully admit that our company is an imperfect work in progress. In the early years of business, I naively wrote things like "keeping culture alive," "preserving culture," and "disappearing craft," which is incorrect and implies a relationship between our brand and the artisans that actually didn't exist. Our relationship was always Cultural Collaboration, but our words and marketing failed to communicate this to our customers and wider community properly. That's my bad, and I take responsibility for it, and we have taken many steps to avoid this happening again. We learned and moved on. These aforementioned problematic phrases we used were actually quoted directly from discussions we've had with some of the artisans we worked with when they were talking about their craft, but we didn't realize that by taking those words out of context and putting them on to our own platform it would have the opposite effect of what we were trying to convey.

One particular and very patient and forgiving BIPOC (Black, Indigenous, and People of Color) activist named Ayden helped us see that our message was construed as white saviors, as if "we're helping the poor defenseless artisans and their dying craft," which is demeaning. The embarrassment and shame that washed over me after he held up a mirror like that can't be understated. Needless to say, our team quickly changed the wording on our website and how we talk about the mission as a whole to be more faithful to our values and accurate to how our mutually respectful collaboration actually works. For better or worse, words hold power. We realized pretty late in the game that we should have invested more time and thought into our written communication and content professionalism early on, but I can't turn back the clock. Regrettably, it took someone else to point that out to us to make the change, but it happened, and lessons were learned.

If you're a social entrepreneur reading this and wish to collaborate with cultures other than your own, don't make the same mistake. You can spend years developing an incredible supply chain that you, your collaborators, and your customers are thrilled with, but it's a few words and turns of phrase that could potentially bring the whole thing tumbling down if you're not careful. I suggest running your written copy past as many diverse people as possible to ensure it's balanced and true to your values before publishing. In parallel, I encourage activists to continue confronting brands like Ayden did with an open heart and give entrepreneurs the benefit of the doubt. Sometimes, as in our case, we were simply being naive and clumsy with our words.

Ayden's action to challenge us was an act of service to the artisans, indigenous communities, and our business. Instead of us both standing rigidly and defensively in our positions or trying to tear each other down, we listened to each other, agreed to disagree on some things, met in the middle on the most critical points, and made changes to what needed to change. He was right; we were wrong, plain and simple. Admitting that and changing made us better. Thank you for your candor, Ayden.

As mentioned, at Ethnotek, we engage in Cultural Collaboration. In the context of produced goods within the fashion, outdoor, and sports industries, the solution to achieve this isn't always easy. Don't steal, that's it. We all know that when we stroll into a supermarket, you can't just grab whatever you want and walk out without paying. The same applies to Interfusing (Chapter 1) someone else's craft and culture into your product.

We've avoided Cultural Appropriation in our supply chain all these years through a document we call our **Sourcing Roadmap.** It's our policy for working with artisans and serves as a checklist of qualifying criteria and questions to ask when we're setting up new sourcing relationships. This is an internal checklist and mostly relevant to those seeking to create products with textile artisans, so if that's not directly relevant to you, bear with us. Hopefully, it'll provide transparency on how we conduct ourselves while sourcing and provide you with some warm fuzzies next time you check out our bags. If you want to read the full Sourcing Roadmap (it's long!), visit our website ethnotek.com/blogs/news/sourcing-roadmap. But here's the truncated version, starting with our **10 Key Points for Responsible Cultural Collaboration.**

1. Find Your Foundation
2. Go There & Be Human
3. Communication & Intent
4. Permission
5. Commercial Inclusion
6. Repeat Orders
7. Know Your Limits

8. Plan For Mistakes

9. Never Copy or Reproduce

10. Credit & Storytelling

A quick side note to the soon-to-be social entrepreneurs: Before taking any of these steps, it's important to know *why* you're launching your product, collection, or brand in the first place. For that, I suggest giving yourself the **"Ethnotek 3Ps Test"** before launching. Is what you're creating good for the **Planet** and **People**, and are you **Passionate** about it? If you answered yes to all three questions, please proceed, young Jedi! If it's not a wholehearted "hell yes," it's time to go back to the drawing board.

The last point may sound trivial, but it's anything but. Passion is the fire your business will run on and the ember you carry with you throughout your business journey. The fire will go out sometimes, and if you don't attend to fanning it, blowing it, keeping it dry, and making sure it's glowing at all times, you'll never get the fire going again. The initial spark of passion is the fuel that keeps the show on the road. Intrinsic motivation is the key to perseverance. For some entrepreneurs, the thought of getting rich is enough, and they'll spin any motivational story to reinforce that goal, but Social Entrepreneurs are wired differently. We must know we are doing something positive and giving back to the world in a way bigger than ourselves. If the brand and business you're building embodies that, it's much easier to endure the ceaseless problems, setbacks, cashflow dips, and late nights. Pursuing your life's purpose is very different from punching into a job, so choose your path wisely. It must give you energy, not take it from you.

The first piece of advice I received on my Ethnotek journey was from a guy I sat beside on a bench at the Action Sports Retail trade show in San Diego, California, in 2010. I had the first Ethnotek bag sample, and he said, "Hey, cool bag, where'd you get it?" Bursting with enthusiasm, I explained the product and mission; it was the first time anyone had asked me about it publicly. I was like a giddy schoolboy. We talked for a while, and he liked the idea. Eventually, I asked, "What's your one piece of advice for me?" He didn't pause for a second and said, "Never lose your enthusiasm. The secret sauce is the energy that just poured out of you when telling me about your bag. I honestly couldn't care that much about your bag, but the passion for which you spoke about it is infectious. It made me lean in and want to know more. More importantly, it's for you. It's your fuel source. If you ever lose that enthusiasm, it's time to walk away." I'll never forget that kind guy's words. All these years later, I understand precisely what he meant, and I pass on the same advice.

1: Find Your Foundation

When researching traditional art to incorporate into your designs, make sure the piece of interest has historical-cultural roots that are still somewhat thriving and have a local population supporting its continuation for assurance of authenticity and supply capability. You want the "goldilocks zone" of local supply and demand: Not so small that you'll be the only producer reviving the sector in the area and not too big to where you can't make an impact or aren't needed. You want to see the opportunity and runway for gradual, long-term growth together. Partner only with those who share your values, and stay with them throughout the lifespan of your company.

2: Go There & Be Human

Show up! Face-time is everything! All worthwhile relationships need a dating period; don't expect to get the best out of people until you first earn their trust. The best way to establish this trust is to share experiences openly. Curiously take an interest in your future sourcing partners, their lives, and their families.

Above all else, be human, be yourself, be polite, be respectful, ask questions, and be lighthearted. Share stories about your personal life. Be vulnerable. Ask about any important upcoming events they have (and mark them in your calendar) so you can say something nice on the day, and be sure to avoid bothering them with work requests at that time. Celebrate their marriages, birthdays, and holidays. Visit in person and have video calls as much as you can. Of course, everyone is busy, but face-time is the thread that connects us all. Your artisan partners are your star players; treat them as such. Create shared experiences together; don't just focus on work the whole time. Those bonds and good feelings will infuse everything in your work, and they will show. Keep each other warm; don't drift too far away into the land of busy.

3: Communication

Unless you're superhuman, it's impractical for you to speak every language fluently of your suppliers, nor is it easy to travel to the countries where they operate for every small thing. That's why it's crucial to find a facilitator to work with you who can honestly and transparently share your vision for how the collaboration will look, both initially and in the long term. This person will become a part of the artisan supply chain, so it's important to know that they not only speak the spoken and written languages between you and the artisans but the language of both traditional craft and modern business. It's essential to develop a close relationship with them to feel a part of the team and have a shared vision. These star MVPs can often be more challenging to find than the artisans and textiles you're looking for, so when you do finally find them, keep them happy. Some of our facilitators get a percentage commission on every order we send to the artisans, and some ask for a flat monthly retainer fee. Let them come to you with a proposed compensation they feel good about. Create a culture of open communication. Your facilitators should always feel safe asking for help, suggesting changes, and reporting problems as they arise. You can't plan for everything, and you learn more through doing, hence why it's important to rely on trust and open communication. You'll need that when surprises pop up. Things will run much more smoothly when the facilitator and artisans are already friends and have done business together. Assigning a facilitator of your own from outside their community can be a challenge and we suggest avoiding it.

I'd like to caveat this by saying that making the long journey to your artisan collaborators alone can be tricky, as can partnering with a trustworthy facilitator on a single trip. In this regard, here are some more words of wisdom from Erin Semine Kokdil.

"If you cannot make direct artisan connections, work with reputable organizations and make sure orders with them are repeatable. Get references before working with them. There are a lot of bad NGOs and sourcing agents out there. I've witnessed and worked for NGOs just creating new dependency models. They tell the artisans and recipients of donations what they need instead of asking, listening to, and working with the people they intend to help. So do your homework.

4: Intention & Permission

At the beginning of the relationship, gather with your artisan partners and facilitators in the same space to state your intentions for the project (ideally after some social time over an activity, meal, or beverage to warm up to each other). Make it clear how you wish to involve their community, combine their art with your product, and what your long-term plans and goals are for the business. Share information about the entire company, not just the aspects they'll be involved in. They deserve to know the big picture and often have cool ideas you might haven't thought of. Remember, they're entrepreneurs, just like you!

When you're all on the same page, and they understand your intentions, ask for their permission to order material from them on an ongoing basis and use their textiles in your products the way you all discussed. Don't ask yes or no questions. Instead, ask open-ended questions; kindly ask them to repeat their understanding of the project to you while you ask for their permission.

If they grant permission, this is your green light to move forward to the next step, but pay close attention and read their body language before jumping ahead. If you sense apprehension, see if you can figure out the source of the apprehension and address it. This is where it'll help to lean on your facilitator's existing relationship with them.

Keep in mind that when the thought of money and future orders are on the table, some collaborators are inclined to say yes to everything, even if they don't feel it's right. This type of arrangement can fester and later manifest itself in harmful ways. Have enough awareness to know the difference between "yes, I'm inquisitive and excited to be a part of this project" and "yes, because I need the money."

If you want to take photos of anything or anyone, ask for their permission first, and after you return home and edit everything, send them a link to access the images and videos to double-check their usage and share the good vibes.

A little tip for getting good photos of artisans after they've given you their permission: Ahead of time, learn some playful greetings, like the word "smile" in their local language, or employ the help of your facilitator to joke around with the person you're taking a photo of. Creating a lighthearted atmosphere and sense of ease often results in natural smiles that show their personality and make the image shine. Ask them what their social media handles are and tag them, if possible. They'll often love using your photos on their social accounts if they have them.

5: Commercial Inclusion

This one is simple: Pay the artisans fairly for their work. You don't set the price; they do. They are not your employees. The artisans with whom Ethnotek works prefer to sell us their handmade fabric. It's a trade relationship. Agree to pay the price the artisan sets for their products and payment terms/timeline that supports the cash flow of all involved. We recommend offering a 50% deposit when placing your purchase order with the artisan so they don't have to finance materials on their own, and then pay the remaining balance when you receive the finished goods and approve the quality. This method supports the artisan, but they also share the responsibility of delivering the promised goods per the timeline and quality standard you've both agreed on.

6: Repeat orders

At Ethnotek, we're firm believers in sustainable supply chains instead of charity. What we mean by that is that repeat business sustained on an ongoing basis through consistent material orders monthly, quarterly, or semi-annually is far better than charity. We know this because the artisans told us! They know how to distribute wealth among their community better than any outside third party. All they want is our help selling more things they create — simple!

"Any day, trade is better than aid."

— Pankaj Shah
Ethnotek facilitator, India.

Even if you follow the guidelines noted here, it's not impactful unless consistent. Repeat orders provide a reliable revenue stream for the artisans. This is the most sustainable way to maintain the relationship. It can also be great for your business. As Shamji taught us (Chapter 2), placing frequent small orders instead of infrequent large orders will be better for everyone's cash flow and release tension in the supply chain. Plan for slow, steady, long-term growth instead of single orders or scaling too quickly. Order consistency, coupled with on-time payments, speaks louder than words. This will allow you to maintain trust between you and your suppliers.

Where the rubber meets the road on this point is forecasting—looking at where your sales projections meet production and material orders and sharing those projections with everyone. This transparency should always be presented with the caveat that these order volumes aren't promised and are only being provided for transparency's sake. When we've provided projections like this in the past, some artisans were proactive in ordering the materials that commonly cause the most delays, usually raw cotton yarn, but not dying or weaving anything yet. Seeing the potential for textile orders months ahead, at the very least, shows our intentions for repeat business and helps them roughly calculate where they fit into the equation instead of a wait-and-see reactive working style.

7: Know Your Limits

It's essential to know the cap limit of the artisans' output. What's their monthly maximum production? What are the maximum widths and lengths of the finished fabric? (This often varies between cultures and techniques and can throw off your die-cutting layouts at the factory level if they are not planned for.) Can they scale their operation if orders increase, and if so, how will they do that, and how can they ensure quality standards throughout the process? It's also important to know if scaling is something they want to do. It may cause undue stress, or they're simply uninterested in it, so ask. It's important to discuss all constraints at this stage of their process. This is the beauty of physically being there so they can walk you through their process step-by-step. Ask questions every step of the way. Ask them about all potential risks to quality, delays, and worker strain. Learn about their religious and public holidays or seasonal factors affecting lead time and delivery.

This is important so you know when you're approaching the limit to ensure you're not straining the artisans or bottlenecking your business. If you take on investors, they'll also want to know this. Growth can be good and bad, so know your limits.

It's also important to know what limits can be pushed. Our artisan partners often ask us for new designs or "songs," as Felipe calls them, to collaborate on. People rarely enjoy doing the same thing forever; we're creative beings, after all. If there are new things to co-create that celebrate the artisan's cultural identity and satisfy the end customer, leading to higher orders, everyone wins. Plus, it's just fun!

8: Plan For Mistakes

The nature of working with handmade goods is that they're always imperfect, which is one of the many reasons we love them. We call these "signatures of handmade" and fully embrace them. As long as you communicate in your marketing and customer service the variations customers can expect, there shouldn't be any unwanted surprises. That said, it's good to set a tolerance for your design standards. What degree of imperfection will you accept? Communicate that to the artisans. Our acceptable variation tolerance is 10%, which seems to work well. If the handmade fabrics are 90% similar to the original samples and production run before it, we're good with that.

9: Never Copy Or Reproduce

Artisan creations often contain deep cultural meaning and identity and must be cherished and respected as sacred objects. Founders must promise the artisans to refrain from copying or reproducing their creations with other artisans or manufacturers. Doing so is plagiarism and opens you up to litigation and public scrutiny. Keeping production in the hands of the original creators will keep the narrative positive.

10: Credit & Storytelling

In a responsibly run artisan supply chain, the stories of your collaborators and their cultural heritage can be the most valuable thing if they choose to share it. At the basic level, crediting the artisans who created the original work is necessary (if they want that). If they're open to you re-telling their broader cultural story, ask as many questions as you possibly can and circle back regularly so you can validate that these stories still hold true. It's common for some artisans to leave the craft for various reasons, so it's good to refresh the roster to acknowledge the new folks crafting your handmade goodies. At scale, this can be a little tricky to do. When our supply chain is at full tilt, we must name up to 500 people across five countries throughout our various products and marketing channels. That's a lot of names to fit on a hangtag, woven label, or collection page, but that's where creativity comes in. We are in the process of building a database, which you'll learn about in partnership with Tip Me in the last chapter.

Side note: Tread lightly with the wording of your credit-giving; the wrong words can disparage your excellent work if you are not careful. Start by asking your artisan partners how they'd like to be credited and do just that. If you have further ideas for storytelling, brainstorm with them and get their sign-off. It's yet another fun opportunity to co-create. In our experience, our artisan partners view themselves as we do: equals and business partners. Speak to that level playing field whenever writing copy online and in print. That's why we say "artisan partners," not "our artisans" ("our" implies ownership and is a big no-no). They mustn't be portrayed in a light whereby we're providing some sort of aid or exposure to opportunities they couldn't otherwise access themselves.

In some cases, this is true, but it's better to omit that from public storytelling because it can be misconstrued as projecting power dynamics and goes against the grain of what we're here to do. Each of us brings something different and valuable to the table to achieve a shared goal, and that's it: "Trade, not aid." Our writing and credit-giving should capture this collaborative spirit.

This abbreviated Sourcing Roadmap provides a glimpse into our process, and we hope to keep adding to and refining it as we learn and grow over time. We're not masters by any means, far from it, but we're trying our best and we've learned a hell of a lot along the way.

Now, I'd like to point our attention to some other key players worldwide who are demonstrating Cultural Collaboration on a much larger scale than we are.

One of the **Good Guys** in this space is the well-known household name IKEA, which has collaborated with artisans since the 1960s. This is relatively unknown to most consumers because IKEA doesn't heavily feature these stories in their marketing, but quietly, on a mass scale, they are engaging in Cultural Collaboration. I visited some of their artisan rattan workshops in Java, Indonesia, in 2011 with Iwan, and the conditions were great. It appears that IKEA is starting to come out of its shell and more openly discussing its artisan collaborations. The craft and community they were highlighting at the time of writing were their rugs, made in collaboration with artisans in India and Bangladesh. They've also committed to having a 50% female workforce by 2025, they've built two schools for their workers, pay them while they're learning, and are building weaving centers closer to artisan's homes to reduce commute distances.

From weaver Shashi Devi, who works for IKEA:

"I was a teacher; then I applied for a weaving job. Now I'm learning a new craft, earning much better, and can spend more time with my children."

Taking this mission one step further, IKEA invests in social entrepreneurs worldwide. These collaborators include Doi Tung DP in Thailand, Jordan River Foundation in Jordan, Saitex in Vietnam, and Dun Anyam in Indonesia. Good job, IKEA. It's great to see Cultural Collaboration happening globally in the home goods sector and to see more and more end customers bringing artisan craft into their homes. This sets an example for other big box retailers worldwide who will hopefully follow suit.

Next up is Nest, a non-profit organization that stands out for its commitment to fostering the artisan and maker economy's responsible growth and creative engagement, emphasizing gender equity and economic inclusion. This organization supports over 1,500 artisans across 120 countries, bringing visibility and opportunity to the informal handworker economy. By focusing on traditional crafts and handwork, Nest is critical in elevating cultural practices and ensuring they are respected rather than appropriated.

A significant aspect of Nest's impact is its collaborations with major brands. They have connected artisan producers with notable companies like Patagonia, Target, and Williams Sonoma, leveraging these partnerships to advance ethical practices in the handmade sector. These collaborations help Nest to integrate its ethical standards into mainstream supply chains, thereby broadening the impact of its mission.

Nest's Ethical Compliance Standards for Home and Small Workshops were developed to ensure ethical practices when work happens outside of the factory — at home or at community workshops. Additionally, the organization works with companies and artisans to follow best practices in design collaborations to avoid Cultural Appropriation.

Their founder and executive director, Rebecca van Bergen, shared some great insights about cultural appropriation and advice for social entrepreneurs.

"When it comes to avoiding cultural appropriation, the simplest and often overlooked aspects of these collaborations are consent, artisan leadership and education. It's imperative that brands share their long-term vision with artisans and receive their permission before proceeding with any production. The collaboration must be artisan-led or ensure both parties are equal contributors. Artisans are not contract manufacturers; their culture and livelihood are woven into these crafts, and they need to be sure that any brands sourcing with them understand and respect that. A lot of Cultural Appropriation happens unknowingly. It's all too common that an intern at a brand is scrolling Instagram for inspiration and puts an image of something artisan-made on a moodboard that eventually gets interpreted into a finished product that doesn't involve, credit, or compensate the original artisan. It's hard to fault the intern for that, and this is why we need to take several steps back and make artisan collaboration and rights a fundamental part of design education. That's essential. As far as advice for young social entrepreneurs at the start of their journey, I'd say two things: get crystal clear on exactly where you want to position yourself in the market and what type of business structure and entity to register to support those goals. Know what product you're making in collaboration with your artisan partners, how it's different, and who specifically it serves. We all want it to succeed long-term, so take your artisan partners' advice and create something unique. Good sales benefit the whole ecosystem. Also, consider whether you want to be a for-profit social enterprise or a nonprofit 501(c)(3). Having an artisan-based business is hard. Things will go wrong, and it won't be profitable in the first few years, if ever. The impulse is to go straight to for-profit, but managing the dips with this type of entity can be hard. So much learning and development has to go into building a successful supply chain. That is sunk cost. If you're not a non-profit and can't get a grant for that, then you are bleeding money, at least at the beginning. You'll need to invest in education and community project building, which aligns with non-profit values and mission. So, if you have an affiliated non-profit, there are ways to raise 'gentle capital' that can help offset some of those major investments you must make to build up the expertise and talent of the kind of artisans you're looking to support."

That's sage advice, Rebecca! Many thanks.

Nest exemplifies how cultural collaboration can be ethically and effectively achieved in the global economy through its work and partnerships. It demonstrates a commitment to advancing the artisan and maker economy in a way that honors cultural heritage.

Another one of our shortlisted favorites of Cultural Collaboration at scale is Powered By People (PBP). They are a digital wholesale marketplace that connects independent, diverse artisans and retail buyers. It focuses on small-batch and responsibly made products. Unlike Nest, which primarily focuses on elevating artisans through ethical practices and cultural awareness, PBP leverages technology and financial solutions to streamline artisans' manufacturing and selling processes. This approach removes the complexities often associated with wholesale transactions, making it easier for both buyers and makers. PBP's values center around creativity, responsibility, innovation, diversity, transparency, and self-sustainability. They emphasize the ingenuity and collaboration of people as their driving force, and they are committed to causing no unnecessary harm to the planet while progressing for people. Their innovative approach looks for new ways to improve makers' lives and earn buyers' trust. Since its launch, PBP has grown into a global company with team members and over 700+ artisan partners across 70+ countries. They also partner with global brands like West Elm, Liberty, and Banana Republic Home, expanding the reach of these artisans. They also focus on environmental sustainability by encouraging makers to reduce greenhouse gas emissions and increase resource efficiency.

Since we're all about merging traditional with modern at Ethnotek, let's touch upon how technology can play a crucial role in the future of social enterprises.

Last on our list is the International Social Impact Institute (ISII). They're at the forefront of training entrepreneurial changemakers by leveraging Artificial Intelligence (AI) to support their missions and streamline business operations. Since its inception, ISII has made a significant global impact, training 600+ leaders, reaching 33,000+ participants through 100+ educational events, and forming partnerships with over 100 organizations.

I spoke to The ISII founder and CEO Liz Ngonzi, who had a range of great insights, including thoughts on the Cultural Appropriation debate.

"Cultural Appreciation isn't enough. Brands must bring their artisan partners and beneficiaries to their social mission for the full ride. It has to be a collaboration, not an extraction. Both parties with equal input."

Liz also made some excellent points about messaging in marketing.

"Social Impact brands need to be as transparent as possible. Naming your artisan partners is a great start, but it's also important to share your whole business structure, especially if you have someone taking care of business on the ground in each country as a project manager or facilitator. I see brands naming the collaborators that make the beautiful art (textiles, pottery, baskets, etc.) all the time, but the roles in each country on the business side are equally important. This shows you care to employ people who not only speak the two languages of modern business and traditional art but are a filter to ensure all business is conducted with cultural sensitivity."

In addition to AI-powered solutions, The ISII also helps small retail brands develop and amplify their stories to engage conscious consumers. Through the "Balancing People, Planet, and Profit" webinar series, developed in partnership with NY NOW, Liz shared best practices, case studies, and practical tips on creating unforgettable consumer experiences by balancing social and environmental responsibility with profitability. By emphasizing the importance of digital storytelling, strategy, and effective communication, The ISII equips brands with the tools they need to differentiate themselves, inspire loyalty, and drive meaningful impact.

"Don't follow in the footsteps of companies like Prada, Gucci, Dolce & Gabbana, etc., which have taken cultural appropriation missteps. I suggest taking inspiration from authentic smaller brands like Zuri Kenya, my favorite retail social enterprise right now."

Liz also gave some advice to social entrepreneurs at the start of their journey.

"Make your business AI native and work for an existing social enterprise that solves similar problems you want to tackle before starting your own business. Social enterprises usually have to bootstrap in the beginning, and AI greatly reduces overheads and manpower usually required in old-school business structures. But don't introduce tech for tech's sake. First, identify the exact problems you want to solve and start integrating tech to achieve those means after the roadmap is set. When you get to that stage, be careful what tech you bring into your organization. There are a lot of free AI tools out there that might be exciting to use, but getting hacked is quite easy. Review a company's privacy policies and AI code of ethics carefully, and if in doubt, work with experts like The ISII to get you started in the right direction."

Liz had this to say about efficiency.

"Duplicated effort is unfortunately very common. Social entrepreneurs are passionate people, but passion for your mission isn't enough. What budding entrepreneurs need is business grounding. Join a social enterprise and learn on their dime; see how they solve the problems you're passionate about so you can pick up where they left off by spotting new opportunities. Taking learnings and transferring them from one sector to another. I spent years working in the tech private sector and later converted that knowledge into the social sector, which I'm doing now with The ISII. It gives me a competitive advantage and maximizes impact by leveraging my unique skill sets and experience in new ways to benefit small businesses and their stakeholders. It would have been much riskier if I had launched a business before my previous work experience. I'm not sure I would have built something as unique, successful, and fun as The ISII."

As we near the end of this chapter, it's time to leave with some good vibes. Is there a reason for **Optimism** for social entrepreneurs working in cross-cultural collaborations? Simply, yes. The optimism I feel as an entrepreneur and company working in this space is partly due to the demand for artisan-made products driven by a rise in conscious consumerism. This is the single greatest driver for optimism. That demand comes from one source: well-intentioned conscious consumers and social entrepreneurs like you!

While Cultural Appropriation is a serious topic in our globalized world of consumerism, it can't and shouldn't stop the positive momentum of Cultural Collaboration and the brands that embody its practice if we aim our attention in the right place. We're out there, strong, helping each other as opposed to competing, and hopefully, that's all the encouragement an aspiring social entrepreneur and their customers need. Look to the positive examples, brands, artisans, and conscious consumers who are making a lasting positive impact. Join this movement. Get involved. Buy from ethical brands and show you care about handmade artisan trade and products.

As we leave our wandering conversation through Collaborate Don't Appropriate, I hope I've been able to provide some useful insights that may help you and your business avoid these pitfalls and steer clear of unethical practices and behaviors. In many cases, these can be easily avoided *if* your intentions, values, mission and ethical business practices within the Direct Trade model of businesses are respected.

Collaborating between cultures in business in today's often highly charged environment can be tricky. But if you know and trust your ethics, stay true to your values, honor and celebrate the communities you work with, you can navigate any criticism and collaborate freely with trust and integrity.

8

Changing Threads

"The only way to make sense out of change is to plunge into it, move with it, and join the dance."

— Alan Watts

Ho Chi Minh City, Vietnam, 2015

I was sweating bullets. My butt was sore, and my throat was on fire from an afternoon of breathing in fumes while stuck in peak Ho Chi Minh City traffic. Eventually, I arrived at my destination. A small modern angular tower with glass doors on the ground level and a residential space above with rusty window frames and laundry hung on the balcony, as is common with shophouses in the city, with the business on the ground floor and living space above. A few moments later, Ái, Ethnotek's head developer, screeched into the driveway on his motorbike, parked next to me, and gave me a cheeky wink. We ducked inside the building through double doors and emerged into an air-conditioned oasis, a welcome respite from the stifling heat. The immaculate white-walled interior was silent and still in stark contrast to the bustling streets outside. The walls were lined with floor-to-ceiling bookshelves containing more knowledge and inspiration than a single human could digest in a lifetime. This was the city's little-known Artbook Design Bookstore, which was a candy store for a designer like me. We were here on a special scouting mission. To search for an up-to-date Pantone color swatch book for an upcoming textile collection I was working on in collaboration with Shamji and the weavers of Bhujodi, India. We had an idea to co-create a new collection to boost fabric orders, driven by demand from our Japanese distributor. This would be the first time we'd try custom colors dyed into their traditional motifs. None of us had thought of trying it before — but we were excited about the possibilities of creating something new.

Threads of Change is the name on the cover of this book because the nature of our business is constantly changing, whether we like it or not. Adaptation and evolution are part of human life, including companies and social enterprises. As such, culture is constantly growing. It's eternally alive in the hearts and minds of the people. And so, traditional craft innovates over time. Recognizing this ever-moving timeline is essential when working with artisans to stay relevant and embrace change while balancing traditions holistically. At Ethnotek, we have worked hard on embracing the new with the old, meeting the modern world while preserving traditions. It's not always easy, but it's a part of our business that we've put a lot of effort into, and it's here we'll now take a break on our journey to chat about this much-needed and timely balancing act of where modern meets tradition.

As discussed in Chapter 1 with our Interfusing business concept (handmade artisan textiles meets high-tech backpacks) from the outset at Ethnotek, we've placed innovation and adaptation at the center of our work. We like to think of what we do, specifically in textiles, as **New Beginnings for Ancient Motifs**. Now to expand a little on this point, we have to go back to Vietnam.

In the weeks before my visit with Ái to the Ho Chi Minh City bookstore, we had been experiencing stagnating sales of Ethnotek bags featuring Indian fabric styles. After a jam session with our facilitator and head weaver, Pankaj and Shamji, they said they were open to experimenting with new designs. However, a rule I made for Ethnotek early on was never to change the artisan's traditional art (also a wish of theirs), which came to define much of our mutual respect for one another. However, there was (and will always be) an exception to this rule. If the artisans suggest a change or update to their textile, we'll entertain and happily support them because it's their right to do so — after all, it's their family's art and heritage.

During this jam session with Shamji, he reassured me that we could use the traditional motifs but develop new colors that might appeal more to foreign customers and arrange the patterns in new ways. This meant that the weavers' community identity would be preserved. Still, the fabric design would take on a new life and hopefully reignite interest in Indian textiles with our distributors and customers. Shamji floated the idea to his weavers, who were excited about the new direction. After getting that reassurance, I was all in. It was worth a shot! Little did I know that the simple decision to change the Indian threads would lead to the largest order for the artisan weavers in Ethnotek company history. Wowza!

Okay, let's back up to see how it happened. In the HCMC bookstore, Ái and I were armed with two new trusty sets of Pantone swatch books fresh out of the package. We were like giddy schoolboys as we loaded our bikes with our new colorful books and set off into the early evening traffic headed for the Hoa Hao Fabric Market across town. We planned to send one Pantone book to Shamji in India and keep one for our production crew in Vietnam. We would also send printouts of the new textile design briefings and yarn trimmings that were the closest match to the colors I would select. Pantone is handy because it adds a layer of professionalism to our color process since it's what most dye houses use. Also, having physical color references on hand is a quality control measure to ensure accuracy. Shamji sent me numerous photos of textile options from his showroom via Whatsapp (and I had photos of other styles we had been working with), which I then rendered into Adobe Photoshop and Illustrator to digitize into 1:1 scale on our bags. I produced ten new designs, and I was happy with the result. What I was going for was to rearrange Shamji's classic motifs in a way that would work on our biggest and smallest products. Typically, there are large blank sections in the artisan's textile designs because they are often used for large items like shawls and rugs. If we didn't reduce the blank spaces, some small wallets and pouches couldn't feature the motifs due to the random nature of die-cutting in bulk during the production stage. The motifs we were working with were *Kungri*, *Damaru*, *Hudadhi*, *Vankiyo*, and *Five Faces*.

The colors I chose were based on feedback from our Japanese distributors (who were into indigo at the time) and my intuition to fill the color gaps in our existing collection. We had a white neutral tone at the time but needed a darker black base, so I added that. We also needed red and some earth tones, like brown and olive green. We usually apply color codes to our artisan partners' fabric variants by country name and style number; in this case, these new styles would be known internally as India 10-19. After deciding what colorways to move forward with, my job was to arrange these beautiful motifs in rows that would be possible for the weavers to create on the loom and in sizes that would look great on all Ethnotek products, big or small. Each page of the briefings I prepared had a large zoomed-in section of fabric with measurements, Pantone code callouts, stapled yarn trimmings, and a rendered mockup of the Raja Pack with the new textiles. I put them all into an Ethnotek branded folder, boxed it up, and sent it to India via secure post. It arrived a week later, and Shamji and the team promptly got to work on making samples. The urgency was that I had shared the new design renderings with our biggest distributors, and the feedback was resoundingly positive. I asked them to narrow the 10 styles to a smaller collection of six to make it easier to manage, but they wanted them all! On one hand, this was incredible news. We successfully reignited the spark of interest for the artisans' India textiles from one of our biggest distributors. Job done – well – almost! Because, on the other hand, we had no idea how to fulfill the order! After six weeks of back and forth with the team in India virtually, we nailed the colors and new designs. They shipped five meters of each design to Ái and me in Vietnam to start building a complete set of sales samples for our distributor's trade show, which was only three weeks away. We had under one month to make over 60 samples.

When I gave them the brief, our sample room team looked at me like I was insane. We only had two sewing workers and one pattern maker. Meanwhile, making 65-70 finished bags was like producing an entire run. I politely insisted and stayed with the team when we had to work overtime. Amazingly, we managed to pull it off. The result was the biggest order Ethnotek had ever received, even to this day.

I was on the next flight to Ahmedabad, India, to join the crew while producing this new monster order. The next few weeks were a blur, and we fulfilled that order on time, resulting in happy distributors with a new appreciation for Ethnotek bags and textiles. Sure, the cash infusion helped us all, but the more impactful lesson was that we creatively pooled our resources, changed how we did things and stepped out of our comfort zone to try something new. We swung for the fences and hit a home run on the first swing. This strengthened the relationship with the team in India. It reenergized them and injected some new inspiration. It also set the tone for how we'd modify traditional textile designs to infuse modern Ethnotek flavor in the future, taking extra care to maintain the original identity of the artisan's textiles, which falls in line with the careful balancing act we need to walk between change and tradition.

The Ethnotek Way is at the crossroads of traditional handmade art and modern tech. And this intersection is also where many of our artisan partners seem happiest working. Remember Iwan's story about his funky new take on his family's *batik* in Indonesia (in Chapter 4)? Many examples on the Ethnotek journey exist where artisans, production facility crew, marketing, customer service, and admin teams have sought to break the status quo in their respective fields. *What if?* That question beats through our company from our curious band of creative souls. These small, incremental choices have created a rich tapestry of innovation woven from many threads of our change-welcoming community who are happy walking (and trailblazing) the Ethnotek Way. What's more, we use our commercial vehicle and global audience of supporters to help us constantly bring new energy to traditional techniques led by the artisans.

Shortly after that mega order from our Japanese distributor, Pankaj, our facilitator in India, coined a new phrase for both the weavers' move into innovative new textiles and Ethnotek customers as a whole: "From nomads to newmads!" He was referring to the original use for many of the Indian textiles we use in our bags that were once versatile garments used by nomadic pastoral herders either as shawls to shade from the desert heat and to keep warm at night or as slings to carry their wares while roaming with cattle or as rugs at home. But today, our Indian partner artisans have given new life to these textiles, from the traditional nomads of Kutch to the "new nomads" roaming major cities worldwide. This example from India shows how innovation and tradition can meet in the middle at the intersection we call home — The Ethnotek Way!

For as long as I can remember, I've sought to embrace change, and I believe this is an essential skill for any entrepreneur. After all, **Change Comes To Us All**. Life is constantly moving, evolving, and changing into something entirely new. It's just part of life, which is true of culture.

"Culture is constantly changing, constantly evolving, constantly dying, and constantly being reborn."

— Octavia Butler

At the start of this chapter is a quote from the late philosopher Alan Watts, who said, "The only way to make sense of change is to plunge into it, move with it, and join the dance." Absolutely right, good man! This quote resonates with us at Ethnotek because if there's one quality that led to our ongoing growth, it's our ability to go with the flow. While our route may have zig-zagged and occasionally gone off course into sideways explorations into the unknown, we have always adapted and found our way back as a team to the path of progress. That's possible because of our collective ability to embrace change as a company and community — especially the artisans.

One example that highlights this point happened in 2023. Because we had such success co-creating the Ethnotek Way in the past, I bet big and took a risk by breaking my only rule when introducing new artisan textile designs. That rule was to test the "new" designs in a **Capsule Collection** before distributing them. You may be thinking, *What the hell is that?* Well, at the core of our Capsule Collections lies the collaborative creation of new textile designs with artisans. These designs are thoughtful evolutions of traditional patterns tailored to resonate with our customers and adapt seamlessly across our diverse product range. We've developed a process for these collections and implemented specific steps so that we stay true to our artisan mission. It goes a little something like the following: We kick off our Capsule Collections with **Textile Explorations.** Our journey begins with a meticulous textile testing phase. Upon confirming the color, quality, strength, and consistency and understanding the production constraints, we initiate a modest test order of five meters per style. This preliminary step is crucial for gauging lead times and setting the stage for larger production runs.

Next, we **Learn Through Mistakes (Round 1)**, which may sound like we're setting ourselves up for failure, but it's an essential part of the process. Our test orders provide a gateway to uncovering the unexpected. New designs often bring unforeseen challenges, such as overly complex techniques requiring adjustments to motif layouts or loom setups, color discrepancies, extended production times, or unexpected costs. These insights enable us to make informed decisions, whether crafting an online exclusive limited edition or adjusting our distribution strategy.

Then, it's time for our **Prototype-To-Product** stage. Armed with the initial textile samples, we craft the first Ethnotek bags. This real-world testing illuminates discrepancies between the envisioned design and practical application, particularly how new textiles integrate with our existing bag designs.

Learn Through Mistakes (Round 2) is up next. This is where real-world tests happen. Some things we've encountered in the past are issues with fabric thickness that need further adjustments to ensure the new textiles enhance our bags' aesthetic and are durable and functional. Addressing these challenges is pivotal for our sales and quality standards.

After post-testing adjustments have been made, we **Place The Capsule Order**. This curated bulk order focuses on applying the new textiles to our bestsellers — usually Raja Packs, Cyclo Slings, and Chiburi Wallets — aiming for a targeted market introduction.

Then, it's time for the fun **Launch Phase**. With the collection ready, it's showtime. From fabric procurement to final product delivery, it's a collective effort to bring the Capsule Collection to our audience. We initially engage our customers and subscribers with a newsletter and sneak peek on social media, anticipating a swift sell-out of the limited edition line.

We then try to **Scale Success** by leveraging insights we have gained from the launch. We expand the new styles across our full collection, presenting them to distributors and showcasing them at global B2B trade shows to make maximum impact. Finally, we always reserve time to reflect at the end of the Capsule Collection process. This allows us to learn from mistakes early on and refine our approach before introducing the products to B2B customers.

But remember, I mentioned a risky bet. Well, in 2023, I bypassed our Capsule Collection rollout process. I know, I know, what a renegade! While I joke, it *was* a risk, even if it was calculated. Instead of following the process mentioned above, I made an impulsive decision (with the team's backing) to roll out a new complete collection of textiles lovingly woven by the Sic Tzunun family in Paxtoca (remember them from Chapter 3?). The reason was that I had collected some reference samples of four new Guatemalan fabric designs in colorways and patterns we hadn't worked with yet that I had a powerful feeling about. So I whipped up some renderings, built a pitch deck, showed it to select distributors and our internal team, and the response was overwhelmingly positive. We all got a bit overexcited, and because I was already in Guatemala, living there for a few months, and super confident in our team on the ground, I figured perhaps we should skip the whole Capsule Collection process and go straight to market. So that's what we did. I warned the team of the potential risks of skipping the process, but amazingly, they were on board. And so we rolled the dice and marketed this new collection in our Fall-Winter '23 B2B offering, and away we went. After our team gave us the go-ahead, Averie, Flory, Heriberto, and I drove from Antigua to Xela. The plan was to visit Alirio (we met him in Chapter 3) and his family to present the new designs and see which styles they felt confident weaving. After finding the answer, we visited Manuel and the Sic Tzunun family in Paxtoca, who would take on the rest of the weaving responsibilities for the new super-duper-fast-to-production Guatemala collection. At first, Alirio took on two of our four new designs because of their expertise in *falseria,* and Manuel took on the other two styles, which were *jaspe* techniques. Again, refer to Chapter 3 to refresh your memory on those techniques, or jump to the Appendix to learn about all the artisan textile methods.

Meanwhile, Alirio's textiles were flawless but much more expensive and time-consuming than anticipated, and the projects with Manuel completely unraveled (excuse the pun). Manuel's family of weavers was an incredible artisan partner for Ethnotek for over a decade despite their famously slow and challenging communication. While we did address the communication issues, problems unfortunately persisted. Things took a turn for the worse when Flory visited them several times while producing their first few meters of the new styles and discovered that the colors were way off. What made this new order of designs tricky is that on our last visit with them, they had put in place a new requirement of 50 meters minimum for trying new fabric designs.

That's a big commitment for something unproven, but it was a risk we had to take. When you set a loom for weaving, you need to spool the warp yarn for the entire length of the production. In this case, 50 meters of the wrong color! We'd have to tear down the loom setup to start over and still pay them for the materials for the whole order. Instead, we got creative and decided to keep the black warp yarn* but introduce a light blue weft yarn* for every bobbin pass to create the illusion that the base fabric was the correct indigo blue. It was pretty cool and worked, but it delayed our delivery by a few months.

Side note: If the last few sentences sent you into a rabbit hole of weaving vernacular that made your head spin, worry not! See the Appendix for all these definitions; it should fill in some blanks. Occasionally, my textile nerd needs to be unleashed to detail some of our decisions. I'm sure you understand.

Back in Guatemala, we also discovered that weaving was not the Paxtoca weaver's priority during our order process. Manuel has a background in finance, and his main gig was actually micro-lending in the community. On top of this, most of his weavers had day jobs in the agriculture sector, meaning they only weaved in their free time as a side hustle. At the same time, Ethnotek had grown to a scale that was way too much work for them to handle on a side hustle basis, and they were also unenthusiastic about continuing with our new and more complicated design order that we had just submitted. All these facts came to light just four weeks before the delivery of our fast-to-production-brand-spanking new collection was due. Cue scary music. Uh-oh! The pressure was now on. But rather than panic, we thanked Manuel and his team wholeheartedly for their work and the good memories over the years, wired them payment for the order, plus a little extra on top, and then we mutually parted ways.

But now we had to pivot and adapt — fast. Thankfully, Alirio agreed to take on one of the two new designs Manuel's team had been working on. Then Flory stepped into action. She made contact with a new weaver, Arlindo, whom we hadn't worked with before but who came highly recommended. It was now up to our A-Team of Alirio and Arlindo to rescue the order, which they did! Not only did they complete it, but the quality was much higher, the colors were more accurate, and they even built us a new loom to double their efficiency. What champs! This little sideways maneuver to enlist the help of Arlindo may have cost us a couple of months in delays and thousands of dollars due to having to air freight goods from Vietnam to satisfy upset and impatient B2B customers – ouch! But while this stung a whole lot, we learned some valuable lessons. Number one was always to follow our Capsule Collection process. On the flip side, the experience did accelerate our movement in Guatemala, which was to find a new weaving group of artisans that had been overdue. As sad as it was to part ways with our long-time partners, it was a change we both wanted. Perhaps we were both too shy and polite to communicate with each other, but it should have happened a long time ago. That was another lesson for us in the value of a missed opportunity for open communication, even for difficult conversations.

Despite all the delays for the new collection, we eventually launched it. Thankfully, fantastic distributors are entirely on board with our mission. Of course, there were some complaints, but they rolled with the challenges with flexibility, understanding, and faith that the final results would be worth it. Now that the new Guatemalan designs are out in the market, our European distributor told us that the new collection has been so well-received that it will comprise 60% of their annual buying volume – wowza! That's a big win for our new weaving partner, Alirio, Arlindo, and their families, and it proves, despite all the lost days and dollars, that it was worth it in the end. What felt like months of losses and a mistake on my part turned out to be a big win. Of course, we all wished it had gone much smoother, but sometimes, you have to endure a bumpy take-off before reaching clear skies. Ultimately, it was a lesson to us all that despite the risks and setbacks, the leap of faith in launching a new collection acted as a catalyst for internal growth, adaptation, and renewal.

This hard lesson in Guatemala was also an eye-opening reminder of what Shamji taught us about Bridge Orders (Chapter 2) for our bestselling repeat-order fabrics. The artisans taught us that they need at least three months to complete any order, and for them to deliver high-quality textiles without straining their community with overtime, they need quarterly small orders, not bi-annual monster ones due within two months. The Bridge Orders reduce lead time, strain on artisans and the likelihood of quality control issues. Meanwhile, Capsule Collections helps the business avoid delayed deliveries to B2B customers. They give our team a safe space to try new things, learn, and test the market while reducing wasted materials and time while also keeping morale high due to less stress. The key takeaway here is that while change is necessary and inevitable, changing too fast without due care can be detrimental. Taking calculated risks and doing everything possible to grease the wheels of change to make it smoother is a wise way of working. Setting up protocols and testing before making radical changes is my advice to the Ethnotek team and all you social entrepreneurs working in the artisan space for the good of everyone — customers, distributors, artisans, and the community. Proactive change keeps businesses relevant and growing. But while adapting, we must also be vigilant to constraints and existing processes we built for good reasons or rushing big decisions. Ensuring clear communication with the artisans throughout our company history has led to some of our biggest adaptations and successes. Conversely, our lapses in communication have led to some of our most valuable failures.

"Sometimes the smallest step in the right direction ends up being the biggest step of your life. Tiptoe if you must, but take the step."

— Naeem Callaway

We've been no strangers to change at Ethnotek, and in the last few years, there have been seismic shifts in our company and my personal life. One of the biggest events happened one morning in June 2022 while I was drinking my first-morning coffee and staring at numbers on a spreadsheet through tired eyes. I was back home in Minneapolis after returning stateside after spending COVID lockdown in Bali. It was the end of the company quarter, and I was doing what I usually do at this time of year. It's my routine to pause and reflect, analyze the business's heartbeat, envision new pathways for expansion, and sketch out a roadmap. I would then join the scrum, eager to make a plan with the team. But this quarter was different. A subtle yet profound shift had occurred within me. Sometimes, a founder's most profound decisions arise not from external pressures but from an inner voice. Introspection can help illuminate the path forward or, consequently, a different direction. And so, during this end-of-quarter rumination, as I looked over the business numbers, I realized that I'd grown the company from an idea scribbled in my notebook on a hike in the highlands of Vietnam more than a decade ago into a business that had grown beyond my wildest dreams. Then, the next thought that floated into my head: *I'm happy with how far we've come, and I think I'd be okay with someone else taking over from here.* That was the first time I'd considered stepping aside from the company I had built. But once the idea entered my head, it wouldn't go away. It had been an incredible run, and I am so proud of what hundreds of amazing people and I have created. But at that moment, something in me said, *It's time*. Right then, I knew it was my time to let go and hand the business' leadership role to someone who could inject new energy and take the company to new heights. And so that's precisely what happened – and fast.

In the following months, I stepped into the role of Creative Director at Ethnotek, where I dove back into design and building a plan for my replacement, who would take our mission to the next level. It was quick, felt right, and on we went. Our lead investor, Chris, and I put our heads together for a strategy to merge Ethnotek with a larger organization that shared our values but had a more substantial global reach. It was testing but also an exciting new headspace to wander into. As I'm sure many founders will be able to relate, I felt a deep personal connection to the company, and letting go felt like losing a piece of my identity. But I also felt excitement for Ethnotek's future. I felt responsible for this creation that so many great people believed in and cared about over the years. I felt I had to initiate a transition to help the company outgrow me. As soon as I made peace with the decision, things moved like lightning. We pitched a few individuals and companies, and within a month, we negotiated a company merger, had a new Managing Director, and signed the contracts. And so I'm thrilled to say that in August 2022, Ethnotek merged with our long-time German distribution partner Gustavo Trading GmbH & Co. KG. While this merger is largely about amplification at a business level for me, it's all about values. Gustavo and its founder, Jim Tichatschek, are the real deal. They are a B-Corp with a score of 111.2 at the time of this writing, while the median score for an ordinary business who completes the assessment is 50.9. They have also won the Green Product Award in 2019, were nominated for the German Sustainability Award Design Prize in 2021 for their in-house brand Kushel, and are a climate and groundwater-neutral company.

Here are a few words from Jim: "I'm honored and thrilled to have been a part of the Ethnotek mission since 2015 as a distributor and now in the new role as its Managing Director. I intend to carry Jake's original vision forward while adding a few tricks of my own. My goal is to maintain the highest quality standards while showcasing the beauty and craftsmanship of artisan fabrics. We understand that our customers expect nothing less from us and are committed to delivering on that promise. Our vision for the brand's future is to stay true to our roots, even if it means remaining a boutique brand.

In the coming years, we are focusing on enhancing the repairability and modularity of our designs. A backpack should be a long-lasting companion capable of enduring decades of adventure. As for our team, we plan to grow organically in line with the demands of our customers and the market. As a social enterprise, we understand the challenges of maintaining high standards while making a profit. With our company's steady growth, we are committed to addressing these challenges and creating equal opportunities for indigenous entrepreneurs in lockstep. Your input and ideas are invaluable, and we strive to incorporate them into our product development process. If you have any specific suggestions or ideas, please feel free to share them with us. We are always eager to hear from our customers and involve you in shaping the future of Ethnotek. Thank you for your support and being a part of our community."

— Jim Tichatschek

Well said, Jim. I'm mighty proud to have such a good person take the leading role. At Ethnotek, I can see the great things on the horizon for the company and community under your stewardship. And so, while my time has come to step aside from Ethnotek, with my last day coming in the summer of 2024, I feel inspired by what's in store for the company. I feel only love for all of the community and for what lies ahead because there's so much to look forward to. But before I go, there's still time to peek into distant roads and decades as we end our adventure through the Ethnotek story with a wander into the wisdom of our **Future Threads.**

Conclusion

Future Threads

"The future is not something we enter. The future is something we create."

— Leonard I. Sweet

Big Cottonwood Canyon, Utah, 2023

The sound of a babbling brook stirred me awake. Leaving the warm cocoon of my sleeping bag, I zipped open the frosted tent flap and a gust of frigid air stung my face. I peered over a majestic view just as sunrise sliced through the aspens and ponderosa pines of Big Cottonwood Canyon in Utah. I was at the tail-end of a six-week road trip, and winter was rolling in earlier than expected, meaning my plans to continue my "writing in the wild trip" north to Glacier, Montana, now felt a bit unrealistic. I fired up the jet boil with my portable battery cell and laptop, made myself a cup of coffee, and continued writing the final chapter of a book called ***Threads of Change*** — and the words you are now reading.

I have been writing this book for nearly two years. Reliving the memories and experiences of building Ethnotek into the company it has become, and at the same time, helping me grow into the man and

(I guess) business person I am today. I've giggled, cried, and cringed through these anecdotal tales and memories. Only now do I realize the magnitude of how far Ethnotek has come, from an art project to today's thriving international company and community? If you had told me in college that I'd eventually build a social enterprise that spanned several continents, supported by hundreds of thousands of enthusiastic customers, and had millions of dollars in cash flow through it over the years, I'd look at you like you were insane and tell you you've got the wrong guy. I'm a dreamer, but the type of self-confidence to hold that idea and say, "hell yeah, I can do that," isn't my usual inner dialogue. I've got self-doubt and criticism in spades, though. But perhaps those aspects of myself brought me to where I (and Ethnotek) are today. I'd hazard a guess that they played a role.

On the trip, I now found myself. I'd driven from Minnesota to Utah, taking in the sights and visiting as many nature spots as possible to write along the way. While writing this chapter, I'd been at Big Cottonwood Canyon campsite for a few weeks. Every few days, I'd drive into Park City to refill my groceries and attend a hot power yoga class. It was the perfect place to warm up, work out, and, most importantly, grab a free shower afterward. After several trips to town, I remembered how much I loved the city. And it's also when I realized something serendipitous. This was also where so many good memories had happened with Ethnotek in our fledgling days of inception. It was where we had our first-ever trade show at the Outdoor Retailer show in Salt Lake City (Chapter 1). Eleven years later, I had unintentionally returned. While I hadn't planned to be here or fall back in love with the Wasatch Mountains, it had happened nonetheless.

A few weeks earlier, during my road trip out west from Minnesota, I stopped in Nevada to pick up my dad. Living in Bali during the lockdown had made it challenging to visit family, and it had been three years since I'd seen my dad, Kevin, in person. We had been talking over the phone and thought it'd be cool to do a road trip together to catch up and bond, as we had never spent that much time together as adults. We usually gathered for only a few days during the holidays, often filled with delightful but distracting other family members and festivities. And so, father-and-son quality time was a rarity for a few years. Before the trip, we both joked that we hoped we wouldn't run out of things to talk about. After all, it would be a lot of time in the car and nature. My pops only had a week he could take off between work and getting an operation on his bum knee that was starting to age after all his years of marathon running. Because time was limited and he was based in Henderson, Nevada, it made sense to drive north to the bordering state of Utah, which had some legendary national parks. He wanted to see Zion, Bryce Canyon, Arches, and end the trip in Park City, where he knew a good burger and beer spot. After the trip, I'd drive him down to Salt Lake so he could fly home while I continued my hair-brained scheme to write a book in the wild. The trip was truly epic and exactly what our relationship needed. In fact, I get choked up even writing those words right now. That's how meaningful that trip was for me. And without fail, he's called me every week since we left each other on the trip. Big love, Dad!

After a couple of weeks of canyon camping, cold river plunges, pecking away at this book, and poaching free showers at yoga studios, an idea popped into my head: "What if I moved here?" Technically, I was homeless. My wife and I uncoupled a year before, and I was on a walkabout to find where I would settle next. I tried Portugal for a couple of months, but it didn't feel like the right time for me. I tried Minnesota, Bali, and Vietnam, but that felt like going backward. I did a Yog Dhyan retreat in Pokhara, Nepal. Shortly after, I moved into a small house on Lake Atitlan in Santa Cruz La Laguna, Guatemala, which was incredible but not a long-term fit. And this brought me to the summer of 2023 and this road trip, where I am writing to you now.

I figured I'd scout some potential places to live out west. I've always wanted to live in the mountains, although I always saw myself ending up in Colorado. So, this is what I'd been up to and how I'd come to find myself camping in Utah. It didn't take me long to move to Park City full-time. I'd made it happen four weeks after that morning epiphany to relocate. I found an apartment to rent and drove back to Minnesota to pack up my life. Before leaving Park City, I had coffee with Ethnotek's former Chief of Marketing, Megan, who had moved there post-divorce and had parted ways with Ethnotek many years before. When I told her I was moving to Utah, she laughed.

"Sounds familiar," she said with a cheeky wink. We caught up and reminisced about the good old days with Ethnotek: the struggles and misadventures. We also caught up on each other's lives and celebrated her becoming a new mom. She and I always had a strong relationship but naturally drifted away after the split with the company, so it was great to reconnect and hear old stories as I put the finishing touches to this book.

On the long drive from Park City, I called a lot of people. I felt a twinge of buyer's remorse after paying the deposit for my new rental place in Utah. My usual self-doubt was getting the better of me, so I needed to sound it out with friends and family to keep the existential panic at bay. One particular call with my buddy Aaron resonated.

"It's pretty cool and kind of poetic that you're moving to where the Ethnotek journey started when you're now at the end of it."

It was a thought that never once crossed my mind until he said that. It's weird how the universe works. Perhaps my subconscious had this planned all along? Either way, it feels perfect to be writing this final chapter from where this grand adventure began, then closing the book, putting a stamp on it, sharing it with the world, and taking my first step into the unknown. You have to love it when things come full circle.

I've always been a bit of a dreamer. I can't help myself, and I'm happy to say Ethnotek is a company full of fellow star-gazing creatives. Now that the company is in good hands and the healthiest it's ever been financially, I think it's time to share a vision for the future— and our **Big Dreams.**

I'll start by saying that we've always wanted these dreams to become a reality. Some of them are already happening, while others might not be achievable. By no means is this chapter a promise of things to come. Still, at the very least, it's super fun to share the excitement and paint the sky with a constellation of concepts and opportunities to widen the scope of how far out we could potentially expand the Ethnotek mission together. This is also an open invitation to keep the conversation going. We want to hear from you. Send us your feedback on any or all of the ideas in this chapter or anything else that came to mind while reading this book. Also, I will list a few ideas here and put more at the QR-coded link in the Appendix. After all, it's time to wrap this thing up, and a single book can't encapsulate every ounce of the Ethnotek story. There's so much more to share now and in the future.

The **Ethnotek Summit** is a dream many of us have had for a long time. Shamji said he'd love to meet the Ethnotek teams in other countries, learn about their techniques and cultures, share ideas, and collaborate on new products. We've always wanted to do this as well, and we're starting to make plans to not only take our mission to the next level but invite other businesses and creators to join the cause. We envision this being an annual summit for social entrepreneurs and key players in the artisan sector. This won't be your usual trade fair. Think of it as an incubator or accelerator program, whereby at the end of it, we'll create something tangible and actionable to be implemented and launched throughout the year. This is not an artsy-fartsy project. On the contrary, it generates millions of dollars and happy customers. We push the boundaries of Cultural Collaboration! I've been to so many craft fairs and tradeshows. The handicraft fairs are small, stuffy, and – well – small. Whenever I'm at one of those places, I feel like the world isn't taking us seriously. The B2B trade shows like ISPO, Bread & Butter, and MAGIC are so massive that it's no wonder where much of our human-produced environmental damage comes from, and it's hard to imagine how to cut through that noise to make meaningful change.

We want to create ***the*** forum for cultural exchange in commerce. It'll be intentionally small but have a massive impact in the end. Everyone should walk away fully energized and ready to take action, knowing that it's achievable and that they have artisan production partners, distributors, marketers, and influencers to help them do that.

The potential event breakdown would be that the first five summits would take place in each of the five countries of our existing artisan partners. Then, we would branch out to our other collaborators and event sponsor countries – and make it a roadshow! There would be hands-on workshops where various artisans teach us how to hand-make their art. We will fly in all materials so they can do that effectively, and participants can have fun trying their hand at weaving. Expert seminars and brand presentations will highlight what's happening globally in the world of artisan production at scale and the artisan economy at a macro level, as well as talks on material science.

To break things up, attendees can enjoy our cultural exchange breakouts, which will be intimate classes and gatherings for wellness, food, art, and language. The festivities will conclude with a full music, dance, and party celebration. It will always be held somewhere beautiful, remote, deeply immersed in nature, and, ideally, without Wi-Fi or cell service.

This summit will make waves, challenge the status quo, and set a positive example for the fashion, outdoor, and consumer product industries. Creating a fun and vibrant event with influencers, famous bands, performers, opinion leaders, podcasters, and artists centered around celebrating culture and diversity will shine a bright light on the cause. Doing good and giving back is cool; we want to help ignite that existing fire even more through these events.

Another dream on the horizon is **New Songs**. Don't worry, I don't mean we are starting a band, although that would be fun. While writing this book, I've been on a whirlwind tour visiting our artisan communities to apply the Ethnotek Way (Chapter 8) of Cultural Collaboration to develop a new spin on traditional textiles with our artisan communities worldwide. Or, as Filipe (Alirio's father in San Marcos) would say, "We're making new songs." I love that idea. Our plan to combine the textiles of our international artisan partners, in a sense, will borrow beats, rhymes, rhythms, and musical elements from across the world and weave them together into a new fabric with a heart that will strike a chord with our ever-growing community. Our New Songs textile concept has also got our internal team nodding their heads and tapping their toes in excitement. The idea of the new songs would be complex, but it would be hugely impactful. There will be announcements on this project in the coming months, so stay tuned.

There's a dream we have for an **Indonesian Batik Design Competition.** After COVID-19 travel restrictions opened up, I returned to Indonesia to visit Iwan in June 2023, primarily to develop new textile designs and catch up with each other. But I didn't expect the awesome surprise he had in store for me. I landed at the Adisumarmo International Airport in Solo from Bali. Upon my arrival, Iwan was waiting for me outside. I hadn't seen him since 2018. I didn't know what to expect. But seeing him from afar was so comfortable and familiar. I couldn't wait for the bear hug I knew was coming. Iwan is a strong, stocky guy. As soon as I exited the airport, he promptly sauntered up to me with a lit clove cigarette in one hand, a smile on his face, and delivered the expected bear hug so firmly it cracked my back in a strangely satisfying way.

As we sped across Solo in Iwan's car to his workshop, the sun set over the rooftops of mosques and shophouses, and the call to prayer rang out over a city winding down for the day. Iwan and I caught up on events of the past few years during the pandemic, and by the time we rolled to a stop at his shophouse, it felt like we were old friends arriving back home. He showed me around the workshop that I was so familiar with, but I noticed some big changes. Half his *batik* workshop had been converted into a food prep station for his new restaurant and hookah lounge — you have to love that entrepreneurial spirit! He explained that he had to pivot his business due to dwindling fabric orders during the pandemic. He decided to convert part of his family's compound into a gathering space for the community: a late-night hang-out spot, classic Solo style. The next day, Iwan said he wanted to take me on a drive somewhere special, so off we went. As we drove across the city, I could tell Iwan was excited about something. Eventually, he explained what we were up to. It turned out that during the pandemic, Solo City officials had made huge investments to revive traditional arts and crafts production to drive demand and supply capability. They also built Industri Kecil Menengah (IKM), a craft industrial area in Semanggi Village, Surakarta, on a 5,000-square-meter plot of land that opened in September 2020. IKM was built to become one of the main facilities for artisans in Solo and a creative cultural hub on the island of Java. Moreover, artisans from around the region could access facilities, furniture, infrastructure, and tools to continue their craft and scale their businesses. Crafts produced at the new industrial site included *batik* textiles, traditional shadow *wayang kulit* puppets, mask carving, and more.

Soon after, we arrived at the massive site and parked outside one of the hundreds of studio spaces. Iwan jumped up, fiddled with some keys, clicked open a padlock, and rolled back a large shutter. Ushering me to follow, we ducked inside a large, dark space. There was some shuffling in the blackness, and lights flickered on, revealing a colossal warehouse.

"Welcome, come on in," Iwan said, smiling, a clove cigarette clenched between his teeth. He pointed to a giant glass showcase containing thousands of copper *batik* stamping chops*.

"Is that what I think it is?" I asked.

He chuckled and didn't reply. Instead, he opened all the little glass doors on the showcase and motioned for me to come in closer for a look. I could tell he was relishing the surprise. He knows what a geek I am for this type of thing. Casting my eyes over the treasure trove, I took a long time examining the blocks. Many had cobwebs and were covered in years of dust and dirt from decades of abandonment. The display cases provided by the IKM were new and fresh, but their contents were steeped in history.

Without noticing, Iwan had left me alone to look over all the *batik* blocks. I don't know how much time had passed, but it could have been a few minutes or an hour when he reappeared—I lost track of time. While he was away, I selected a few blocks that could be incredible for use in a new collection of designs for Ethnotek textiles, possibly even the New Songs collection. Iwan smiled when he returned carrying two steaming cups of tea for us. He could see how excited I was to be introduced to this archive of *batik* artifacts.

"Come with me," he said, giving me a nod and another sly smile.

I followed my friend, tea in hand, into the back of the warehouse, where he fiddled with some keys, unlocked the door, and led me into a bright white empty room. Then I saw it. In the middle of the floor was a giant metallic machine that looked like some kind of robot.

"What is that thing?" I asked Iwan.

"The future," he said, smiling the biggest goofy grin I'd ever seen from him.

After a few moments, I realized what this thing was before us. From my experience in industrial design and woodworking, I knew I was looking at a CNC (Computer Numerical Control) machine. Iwan explained that students from the local technical college and our longtime punk friend Tino had devised a way to program the machine to create *batik* designs.

While coding a computer to follow a design path is easy these days. What blew my mind is that these students had constructed a hop feeder system* to get the same seven-ingredient *batik* wax recipe while keeping the ideal temperature for perfect printing. You could create 2D *batik* designs in the software and send them to the machine to print. I realized this machine had replicated the handmade process of *batik*-making, which I thought was impossible. I was baffled and impressed.

"Cool, right?" Iwan asked.

"Why did you guys build that thing?" I asked, a bit perplexed.

Why would Iwan, a handmade batik artisan specialist with a rich family history bound to his art, be tinkering with technology to create the same art electronically?

"Because we can!" he said, grinning.

Over the next half hour, Iwan explained all the many ways this machine would help, not hurt, his family's *batik* business. By the time he finished, I was blown away. This was an experiment to see if it was even possible to replicate complex *batik* prints. He outlined that the goal wasn't to replace artisans (far from it!) but to inspire the younger generation by using technology and engaging them in discussions about the future of the craft. It did sound like a great way to get young people involved.

"We're not trying to replace artisans with an automated process. It's a good way to get the younger generations excited about the craft," Iwan said, taking another puff on his cigarette.

Side note: Iwan's enthusiasm is understandable when you consider that the domestic demand for classic *batik* is strong, so technological experiments like this are not seen as threatening the tradition. With this in mind, Iwan's attitude to this new machine didn't seem so odd. He saw it as a helpful way to motivate young people from Solo and across Indonesia to enter the *batik* industry. This had been a key issue for all our artisan partners worldwide at the time of writing. According to Iwan, the bridge that could serve as an entry point for young people into the weaving industry might be technology.

After several coffees, we came up with what we thought might be a great idea to help test the potential of the *batik* machine. We would create an Indonesian Batik Design Competition using the machine to get young people to experiment with *batik* making for the first time.

"We should make this a global competition," Iwan said excitedly.

"You mean for Indonesians around the world?"

"No, for anyone! This way, we can teach other nationalities about our motifs, culture, and process and let them participate. The machine can produce hundreds or thousands of ideas and styles, and people can experiment and unleash their creativity using the traditional motifs of our culture. That could be really interesting, right?"

I had to agree. Iwan's idea was a great opportunity to widen the scope of interest in *batik* to a new generation of young people who otherwise would have no access to the craft. This was a way to engage them and spark their creativity and interest, which could then lead them further into *batik* and its origins. And so, at the time of this writing, we are beta-testing the project and speaking to our community to see if they think it's a good idea. So how about it? What do you think? We'd love to hear your thoughts, so write to us after you finish reading.

Something else we are very excited about in the future is our **Road To Certification**. Our production facility in Ho Chi Minh City, where all Ethnotek bags are produced, recently became audited and certified by Amfori BSCI. At the same time, we are also on our way to Fairtrade status along with a few other third-party accreditations. This is important because it proves we're walking the talk. Seeing is believing, and we've always maintained that transparency is more important than a superficial badge from someone outside the company. However, sometimes we have skeptics who want to support the company but need proper validation that it's, in fact, scandal-free before doing so. Fair enough. This creates a lot of extra administrative work for us, but we believe it's worth it.

It took a year to move our 90-plus team, all our machines and materials from our previous workshop to a new facility, upgrade our safety protocols, give staff training, sort through stacks of accounting documents, and endure a nerve-racking audit, but we're proud to report that our production facility became BSCI certified on October 11th, 2023. Amfori BSCI is short for Business Social Compliance Initiative, which provides a recognized methodology for identifying and remediating risks in global supply chains. Amfori is one of the most reputable human rights and sustainability compliance consultancies serving the manufacturing industry on the planet. Receiving the stamp of approval is a rigorous process, which is difficult to get but holds a lot of weight when you become an approved member. Amfori believes companies can simultaneously focus on people, the planet, and profit. They help companies like ours to navigate the complexities of increased sustainability expectations. Founded in 1977, Amfori has evolved into a leading business association for sustainable trade, supporting more than 2,400 companies across the globe to operate successful and responsible businesses by improving the environmental, social, and governance performance of their supply chains. For full transparency, here are the areas of our production operation and supply chain in Vietnam that were audited with scores for each.

- Social Management System and Cascade Effect (C)
- Workers Involvement and Protection (B)
- The Right of Freedom of Association and Collective Bargaining (A)
- No Discrimination, Violence, or Harassment (A)
- Fair Remuneration (B)
- Decent Working Hours (D)
- Occupational Health and Safety (D)

- No Child Labor (A)
- Special Protection for Young Workers (A)
- No Precarious Employment (A)
- No Bonded, Forced Labor or Human Trafficking (A)
- Protection of the Environment (A)
- Ethical Business Behavior (A)

While this isn't all As, this is actually an impressive win for a small production team like ours.

> *"We have always known our working conditions are good, fair, and safe, but for our small Vietnamese-owned factory to receive this validation from Amfori BSCI feels really good. We are very proud, and it will be nice for our customers to be reassured by this certification. We are already preparing for next year's audit and making improvements to get all our scores to A-level."*
>
> — Cao Thành Tú
> Kim Ta factory co-owner

The full details of our audit can be accessed by scanning the QR code in the Appendix. For all you budding or veteran social entrepreneurs out there, I encourage you to contact Amfori and go through this process.

Now, we can't talk about the future of Ethnotek without mentioning our involvement in the **Tip Me** initiative. Let me ask you a question: Have you ever sent a tip to the people who make your products, similar to how you tip a server, barista, or bartender? Well, it's absolutely possible. It's just that most brands don't do it. We are proud to say that Ethnotek is now the first backpack company on the planet to enable tipping directly to the artisans and sewing workers who made your bag!

We're mighty proud of this feat, and our artisan partners are too. As you know, we prefer trade over aid (Prologue), but we've decided to bend that rule slightly to advance our mission of promoting artisans' work. This slight tweak happened during the pandemic. The world seemed to change to a new normal in a matter of days. All industries were affected, including our own, and we had a slump in sales and order issues caused by the worldwide lockdown, which had a knock-on effect on our artisan partners. It showed us that textile orders weren't guaranteed based on unpredictable circumstances beyond our control. It was during this time that we implemented the Tip Me initiative. We wanted to implement a system to continually drive income to artisan communities during dry periods between textile orders when unexpected events happen. This slight pivot related to our conversation in the previous chapter about businesses' adaptability to change, which the pandemic made all of us reflect upon. We didn't want to ever find ourselves in a position where if the unthinkable happened, our artisan partners' work would dry up, along with their livelihoods. So, the Tip Me initiative protects against these unforeseen circumstances. It's also just a really cool way to add a tip, even in good times. Who doesn't like tips for great work and service?

Tip Me is an NGO founded in Germany in 2018 to increase the financial well-being and visibility of garment workers around the globe. To date, Tip Me has collected more than US$80,000 in tips for 1,000 workers in countries such as Kenya, Pakistan, Turkey, Ukraine, and Vietnam. Tip Me supports Ethnotek in collecting and distributing tips to ensure that 100% of your contribution goes directly to each individual you're tipping.

To show appreciation to the workers who make your bags, you can send a small amount of money to our local team. The money is usually spent on groceries for the family, educational expenses, or bills such as rent, electricity, or medicine. A global tip is not a substitute for a salary; it serves, above all, to show appreciation for their craft. Not only are we the first bag brand to enable artisan tipping, but within the first year of collaborating with Tip Me, we've become the top tipping company among all their brand collaborators. That means our community of customers not only loves the idea, but they're heavily backing it with their well-earned cash! The Ethnotek community never ceases to amaze me.

Another positive thing about working with Tip Me is their thorough documentation. Part of their charter is transparency, and they track every penny of your tip to know precisely where it goes, who it goes to, and when. Mainly to ensure no foul play and clean accounting, but also to create and celebrate the individual recipients. They are building a database of Ethnotek's 500+ artisan partners to properly introduce you by putting a face to each awesome person's name and a short bio. This will take time to develop, but Tip Me co-founder Helen is on it and is excited to share the results soon.

The future of Ethnotek really is looking bright and sun-filled. And we are looking skyward for a little help in the future. We have high hopes to be **Powered By The Sun** in the years to come. Solar-powered production has always been on our minds, and plans are finally heating up. Thanks to the cost of photovoltaics becoming more affordable, we're planning for our workshop in Vietnam to be entirely solar-powered by 2028. We also think our rig can capture so much energy that we can even share it with our neighbors — now that should keep the good vibes in the neighborhood.

When it comes to matters of **Material Science**, the future is full of possibilities for Ethnotek. There's so much innovation happening inspired by climate-conscious consumers who are also saying no to waste and pollution. This has led to an explosion of new developments in materials that are less detrimental to the environment. We're always looking for eco-progressive substitutes that can revolutionize backpack design and manufacturing. Here are some fascinating materials that are not just rooted in sustainability but could also hold great potential for the future of our bags.

Mushroom Leather, particularly Mylo™, is a game-changer. It's made from the root structure of mushrooms (mycelium) and is versatile, durable, biodegradable, and compostable. Brands like Ganni and Stella McCartney are already making strides with this material in fashion.

Cactus Leather is made from the Nopal cactus plant. It's breathable and partially biodegradable, an exciting alternative to animal leather. It requires minimal resources like water and pesticides for growth and is already being used in various industries.

Recycled Nylon from Fishing Nets, especially Econyl®, is an innovative material from recycled nylon yarn sourced from old fishing nets and other synthetic waste. According to the manufacturer, the regeneration and purification process makes Econyl® infinitely recyclable without losing its quality, substantially reducing global warming impact compared to conventional nylon. Our friends at Bureo have been doing amazing things with this material for years. They recycle recovered fish nets in Chile and upcycle them into various products like skateboards, hats, sunglasses, and apparel through their program called Net Positiva®. They recently collaborated with Patagonia, Jenga, and Trek on product lines using their recycled nylon from ghost fishing nets.

Our meander through innovative materials doesn't stop there. **What About Potatoes?** I'm being serious. Another intriguing development is Parblex®, a bioplastic created from potato waste, particularly peelings. This ultra-strong material incorporates other agricultural waste like wood flour or walnut shells, making it biodegradable and recyclable. This material opens new avenues for eco-progressive design in various industries and is worth keeping an eye on in the coming years.

From potatoes to **Algae**, many fashion companies have been testing the potential of fabric and dyes made from this water-based organic material. Companies like Algaeing are transforming the industry through vertical algae farms supplying the textile industry. Algae is energy efficient and requires significantly less water than cotton production. In a conversation with TenTree co-founder David Luba at the Outdoor trade show in Friedrichshafen, Germany, he explained that their Mobius backpack (claimed to be one of the most eco-progressive backpacks in the world) uses ALGIX® Bloom foam, which is padding made from algae for their laptop compartments, back panels, and shoulder straps. As you can imagine, this usage interests Ethnotek, and we'll keep a close eye on the innovation happening with this fascinating material.

Next up, be on the lookout for pineapples making manufacturing headlines in the near future. I'm absolutely serious. Piñatex is a non-woven textile made from **Pineapple Leaf Fiber** waste. It provides additional income to pineapple farmers and offers a more eco-progressive supply chain. Brands like Svala are already utilizing this biodegradable textile for eco-progressive fashion lines.

Another material I'm interested in is **Coffee Grounds Textiles**. It's fast-drying, UV-resistant, and helps reduce odor. It could be an excellent choice for backpacks, especially for active and outdoorsy people — and who doesn't love the smell of coffee?

Banana Fiber is another exciting material derived from tree bark. It's strong, biodegradable, and has a natural sheen, similar to bamboo fibers, making it suitable for stylish bags and backpacks. Swiss brand QWSTION created their own blend of this called Banantex®.

Of course, **Recycled Cotton and Plastics** and **Upcycled Fabrics** will also be key in the future of materials over the next decade as we try to meet the UN climate targets and reduce waste blighting the planet. According to Reuters, the fashion industry creates 2-8% of global greenhouse emissions. Varying estimates predict that by 2030, the textile industry will create 134 million tons of waste annually, with much of it being sent to landfills. This is why urgent innovation is needed in the materials sector. Ethnotek will do all we can to ride the waves of change and use ever-more sustainable materials across our business. These materials are not just about creating products; they represent a movement toward a more responsible way of living. They show us the potential of what can be achieved when innovation meets environmental consciousness.

As we near the finale of our wander through the dense forest of Ethnotek, we are close to the end of the trail. But before our journey ends and we all wander off into the sunset, there are a couple more things I'd like to say. First, I think it's essential to **Keep The Spirit of Adventure Alive**. We're always mindful of the dangers of line extensions, but as you can tell by now, we like to push the boundaries of our own rules sometimes; it aligns with or pushes our ability to serve our mission. One such example of keeping this adventurous spirit alive is taking heed of one of our most recent survey findings, which clearly told us that our community wants us to release more bags in the outdoors and adventure space. With this in mind, we plan to release a big 55-65 liter adventure pack and duffel bag. While we don't think this could be a high-volume business segment, the survey results tell us that our customers want them and see us as an aspirational adventure brand.

Diving deeper into the realm of adventure, we want to meet our customers where they are in their lives. Many of our community members are yogis, climbers, hikers, cyclists, trail runners, skiers, and snowboarders. One day, it would be a dream to design performance products for these folks under an umbrella called ETK-Aktive.

At the opposite end of the spectrum, we could go ultra-premium. I believe handmade textiles and artisan-made goods are the epitome of luxury. If we see intricate artisan-made Swiss watches as luxury goods, why can't a handbag made from hand-embroidered textiles and vegan leather also be that? I can envision a Highland Luxury collection for those fancy folks in our community. We don't always have to be so sporty, right? Perhaps this is too far of a deviation from our core. We want to avoid alienating our OG customers while exploring premium spaces like this.

Our core niche is urban bags that work well outdoors and on trips. We dream big but must also be careful to stay within our core customers and community when exploring new ideas. This is a useful note for our internal team at Ethnotek and social entrepreneurs working with artisans. While experimentation is pivotal, it can go too far and alienate your main supporters. As such, we will test, test, test and follow the Ethnotek Way when rolling out new collections, starting with our Capsule Collection process (Chapter 8).

A parting thought for anyone considering building a social enterprise is to **Build A Company That Outlives You.** When I think back to the start of Ethnotek, to that day hiking in the Bắc Hà highlands with muddy boots on my feet and inspiration buzzing in my mind, I can see my younger self scribbling down the idea for the company I've built, and it feels like a distant dream.

I wrote down that initial idea: "Collaborate with artisans worldwide to combine their traditional handmade textiles with high-tech bags and backpacks." That's exactly what we've been doing for more than a decade. I couldn't have known at the time that Ethnotek would grow into the size it has today or be able to merge with another business that embodies that mission, but it's all happened. I can see one constant thread that winds its way from the present day back in time to that young designer sitting atop a mountaintop pen-in-hand scribbling down ideas. That thread is the simple mission I set out on. It has remained an unbreakable bond to this day. One that I believe has served as a guide and helped us navigate through all the challenges we have faced over the years. Putting the artisan's work at the center of everything we do has been our guiding principle, and it has helped us stay on track and grow exponentially. Definitely, more than that young kid ever dreamt possible. From that initial idea in 2007, the company has turned over more than US$10 million in revenue from 150,000 customers. We have partnered with over 500 artisan partners in five countries, proving that profit, purpose, traditional handmade textiles, and modern business can co-exist and create a brighter future.

So here's my humble advice if you care to take it. When you start a new project or business, the healthiest mindset to adopt is building something that directly aligns with your values and gives back to the world in some way. The mission should be able to outlive you, the founder. It's about the bigger picture. If you can create something that people can get behind, that's about the community, not the company, the group, not the individual, then people will come along for the ride. When it's not about money but instead about creating something useful, beautiful, and beneficial to everyone who touches it, people will be happy to support you. That's what I've learned along the way on this crazy adventure.

I also think it's important to note that while I started Ethnotek, it's not about me, and it never was. I gave birth to the idea, made the right connections, and then helped it grow into the beautiful, flourishing collective of humans it is today. This is why I'm happy to step aside and let it thrive. The company needed a risk-hungry creative like me to get to where it is today. Now that the enterprise has matured, my services are only occasionally required on an advisory and visioning level. I intend to stay on the company board in this capacity for as long as everyone wants me here. The organization needs a conservative, numbers-focused leader whose primary objective is operational excellence, happy customers, and financial health. I'm happy to say we have the right new leader to do this. So, best of luck, Jim!

The company is a highly efficient organism now and has a backlog of design ideas from yours truly. I've deliberately worked myself out of a job. The goal has always been to have the brand and mission outlive me, and now it's time to prove my commitment to that goal by gently placing it into someone else's capable hands, stepping aside, and letting go. I suppose this is similar to how it feels when parents send their kids off to college. It's both a proud and sad moment, but it's time to let my baby bird fly on its own. I am so unbelievably proud of what hundreds of incredible, talented, hardworking, and creative people have built over the years through dedication, inspiration, and our fair share of laughs, love, sweat, and tears. Now, I can walk away knowing I gave it my best and created something unique, impactful, special, and fun. I'm excited to see the new heights of Ethnotek's journey from here. My heart is full, and it's from every fiber of my being; I say farewell and thank you.

And for all of you thinking of starting something similar, I say, ***Go for it!*** It just could be the best thing you ever do.

Wow, what a ride!

With love

Jake

Appendix

Thank you for reading ***Threads of Change***. We hope you loved it! The fact that you're here means you're still interested in learning more, and that's awesome. Scan the QR code above to access the goodies that were moved from the book to this webpage to save paper and give you a further interactive deep dive into the book's supporting content. Inside, you can hear directly from the artisans, dig into our background research, references and citations, and much more. Thanks for being curious and following the thread into our world.

If you haven't used QR codes before, simply open the camera app on your phone and hover over the square code above. A link should pop up. Tap on it, and it'll take you where you need to go.

Artisan Interviews

Ghana

Reiss Niih Boaofo

How did you get into the textiles business, and what excites you about it?

I wanted to make money to support myself when I started tertiary education. My parents have always been in business, so they influenced me. I initially started selling traditional handmade recycled *krobo* glass beads online. Then, I included *batik* fabrics, wax prints, *bolga* baskets, and woven *kente* fabrics. Weaving *kente* initially started as a way to make a living, but later, I became proud that I could introduce Ghanaian-made arts and crafts to the entire world through the internet. I love how I have improved the lives of these artisans and their families. Collaborating with Ethnotek and other clients, we have helped improve the livelihoods of our artisan partners. Today, I'm fulfilled by seeing the smiles on the faces of the artisans' children. They live better and happier lives than before Ethnotek came into the picture.

Shared Answers From Charles & George

Can you please tell us about yourself, how you got into making textiles, and what this work means to you?

My name is Mark George Ameyaw, and I was born in May 1980 in Accra. I have a Junior High School Certificate (BECE). We are a family of 38 people, including my parents, grandparents, siblings, and me. We are courageous people, and my grandparents raised our family with the money they made from farming and *kente* weaving. I speak English, Twi, Ewe, and Lelemi. I am Christian, and my favorite part of my cultural heritage is the Yam Festival.

My name is Charles Yaw Acquah. I was born in November 1969 in Nima, Greater Accra, and I have a Vocational Level education. I grew up with my mother and three siblings. My mother was a single parent, so it wasn't easy for her to take care of us, but with the help of some good people, we got to where we are now. I like to listen to music to relax and create more ideas for my work. I speak five languages: Ga, Twi, Ewe, Hausa, and English. I follow the Christian faith because it promotes peace and unity. I have been making tie dye and *batik* since 2003. It's our traditional cloth, so I love to see people wearing it in different parts of the world because it makes me feel proud to be Ghanaian. After all, the meaning behind our textile motifs helps us to remember our heritage.

Is the younger generation interested in working in the textile business? If not, what would help motivate them?

They are interested in our culture's textiles, but the process turns them off when they see what happens at our workshop. Working over a fire during the dewaxing process makes them change their mind. Maybe if there was a way to implement technology to dewax the cloth, the younger generation might show more interest.

What challenges does traditional craft face in your community, and what are your recommended solutions?

Some problems are the increasing cost of cotton fabric every time we buy it, water shortages, and the international awareness and cultural importance of our craft.

Guatemala

Francisco Manuel Sic Vasquez

Can you tell us your name, your community, and what textile work you do?

I'm Francisco Manuel Sic Vasquez, originally from the Paxtocá community in Totonicapán. I've been working for almost 30 years in the weaving business. What I like the most is to work with traditional fabrics from my home country. This work has been a gift from God that has helped my family in many ways. We have included many people in our business because of the demand for our textiles. We work with families who weave the threads, another that ties the threads, one that dyes the colors, and finally, a family that knits. Our business relies upon five families' skills in creating one fabric. As a result, we distribute all the money equally, and everyone gets their fair share. This work has helped us so much because the truth is that we don't have other work. The lack of work is why many people are emigrating to the USA. I would like to thank Ethnotek customers for helping us export our products. Honestly, in Guatemala, there are not many opportunities, and when you buy our products, you help us to have work. Thank you.

Can you explain some symbols and meanings behind the colors in the fabrics you work with?

Our fabric designs are full of meaning in Mayan culture. Many motifs come from scenes of daily life that represent who we are as people. We get excited when we see these motifs on products, like Ethnotek bags and wallets, that people buy and share in different countries. It makes us proud of our Guatemalan and Mayan heritage. We love yellow. Every child knows from our parents that yellow represents the sun and corn. Blue represents the sky, white represents the clouds, and these are also the colors of our national flag. Green means the mountains, and red represents the blood of Guatemalans.

Is the younger generation interested in working in the textile business? If not, what would help motivate them?

Our country needs to invest in the future of this industry. I wish the textile market were strong, like when I was young when Guatemalan fabric sold very well. But there's a reason why it is different now. The knowledge of dying is fading because we didn't receive training. In my case, I had to pay an expert to teach me how to dye threads properly. As for the younger generation, most of them want to focus on their studies, which is a good thing. Weaving is hard work, so getting them involved is difficult. But there's hope, some of them work with *cortes* (skirts). The problem is that we don't have a market. The younger generation would be motivated to work in this area if there was a market, but this won't happen without investment. Also, now the younger generation is interested in technology, and so this also has an impact on traditional craft.

Interview with Felipe Santiago García Gonzalez

What is your name, and can you describe your work with textiles?

My name is Felipe Santiago García Gonzalez, and I work on everything related to traditional fabrics. We are located in San Isidro Chamac, San Pedro Sacatepéquez, San Marcos. Our workshop is almost 35 years old, and I started working when I was 12. So, I have been weaving for 63 years.

I feel very happy. I thought my children would not continue this work by the time I died, but now I feel proud that my son Alirio has surpassed me. We are both working really hard to continue our craft. Working with handmade textiles, you never stop learning because we try new things daily.

What do you hope for in the future of your workshop?

My son and I want to create new designs. Our traditional textiles have many options, and it's just a matter of thinking about what we want to do differently. Because If we settle with the status quo, we won't progress. Our designs are like songs, and we are the musicians. I've talked with my son about having new fabrics because if we always keep the same styles, people will not buy them. We don't want to settle and always play the same songs. We want to improve and try new things. For example, if we have three or four new songs, not all of them will be a success, maybe just one or all of them, but we have to experiment.

Interview with Rosidalia García

What is your name, what textiles do you work with, and what excites you about the craft?

My name is Rosidalia García. I work in all weaving areas but specialize in the Mayan Star design. Many years ago, I first learned to wind thread at age twelve and weave at sixteen. Our work excites me. It's an extraordinary art, and you can do anything when you love your work. My parents always taught me to work hard and earn money, but they also recognized the value of conscious work and respecting the weaving tradition. I am passing this on to my daughters now.

What do you want to tell Ethnotek customers about your work?

I would ask them to appreciate the work behind our fabric since it is handmade. This work is impressive, and I hope they will realize the time we invest to create these beautiful textiles. Every detail is special and difficult to make. Also, I would like them to know that Guatemalan women proudly handmade these textiles.

Interview with Alirio García

Can you please tell us about your process and what it's like working with foreign customers?

Realizing that limitations are only in our heads inspires me to create new designs. I'm also inspired by the craft's ability to create job opportunities for others. It's good that people from other countries invest in our work because it creates opportunities for us. It's an opportunity to improve our lives. We feel blessed to make this art, even though it is in decline. And so, I feel proud that I give life to this work. I see something positive now: most customers like Ethnotek are going straight to the artisans. That way, we avoid misunderstandings and ensure the benefits go directly to the artisans.

Who taught you to weave?

My parents taught me the art of weaving. Since I was a kid, they have given me an excellent education and taught me to be fair and not take advantage of others. I learned the weaving process from my dad by watching him work. My passion and talent lie in this work; both are necessary to create great art.

What role does technology play in your work?

This is not technology per se, but I studied computer science in Guatemala City and have taken some ideas from coding and frameworks into weaving. For example, I print out large sheets of grid paper and map our complex motifs onto that, which informs new ways to set up the loom. I am proud that our looms are designed differently than any looms you'll find elsewhere in Guatemala. The most complicated design we have has 39 heddles*.

What are your hopes for the future of this work?

I want to continue to give our community job opportunities. Our vision is that our workshop will grow, and we are confident this will happen, so we have already asked a carpenter to build more looms.

India

Shamji

What are your family's various roles in the textile process?

The Valji family consists of six brothers, all involved in Ethnotek production. We divide the roles and responsibilities among ourselves. Ramjibhai (my elder brother) monitors the color of each loom to ensure that the weavers work according to the color story for each design. Ramji and Dinesh (my younger brothers) look after different weavers' inventory needs across a few villages. Arjun, Hamir, and I are involved in the production planning, coordination, quantity, and quality check once the fabrics from different looms come in, procurement of yarn, etc.

Can you explain the textile design we collaborated on?

The fabric designs we create for Ethnotek are based on our original *dhaba* blanket shawls, which we used to sell to nomadic Rabari herders. These were multifunctional textiles for the herders. They used them as shawls to block the midday sun or as blankets to stay warm while sleeping outdoors at night, sometimes to wrap various items, sling over the shoulder as a bag, or as a mattress to sit on when cooking. We are pleased to see the textile take on new forms, such as backpacks and bags, with Ethnotek customers worldwide.

How has Ethnotek impacted your community and process?

The loom structure has moved from the original designs to *shuttle-operated weaving with changing times and product demand. One village, Kanderai, is where Ethnotek weaving has been happening for 13 years. The weavers in this village still practice their craft using centuries-old traditional looms. Before, the weavers here were losing work because the production method shifted to shuttle looms. When there's no work, they must travel to work in factories instead. Working outside the village, they lose their original customs and traditions, and if they have to relocate their families, their children lose connection with their cultural roots. Ethnotek's work came as a boon to the Kanderai village, and the weavers there benefitted from consistent work for most of the year because of those orders. One of the most significant advantages of regular work with Ethnotek is that the weavers do not have to leave their homes or villages; hence, their traditional way of living and culture is maintained, and their social fabric is kept intact.

How do you feel about our project after seeing Ethnotek products and textiles from other countries?

We admire and appreciate the handwork of artisans in Ghana, Guatemala, Indonesia, and Vietnam, and our work is valuable when seen together with theirs. We now know that we are part of a bigger story.

What's it been like to work with Ethnotek?

When we first met, I didn't think much about it, thinking maybe it was a small project or not so serious. Yet after the first few orders, I saw Ethnotek's commitment, and our relationship grew beyond purely commercial. The bond has grown stronger with a deeper connection. Work achieved through such relationships brings in business and impacts the sector, taking it in a new direction. We wish all our working relationships to grow in this manner.

Dinesh

I am so happy to see a fabric that would normally end up as a rug that people walk over instead of now being featured on backpacks and worn by people in many different countries.

Arjun

It's great to see our weaving being featured on products other than typical shawls, stoles, and fabrics we have made for so many years. We truly respect Jake's knowledge of textiles, sense of design, and how he has used our fabrics for different types of bags.

Rajesh

This is the first time that I have seen a buyer in the last 20 years who has successfully sold one design continuously for more than four years. Working with Ethnotek made the artisans' lives more comfortable because they didn't have to keep changing tracks and could work continuously on just a few designs, which made production more stable. Hats off to Jake for this accomplishment!

Shamji

I look forward to working with Ethnotek for many years to come. I would like to see our weave being used on many different types of Ethnotek products, which can bring more work to our community and sustain our traditions. I want our relationship to grow for even 50 years or more! I would love it if one day Ethnotek brought together all the artisans from different countries to meet in person. It would be useful to share ideas and brainstorm what Ethnotek could do for the future with our traditional crafts!

Indonesia

Setiawan Muhammad (Iwan)

Please give us some background on how you got into the *batik* textile craft?

My name is Setiawan Muhamad, but my friends call me Iwan. I was born in 1971 in Surakarta. I have a bachelor's degree in International Business management. I am Muslim, speak Bahasa and English, and am passionate about design, soccer, and traveling. My wife's name is

Retno, and I have three kids. One daughter is 26 years old and works with the Indonesian Transport Ministry. My two sons are 20 and 22 years old and study at the local university. I am the 6th generation of my family's *batik* business, which started in 1756. Our family's heritage is rooted in the Laweyan village in central Java, established around the 16th century. This region is alive with cultures and art. It was known as the center of *batik* in the Kingdom Pajang era by Ki Ageng Henis. Another important figure is Hadji Samanhudi, the founder of Sarekat Dagang Islam, an organization in Indonesia that previously served as an association for *batik* traders in Surakarta. It later broadened its scope to nationalist political issues. I have been making *batik* since 1988. My father taught me. I love this work because it is creative. *Batik* has existed in Solo since 1546, so we feel part of a long line of cultural heritage. I took over my family business when my father passed away in 2005. Like most young people, I wasn't initially interested in the *batik* business. I loved it, but it was old school, and I was thinking about other modern jobs. But when my father passed away, I felt responsible for continuing the craft. After all, if I didn't, who would? This is my family's heritage, and I'm proud to carry it on. Through commitment to my craft, I fell in love with it. Today, I feel like *batik* is now a part of my soul. It fills me with life, and I love it very much.

How did you feel when you first saw Ethnotek customers wearing your fabrics?

Seeing people wearing our fabric outside of Indonesia on backpacks makes me feel proud because it means Ethnotek customers appreciate our craft.

What is your opinion of working with Ethnotek?

We've known Jake, the founder, for many years and have done business together. I really appreciate Ethnotek using our traditional motifs on their products as it promotes Indonesian craft.

What can Ethnotek improve on?

More fabric orders, please, haha!

Teddy Priyanagroho

My name is Teddy Priyanagroho. I'm the third generation in my family *batik* business. When I was young, I helped my father mix colors and bring finished *batik* to the village. I think it was my destiny to be a *batik* worker. Our workers are farmers in the rainy season, and in the dry season, they become *batik* artisans.

What do you think the future holds for *batik*?

Unfortunately, I think *batik* is a sunset industry. The workers are usually 50–60 years old, and when they retire, there is no new generation to take their place. The government should help us. If they don't, I worry that *batik* will fade away.

What is your opinion of Ethnotek?

Ethnotek's concept of combining traditional culture with modern bags is fantastic!

Vietnam

Lan

Lan is our all-star textile partner in Sa Pa, Vietnam. The Hmong community is dispersed throughout northern Vietnam's vast mountainous landmass, making it difficult for textile artisans to market and distribute their products. Often, their only options are to sell to local tourist markets that compete with counterfeit versions of what they create, which barely covers their material costs. Lan identified this need and started a social enterprise that acts as a centralized location where hundreds of artisans throughout the region can come to create and sell their goods. Lan also embroiders textiles, but she decided to serve the greater community by becoming a distributor. She's a badass!

Please tell us about yourself and how you got into the textile trade?

I am Sùng Thị Lan, of the Black Hmong ethnic group. I was born in 1985 in the Tả Van commune in Sa Pa town, Lào Cai province. I am the fifth child in a family of 11 siblings, six men and five women. Since childhood, my parents took me to the forest to plant medicinal herbs (gac fruit, angelica sinensis, and other herbs). I lived in the Hoàng Liên Son National Forest until 1997 when I was 12 years old. I left school in Grade 12 so my other siblings could get an education. I married in 2007, and we built our own house and had two children. After my kids were born, I returned to school on nights and weekends and continued my education. I can speak three languages fluently: Hmong, Giay, and Vietnamese. Additionally, I know a little Tay ethnic language and some basic English. Returning to where I grew up, I realized the land's potential for tourism and witnessed the difficult lives of Hmong and Red Dao women. Having experienced many hardships and poverty myself, I wanted to do something meaningful for the community where I live. I began to explore making traditional embroidery and how to market it. I have always dreamed of being a strong woman who could be a pillar for many other illiterate women who do not speak the national language and do not know where to sell their products. I wanted my shop to be a supportive hub where women can work together and support each other. Fortunately, in 2017, there was a government project to support female entrepreneurs, which I was accepted to. I learned management and customer acquisition and digital skills. Today, I'm so proud to say I have my own business called Mường Hoa Cooperative. It's now a legally registered social enterprise. Although small, I am proud of my business because it has helped many people in my community and preserves and protects the ethnic and cultural identity.

What are the gender roles in your textile process?

The roles of women and men in the production process are such that women are 100% responsible for everything from embroidery to completion. Men of the Hmong ethnic group do not participate in weaving or embroidery. They only help with cooking or other tasks to facilitate the conditions for women to produce embroidery.

What role do your younger generations play continuing your craft?

Nowadays, many young people are enamored with industrialization and modernization, and many have the opportunity to pursue education. As a result, some may not be deeply interested in traditional crafts due to their intricate nature and the dedication required to learn embroidery and production. We encourage and promote our craft among women and mothers to pass it on to the younger generation. We suggest that government bodies and schools implement policies where students wear ethnic costumes on a fixed day of the week to preserve and honor our cultural pride. Additionally, we propose to support universities, students, and professors in research projects related to the embroidery production process. These can be classes and training sessions to teach the craft to the younger generation, providing maximum support to those passionate about making embroidery.

What does the future hold for your social enterprise?

My hope for the future is that our community continues to preserve and develop our traditions. I wish for more friends and customers, both domestically and internationally, to recognize and appreciate the products and the beauty of our Hmong culture.

To achieve this, I still need Ethnotek's support and partnership to guarantee purchases from our community, which motivates us to continue working and preserving our culture.

Acknowledgments

I'm forever grateful to the incredible humans who helped build Ethnotek into the thriving global social enterprise it is today. This acknowledgment barely scratches the surface in conveying my immense appreciation for all those who played pivotal roles along our colorful journey.

Let me start by thanking Josh and Carrie for welcoming me and the first Ethnotek inventory into their basement back in 2012 after I got fired from my corporate job. Josh, your belief in the vision and partnership in those early days was invaluable in getting this dream off the ground. Thank you to Brad for keeping our finances organized.

Huge gratitude to Megan for your brilliant marketing and storytelling guidance. You helped hone our brand identity and created long-lasting partnerships. The vibrant spirit you infused into Ethnotek is something we've aimed to uphold over the years. Thanks also to Steph for your amazing support at that first trade show.

Thank you Josh F. and Aaron for being our wingmen at those early shows! And Lindsey, hugs for letting us borrow your van, despite it breaking down in the Dakotas — so sorry!

We never would have gained traction without the confidence of our early retail partners who put us on the map. Huge thanks to Russell at REI, Ryan and Meghan at Urban Outfitters, the teams at INS, Midwest Mountaineering, Forage Modern Workshop, Cliche, Mild Blend, the Alt, Erik's Bike Shop, Outside Hilton Head, Vita Trade, Bag Creature, Oribags, Tenkie Box, Suburban HK, Rushfaster, Love Luggage, and Gustavo Trading with Jim and Stefan. Shoutout to our rep dynamos Tom and Terry, too.

I'm tremendously grateful for the wise counsel of our investors and advisors, Brian, Chris, Ned and Benoit. Brian, your steady mentorship from the early days until now has been invaluable. Thank you Pierce for your encouragement as well. And to our first investors, my parents Cathy, Steve, Kevin and Diane, grandparents Roger and Jeanne and our family friend John, thank you for believing in me. Shoutout to the LOHAS accelerator crew Cissy and Adam.

Ethnotek wouldn't be Ethnotek without the extraordinary creative talents who helped elevate our visuals and storytelling to incredible heights. Eternal gratitude to Adina for your passionate graphic design, photography and innovative ideas. Francis, your stunning studio and lifestyle photography took us to another level — the door is always open for future collabs! Thank you Corey for your videography genius on that first crowdfunding campaign. And Tiffiny, you made our social media channels shine while connecting us with so many inspiring collaborators.

When we started getting in over our heads operationally, Jennifer rode in to save the day by rebuilding our systems from the ground up. That herculean effort allowed us to professionalize and scale. Thank you Kevin M., your relentless drive pushed us to launch that first Kickstarter campaign which was an invaluable learning experience. Thank you Anthony (aka Ton Loc) for being our Ops Manager and very important third member of the three amigos with Cori and I all those years, we love you!

At the heart of Ethnotek's social mission are the incredible artisan groups we partner with. In Ghana, huge thanks to Reiss Niih Boafo, George Ameyaw, Felix Boakye, James Atagbolo, William Agbo, Charles Acquah, Nathaniel and family. In Guatemala, gratitude to Averie, Flory, Lesly, Hannah, Manuel(s), Daniel, Claudia, Luisa, Agripina, Lidia, Blanca, Alida, Alirio, Rosa, Etelvina, Felipe and Arlindo. In India, we're indebted to Pankaj and Mina, Shamji and the Valji family, Ashok, Purnima and all the weavers in the Kutch villages. Thanks Arushi for your original sourcing support! In Indonesia, kudos to Setiawan Muhammed, Teddy Priyanagroho, Harjono, Sri and Yatmi. And in Vietnam, thank you Ái, Tú, Bao, Inrahani, Ms. Lan and the incredible Hmong embroiderers and Cham weavers.

A massive thank you to our production squad in Vietnam, Kim Ta Co. Ltd. Your team, mostly consisting of badass women, brings constant inspiration through your creativity and commitment to building excellent products. Also, I'll never forget our joyous parties between production runs!

I owe my mom, Cathy, a huge thank you for fulfilling all those early online orders from our basement. And hugs to the models over the years who made our product shots pop, contest winners, and Kickstarter backers: Arley, Sarah, Aaron, Lindsey, Joe, Shane, Ben, Mallory, Milan, Miguel & friends, Kevin, Pam, Matte & friends, Andy & Merri, Ngan, Chiara, Delta, Kennett, Edsar, Citra, Jamie, Jade, Agi, Tim, Kate, Lilly, Ara, Fabian, Yoi, Adiyoso, Lena, Esa, Frenemy, Dior, Heidi, Fede, Laurenne, Seth, Christie, Shayla, Malik, Nahko, Matt, Griffin, Becca, Ben, Brody, Phoebe, Tommy, Claire, Jess, Petra, Tim, Jim B., Abigail, Shane, Kim, Laura, Marina, Otavio, Oliver, Kirk, and Justin.

Thanks must go to our incredible team of hard-working digital nomads: Ruben, Niels, Joao, Marissa, Precious, Reyta, Emile, Shanice, Vinay and the eQuest crew, Hai, Scott, Clarissa, Jenny M., Sarah, James

H., LoriAnn, Zach, Mary, Austin, Colby, Rich, Mustache Mike, Gianpaolo, Olivia, Meow, Sami, James P., Frank, Trish, Eszter and Fraser. You all bring an infectious energy and your talents have helped take Ethnotek to new heights. I'm honored to have been on this wild ride with all of you!

Also big big shout out to all the Hubud crew in Bali: Peter, Steve, Chris, Vitto, Maria, Sisi, Buana, Budi, Kasyfi, Kintan, Esa, and team. Thank you for the support, events, skillshares, parties and community love during our years there. The "win and help win" culture will be forever ingrained in Ethnotek's DNA.

To anyone I may have inadvertently left out, please forgive me and know that I hold you in my heart. The Ethnotek community is overflowing with incredible souls who have all played an invaluable part in shaping our evolution. I'm forever grateful for each and every one of you.

Eternal love and appreciation to Cori, my ex-wife and permanent family member. For being my partner in crime, dreaming big, pulling me together when I was broken into pieces, and courageously riding the big waves with us all, good and bad, the whole way through. Your kindness, strength, and brilliance inspire me daily, and you still have the best laugh on the planet!

Lastly, none of this could have happened without the unwavering support of our cherished global community of customers and fans. By purchasing our bags and spreading the word, you've created a far-reaching positive impact by helping elevate artisans' textile traditions, families, and culture.

Thank you, I love you all.

Jake

Publisher Info

Gustavo Trading GmbH & Co. KG is a distributor of social brands and sustainable products based in Hamburg, Germany, and is led by their Founder and Managing Director, Jim Tichatschek.

Threads of Change was produced in collaboration with Far Books, a division of Far Features Ltd.

Author Info

Jake Orak is an artist, award-winning designer, traveler, and outdoor enthusiast born in Minnesota, USA, in December 1981. He received a BFA in Industrial Design from the University of Wisconsin-Stout and has designed category-leading products for 3M, Crumpler, and Booq before creating Ethnotek. Jake believes his purpose in life is to create beautiful and useful things with his hands and mind that inspire others and contribute positively to people and the planet.

Printed in the USA
CPSIA information can be obtained
at www.ICGtesting.com
CBHW060003030824
12612CB00037B/1449